Common Knowledge About

中国历史常识

（中英对照）

国务院侨务办公室
The Overseas Chinese Affairs Office of the State Council

国家汉语国际推广领导小组办公室
The Office of Chinese Language Council International

前 言

《中国文化常识》、《中国历史常识》和《中国地理常识》是由中华人民共和国国务院侨务办公室组织北京华文学院、南京师范大学和安徽师范大学编写的一套汉语教学辅助读物，供海外华裔青少年通过课堂学习或自学的方式了解中国文化、历史、地理常识，同时供家长辅导孩子学习使用，在海外反响很好。

近年来，随着中国经济社会的迅速发展和国际影响的不断扩大，海外学习汉语的人数，尤其是非华裔汉语学习者人数大幅度增加。为了进一步适应广大海外汉语学习者了解中国文化的需求，促进中外文化交流，中华人民共和国国务院侨务办公室授权中国国家汉语国际推广领导小组办公室对《中国文化常识》、《中国历史常识》和《中国地理常识》进行改编。

《中国文化常识》、《中国历史常识》和《中国地理常识》改编本是一套面向世界各国汉语学习者的普及型、口语化的文化辅助读物，适用于海外对中国文化和汉语感兴趣的各类人员。在中华人民共和国国务院侨务办公室编写的中英文对照版基础上，此次改编增加了中文与德、法、日、韩、俄、泰、西班牙、阿拉伯语的对照版本。

中国国家汉语国际推广领导小组办公室委托高等教育出版社对《中国文化常识》、《中国历史常识》和《中国地理常识》进行改编，高等教育出版社对原书的部分内容进行了增删，修订了部分数据，重新遴选和修改了插图，并翻译出版英、德、泰语版本；外语教学与研究出版社翻译出版法、日、韩语版本；华语教学出版社翻译出版俄、西班牙、阿拉伯语版本。此次改编力求在原书强调科学性、思想性和实用性的基础上做进一步创新。希望本系列读物成为您了解中国的窗口，成为您通向汉语世界的桥梁。

此次改编得到了海内外诸多专家、学者和教师的关心与支持，他们提出了许多中肯的建议，在此向他们表示诚挚的谢意。

由于时间所限，书中不免会有疏漏和不当之处，希望使用者和专家学者不吝赐正，以供今后修订时改正。

中国国家汉语国际推广领导小组办公室

2006 年 11 月

Preface

Common Knowledge About Chinese Culture, *Common Knowledge About Chinese History* and *Common Knowledge About Chinese Geography* are a series of readers initiated by the Overseas Chinese Affairs Office of the State Council of the People's Republic of China. The readers were jointly developed by Beijing Chinese Language College, Nanjing Normal University and Anhui Normal University. Serving as teaching aids for learners of Chinese, these readers make the general knowledge of Chinese culture, history and geography accessible to the young generation of overseas Chinese by means of either classroom delivery or self-study. These books are also for parents to help their children with the study. The previous versions of these readers were well received.

In recent years, with the rapid economic and social development in China and the rising of her international status, the world witnesses a phenomenal increase in learners of the Chinese language outside China, especially from non-Chinese ethnic groups. To meet the demand from overseas Chinese learners to better their knowledge about Chinese culture, and to foster cultural exchanges between China and the world, a revision of the above-mentioned readers has been decided by the Overseas Chinese Affairs Office of the State Council of the People's Republic of China. They assigned the Office of Chinese Language Council International to work out the new edition of *Common Knowledge About Chinese Culture*, *Common Knowledge About Chinese History* and *Common Knowledge About Chinese Geography*.

The revised version of *Common Knowledge About Chinese Culture*, *Common Knowledge About Chinese History* and *Common Knowledge About Chinese Geography* is intended to be a popular edition of learning aid for Chinese culture in a conversational style. These readers make Chinese culture, history and geography more accessible to all people. Based on the original Chinese-English version edited by the Overseas Chinese Affairs Office of the State Council of the People's Republic of China, the newly-revised version has kept its bilingual format, only broadening the foreign language coverage to German, French, Japanese, Korean, Russian, Thai, Spanish and Arabic.

The Office of Chinese Language Council International delegates the revision of *Common Knowledge About Chinese Culture*, *Common Knowledge About Chinese History* and *Common Knowledge About Chinese Geography* to Higher Education Press, who adds and subtracts parts of the original Chinese version with amendments to some data and illustrations. The bilingual versions of Chinese-English, Chinese-German and Chinese-Thai are developed by Higher Education Press. The versions of Chinese-French, Chinese-Japanese and Chinese-Korean are developed by Foreign Language Teaching and Research Press. The Chinese-Russian, Chinese-Spanish and Chinese-Arabic versions are done by Sinolingua. All revisions are meant to be innovative while maintaining the original focus of being accurate, instructive and practical. It is our sincere hope that this series of readers become windows for you to know more about China, and bridges leading you to the world of Chinese.

We would especially like to express our sincere appreciation to many experts, scholars and Chinese teachers both at home and abroad for their pertinent suggestions.

Developed under a tight schedule, the new editions might be blotted with oversights and inappropriateness. We sincerely welcome readers, especially those better versed in the relevant fields to contribute ideas for the correction and future revision of these books.

The Office of Chinese Language Council International
November, 2006

目录
Contents

中国古代史
Period before the Opium War of 1840

中国历史的开篇 —— 先秦
The Dawn of Chinese History — The Pre-Qin Period

封建大一统时期 —— 秦、汉
The Period of Great Feudal Unity — The Qin and Han Dynasties

封建国家的分裂和民族大融合时期 —— 三国、两晋、南北朝
The Division of China Once More and the Intermingling of Ethnic Groups — The Three Kingdoms, the Two Jin Dynasties and the Southern and Northern Dynasties

封建社会的繁荣时期 —— 隋、唐
The Heyday of Feudal Society — The Sui and Tang Dynasties

统一的多民族国家进一步发展和封建社会由盛而衰时期——明、清（鸦片战争以前）

The Period of Further Development of the Unitary Multi-ethnic Country and the Decline of Feudal Society — The Ming and Qing Dynasties (Before the Opium War of 1840)

中国近代史 Modern Period

现代中国
Contemporary Period

附录 Appendix

Beijing 2008

中国古代史

PERIOD BEFORE THE OPIUM WAR OF 1840

中国历史的开篇——先秦

The Dawn of Chinese History — The Pre-Qin Period

概述

Introduction

“先秦”指的是中国历史上秦始皇统一中国以前的漫长的历史时期。

大约在170万年以前，中国人的祖先就生活在云南的元谋县境内，我们把这作为原始社会的开端。约公元前2070年，中国第一个王朝夏朝建立，其统治时间长达400多年。

第二个王朝是商朝，也叫殷（Yīn）朝（因为商朝初年，多次迁都，最后迁到殷——今河南安阳，并在那里统治了300多年）。商朝是当时世界上的一个大国，统治时间长达500多年，留下了甲骨文、青铜器等许多极其珍贵的史料和文物。

第三个统一的王朝是西周，都城在今天的西安。后来西周的都城被少数民族攻占，周王室被迫迁都到今天的洛阳，历史上叫做东周，西周与东周的时间共约800年。东周分为春秋和战国两个时期。春秋时期，国家分裂成许多小国；到了战国时期，形成了7个力量强大的国家，这些国家通过改革进入了封建社会，并为后来秦国的统一打下了基础。

与世界历史对照，当古埃及、古巴比伦、古印度文明发展进步之时，中国正经历文明勃兴的夏、商、西周王朝。当欧洲希腊、罗马城邦国家繁荣之时，正是中国春秋战国思想文化昌盛的时代。东西方文明交相辉映，地中海地区和中国，逐渐形成世界两大文明的中心。

The Dawn of Chinese History —

The Pre-Qin Period

Introduction

The pre-Qin period refers to the long period before Emperor Qinshihuang's unification of ancient China.

About 1 700 000 years ago, the ancestors of the Chinese people lived in present-day Yuanmou County, Yunnan Province. This period is now generally considered the beginning of primitive society in China. About 2070 BC, the Xia Dynasty came into being. This was China's first dynasty and it lasted for more than 400 years.

Succeeding the Xia was the Shang Dynasty (also called the Yin Dynasty for changing its capital several times and finally in Yin, today's Anyang city, Henan Province). The Shang Dynasty was a great power in the world which lasted over 500 years. This dynasty bestowed to its posterity a great heritage of artifacts such as extremely precious inscriptions on bones, tortoise shells and bronze wares.

The third kingdom was the Western Zhou Dynasty, with Hao as its capital (today's Xi'an city, Shaanxi Province). Later as its capital fell into the hands of the minority invaders, the Western Zhou had to move its capital eastward to today's Luoyang city, Henan Province, hence called the Eastern Zhou Dynasty. From the Western Zhou to the Eastern Zhou Dynasties, they altogether existed about 800 years. The Eastern Zhou was later divided by historians into distinct periods: the Spring and Autumn Period (770—476 BC) and the Warring States Period (475—221 BC). During the Spring and Autumn Period, China was split into many small rival vassal states. By the time of the Warring States Period, these small states coalesced into seven powerful bigger states. By way of reforms, these seven states developed into the feudal society, which paved the way for the later unification of China under the Qin Dynasty.

When the ancient Egyptian, Babylonian and Indian civilizations were progressing, the ancient Chinese civilization in the Xia, Shang and Western Zhou dynasties was already in full bloom. When the Greek and Roman city states were in their heyday, the thought and culture of the Spring and Autumn and Warring States periods was flourishing in ancient China. With a broad view of the ancient world civilization, one may find that the two stars of civilization — one in the East, the other in the West — were shining at the same time. This gradually developed into two centers of world civilization.

中国境内最早的人类

The Earliest Human Beings in China

元谋人(距今约170万年，目前中国境内发现的最早的直立人)

Yuanmou Man (dated back to some 1 700 000 years ago, the earliest human beings ever found in China so far)

→

蓝田人(距今约100万～50万年，已经完全直立行走)

Lantian Man (dated back to about 1 000 000 and 500 000 years ago, was able to walk upright on 2 feet)

→

北京人(距今约70万～20万年，懂得用火和制作、使用石器)

Peking Man (dated back to 700 000 and 200 000 years ago, skilled at making fire, making and using stone tools)

↓

大荔人(距今约30万～20万年，是由猿人向古人过渡的典型)

Dali Man (dated back to about 200 000 and 300 000 years ago, representative of the transition from apes to ancient man)

←

山顶洞人(距今约18 000年，相貌已经和现代人没有明显区别，“假若给他们穿戴上现代人的服饰和我们站在一起，谁也不会用奇异的眼光多看他们一眼。”)

Upper Cave Man (dated back to about 18 000 years ago, resembled modern human beings in appearance)

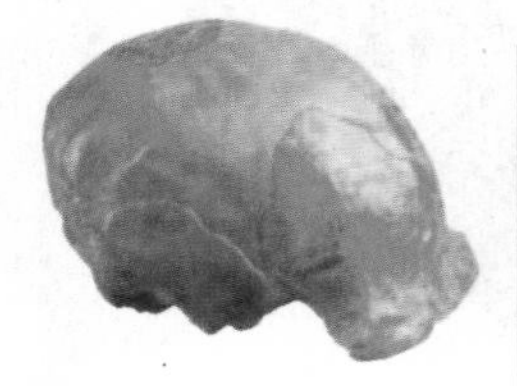

中国是世界文明古国，也是人类的发源地之一。中国到目前为止是世界上发现旧石器时代的人类化石和文化遗址最多的国家，其中重要的有元谋人、蓝田人、北京人、山顶洞人等。

1987年12月，发现北京人头盖骨的周口店北京猿人遗址被联合国教科文组织列入世界遗产名录。

The Earliest Human Beings
in China

China is not only a country with a long history of ancient civilization, but also one of the birthplaces of the human race throughout the world. China ranks first in the number of human fossils and cultural sites dating from the Paleolithic Period, among which Yuanmou Man, Lantian Man, Peking Man and Upper Cave Man are the most important.

In December 1987, the Peking Man Site at Zhoukoudian where Peking Man's crania were found was added to the World Cultural Heritage List by the UNESCO.

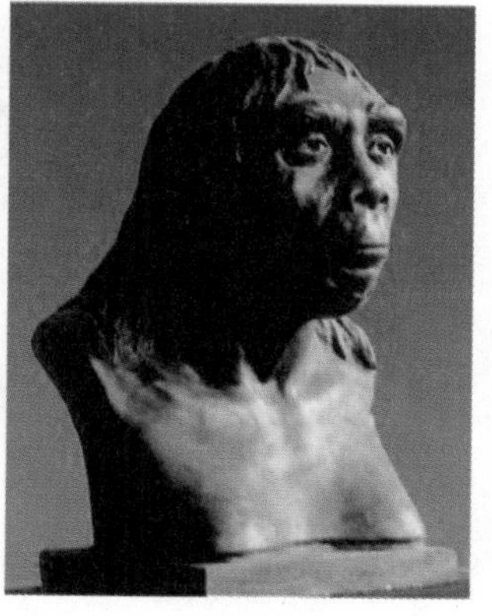

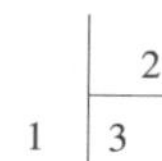

1. 北京人头盖骨和元谋人牙齿
   The skull of Peking Man and the teeth of Yuanmon Man
2. 山顶洞人头部复原图
   A replica of the head of Upper Cave Man
3. 北京人头部复原图
   A replica of the head of Peking Man

小资料 Data

旧石器时代
原始人用石块敲打出来的石器叫打制石器，使用这种石器的时代就叫做旧石器时代。旧石器时代经历了二三百万年，那时人们过着采集和渔猎的生活。

新石器时代
大约从八九千年前开始，原始人已经普遍使用磨制石器。使用磨制石器的时代叫新石器时代。磨制石器更为先进和好用，能够提高原始人的生产水平和生活水平。新石器时代已出现农业和牧业。

The Paleolithic Period
This period is so named in accordance with the stone vessels they used—primitive men used stones to make chipped stone vessels. The Paleolithic Period lasted for two to three million years. People then lived life by picking up wild fruits, hunting and fishing together.

The Neolithic Period
Starting from around 8 000 to 9 000 years ago, primitive people already used new kinds of stone artifacts—artifacts that were ground out rather than chipped, hence the period termed "Neolithic Period". The new stone artifacts were more sophisticated and handier, greatly improving the level of production and life alike. It was during the Neolithic Period that agriculture and animal husbandry appeared.

开天辟地的创世神话

The Great Myth of the Creation of Man in Ancient China

1 | 2
  | 3

1. 神农氏像
   A portrait of Shennongshi
2. 伏羲氏像
   A portrait of Fuxishi
3. 伏羲六十四卦方圆图
   Fuxi's diagram of 64 divinatory symbols

我们人类的祖先究竟是从哪里来的?

据说在很久很久以前，天和地是混混沌沌的一团气，像个大鸡蛋。有个叫盘古（Pángǔ）的人，用巨斧把天地劈开，他站在天地中间，手托着天，脚踩着地，他不断地长高，把天托得越来越高，把地踩得越来越低。这样过了一万八千年，天和地相隔九万里，盘古也成了顶天立地的巨人。盘古死后，他的眼睛变成了太阳和月亮，四肢变成了山脉，血液变成了江河湖海，筋脉变成了道路，肌肉变成了田土，头发和胡须变成了天上的星星，皮肤和汗毛变成了花草树木，牙齿和骨头变成闪光的金属、坚硬的石头和圆亮的珍珠玉石，他流出的汗水变成了雨露。特别是他身上的许多小虫子，变成了人类。这就是盘古开天地的传说，是中国人世代流传下来的创世神话。

还有很多神话传说是古人根据原始人的生活想像出来的。比如教人在树上造屋的有巢氏（Yǒucháoshì），钻木取火的燧人氏（Suìrénshì），教会人们打猎、发明了“八卦”的伏羲氏（Fúxīshì），种植五谷、品尝百草寻找药材的神农氏等等。他们是远古人战胜自然、改造自然的象征，是勤劳智慧的古代中国人的代表。

The Great Myth of the Creation of Man in Ancient China

Where were the Chinese ancestors from? Legend has it that a long long time ago, Heaven and Earth were a chaotic gathering of air masses, just like an egg. A man named Pangu axed the Heaven off from the Earth with a huge axe. Standing right in between the Heaven and the Earth, hands holding out the sky, feet stamping on the ground, he grew taller and taller, hence the sky became higher and higher while the ground became lower and lower. This lasted for 18 000 years. As a result, the Heaven and the Earth were finally driven away from each other to a vast distance of 90 000 li and Pangu became a giant with his head holding up the heaven and his feet stamping on the ground. After his death, his eyes became the Sun and the Moon, his four limbs, the mountains, blood, rivers, lakes and seas, his sinews, the field, his arteries, the roads and ways, his hairs and moustaches, the stars in the sky, his skin and body hairs, flowers, grass and woods, his teeth and bones, the shining metals, hard stones, glittering pearls and precious stones, his sweats, the dews. What is miraculous is that many of the small insects on his body became human beings. This is the legend of Pangu creating the new Heaven and the Earth. This myth has been passed on generation after generation until our time in China.

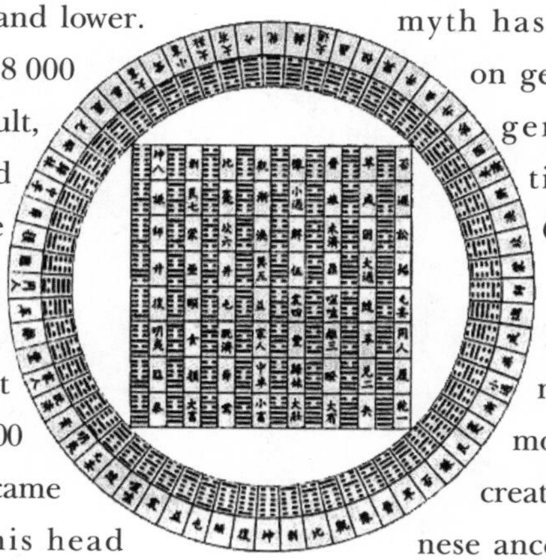

Besides Pangu's myth, many more myths were created by our Chinese ancestors by their imagination. For instance, the legend of Youchaoshi who taught people how to make houses on the branches of trees; Suirenshi who taught people how to make fire with wood out of chiseling; Fuxishi who taught people to hunt and invented Eight Trigrams (eight combinations of three whole or broken lines formerly used in divination); Shennongshi who grew foods and looked for medicine herbs by tasting more than a hundred kinds of herbs and grasses. All of them are the embodiment of the wisdom of our ancient conscientious Chinese people, the epitome of the invincible Chinese people who transformed and conquered nature.

华夏之祖

Ancestors of the Chinese Nation

黄帝和禹传说时期地域示意图
Sketch Map of the Legendary Period of Huangdi and Yu the Great

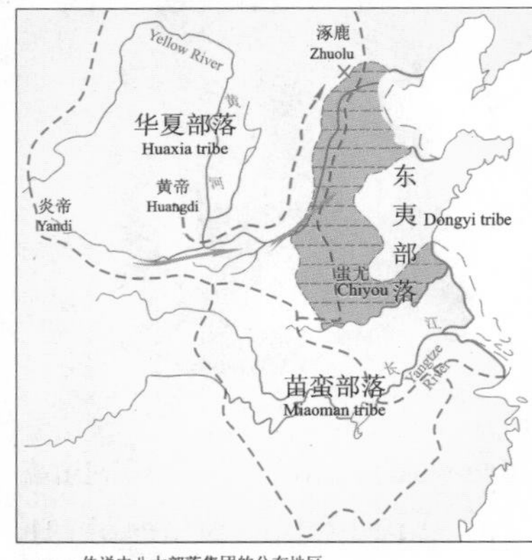

- - - 传说中八大部落集团的分布地区 Distribution area of the eight legendary tribal groups
- - - 黄帝氏族东移路线 Eastward migration route of Huangdi's tribe
炎帝氏族部分东移路线 Eastward migration route of part of Yandi's tribe
传说中洪水泛滥的地区 Legendary flooded area
× 主要战场 Main battle site

1 2 3

1. 湖南株洲炎帝陵
   Yandi Mausoleum, Zhuzhou, Hunan Province
2. 贵州镇远蚩尤陵
   Chiyou Mausoleum, Zhenyuan, Guizhou Province
3. 指南车
   A south-pointing chariot

中国人常说自己是“炎黄子孙”，这个说法跟传说中的人物黄帝和炎帝有关。大约4 000多年以前，中国黄河流域一带生活着许多氏族和部落，黄帝、炎帝就是两个最有名的部落的首领。

当时在东方还有一个叫九黎的势力强大的部落，九黎部落的首领叫蚩尤（Chīyóu），十分强悍。九黎族人会制造各式各样的兵器，打起仗来非常勇猛，常常进攻别的部落。

传说蚩尤部落为了扩大自己的地盘，同炎帝部落发生了战争。炎帝部落被杀得一败涂地，向黄帝求援。黄帝早想除掉蚩尤，就与炎帝联合起来，在涿鹿（Zhuōlù，今河北省境内）的广阔原野上与蚩尤展开了大决战。激战之中，忽然天昏地暗，大雾弥漫，连对面的人也看不见。黄帝使用指南车，帮助士兵识别方向，追击蚩尤，结果蚩尤被捉住杀死。

涿鹿之战后，黄帝和炎帝两个部落为了争夺对其他各部落的领导地位，又发生了冲突，炎帝部落大败，从此黄帝成了中原地区部落联盟的首领。中原地区各部落在语言、习惯、生产、生活等各方面的交流逐渐加强，经过长期的融合和发展，形成了华夏族的主体。

华夏族是汉族的前身，是中华民族的主要组成部分。华夏族把黄帝、炎帝看做自己的祖先，称自己为“炎黄子孙”。直到今天，汉族人和许多兄弟民族还习惯这么说。

Ancestors of the Chinese Nation

Chinese people often refer to themselves as the descendants of Yandi and Huangdi. This refers to the legendary heroes Yandi and Huangdi. Over 4 000 years ago, there lived many clans and tribes in the Yellow River Valley. Among them were the two most prominent tribes led by Huangdi and Yandi.

To the east of the Yellow River valley was the territory of the Jiuli tribe, with Chiyou as its chieftain. It is said that the Jiuli people had all kinds of weapons, and were a warlike group.

Legend has it that the Jiuli attacked Yandi's tribe for larger territory. The latter was defeated, and turned to Huangdi for help. Huangdi allied himself with Yandi, and defeated Chiyou at a place called Zhuolu (in today's Hebei Province). During the battle, a dense mist descended, and all was in confusion. However, on his chariot, Huangdi had an instrument which constantly pointed south. In this way, he rallied the allied forces. Finally, Chiyou was captured and killed.

After the Battle of Zhuolu, conflicts arose between the tribes of Huangdi and Yandi for control of all the tribes. At last, Huangdi prevailed, and ruled over all the tribes of the Central Plains. Eventually, they merged their languages, customs, and production and living habits, to form the Huaxia people.

The Huaxia people were the predecessors of the Han people, and the principal part of the Chinese nation. The Huaxia people regarded Huangdi and Yandi as their ancestors, and called themselves the descendants of Yandi and Huangdi.

小资料 Data

三皇五帝

中国古代传说中远古时期的帝王，三皇通常是指燧人、伏羲、神农；五帝比三皇略晚，通常是指黄帝、颛顼（Zhuānxū）、帝喾（Dìkù）、尧（Yáo）和舜（Shùn）。

The "Three Kings & Five Emperors"

The "three kings" referred to Suiren, Fuxi and Shennong, legendary kings in ancient China. The "five emperors" were legendary emperors of ancient China, later than the "three kings", namely, Huangdi, Zhuanxu, Diku, Yao, and Shun.

大禹治水

Yu the Great Harnesses the Flood

传说黄帝以后，先后出了三个著名的部落联盟首领，名叫尧、舜和禹。传说尧的时候，黄河发大水，洪水冲毁了村庄和房屋，人们只能住到树上和山顶上。洪水给人民带来了极大的灾害。那时，炎黄部落联盟的首领尧任用鲧（Gǔn）治理洪水，鲧采用筑堤堵水的办法治水，遭到了失败。尧之后，担任部落联盟首领的舜杀死了鲧，然后命令鲧的儿子禹继续治水。禹吸取了鲧的教训，改用疏导的方法治水，让洪水顺河道流向大海。禹辛勤地工作，传说他在外面治水13年，三次经过家门都没有抽时间进去看看。最后，禹终于制服了水患。人们颂扬禹治水的功绩，尊称他是大禹。

由于禹治水成功，深受人民的爱戴，舜推举禹为自己的继承人，得到各部落首领的响应。舜死后，禹便成为部落联盟的首领。那时洪水刚刚平息，草木茂盛，野兽危害人民，禹派人教百姓开辟耕地；还派人教导人民耕种田地，收获粮食。人民的生活渐渐安定下来了。禹又对苗族发动战争，阻止他们进入黄河流域，巩固了华夏族在中原地区的地位。禹之后，部落联盟首领的权力大大加强了。

约公元前2070年，禹建立夏朝，是中国历史上第一个王朝。后来禹死了，他的儿子启继承了禹的位置，引起有扈氏（Yǒuhùshì）部落的反抗。启打败了有扈氏以后，他的地位得到了各部落的承认。从此世袭制代替了禅让（shànràng）制。

夏朝从禹到桀（Jié），一共有17个国君，延续了471年。夏朝人制订的适合农业生产需要的历法使用了很长时间。夏人还模仿动物的形象铸造铜鼎（dǐng），使中国历史从石器时代进入到了铜器时代。夏朝最后一个王叫桀，他是个暴君，人民都非常痛恨他。那时黄河下游的商国强大起来，起兵灭夏，大约在公元前1600年建立了商朝。

Yu the Great

Harnesses the Flood

It is said that after Emperor Huangdi there appeared three famous tribal leaders: Yao, Shun and Yu. According to legend, the Yellow River flooded during the reign of Emperor Yao, and the people were forced to abandon their villages, and went to live on trees or on mountaintops. The flood brought great misery to the people. Emperor Yao, the chieftain of the Yan-Huang tribal alliance, appointed Gun to harness the flood. Gun built dikes to keep back the water, but failed. Shun, who succeeded Yao, killed Gun, and appointed Gun's son Yu to continue with the flood-harnessing work. Yu adopted the dredging method to lead the flood waters to flow along river courses into the sea. Yu worked very hard. It was said that during the 13 years he spent on taming the floods, he passed his home three times, but did not enter until his task was completed. As a result of his successful efforts, the people bestowed on him the title Yu the Great and Shun chose Yu as his successor, with the approval of the tribal chieftains.

Following the taming of the floods, vegetation and wild beasts grew rampant, threatening the survival of the people. Yu taught his subjects the art of agriculture, and thus how to dominate the land and feed themselves in a regular and organized way. He also repelled invasions by the Miao tribe, and consolidated the Huaxia people's supremacy in the Central Plains.

Around 2070 BC, Yu established the Xia Dynasty, the first dynasty in Chinese history. After Yu's death, his son Qi succeeded to the throne. Crushing an attempt to overthrow him by the Youhu clan, Qi established the system of hereditary rulers instead of abdicating the throne to another person.

The Xia Dynasty lasted 471 years with 17 empires from Yu to Jie. The calendar of Xia fit well for the agricultural production, so it was used for a long time. They also cast bronze cooking vessels (ding) by imitating the image of animals. Thus China shifted from the Stone Age to the Bronze Age. Its last king, Jie, vilified in the ancient records as a tyrant, was overthrown by the leader of the Shang kingdom along the lower reaches of the Yellow River in about 1600 BC.

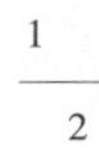

1. 大禹像
   A statue of Yu the Great
2. 浙江绍兴大禹陵
   Yu the Great Mausoleum, Shaoxing, Zhejiang Province

小资料 Data

禅让制

古代部落联盟推选领袖的制度。相传尧在位时，各个部落推选声望很高、能力很强的舜为继承人，尧对舜进行考核以后，认为舜确实是一个能干的人，就把首领的位子让给了他。

Abdicating and Handing over of the Throne

In ancient China, power was passed on to the next generation by means of abdication by the ruler of the alliance of tribes. According to legend, when Yao was in power, Shun, chosen by other tribal chieftains, and examined by Yao, was acknowledged as an able man. So Yao abdicated and handed over the throne to Shun.

武王伐纣

King Wu Attacks King Zhou

商是黄河中下游的一个古老部落。商的祖先叫契（Xiè），传说他的妈妈吞吃了玄鸟的蛋之后生下了契。商部落早期经常迁徙（qiānxǐ），自从盘庚（Pángēng）把国都搬迁到殷（今河南安阳西北）之后，商朝出现复兴的局面。在武丁做国君的五十几年间，商朝进入了最强盛的时期。

商朝的最后一个王叫纣（Zhòu），只知道自己享乐，根本不管人民的死活，是个残暴的君主。商纣王养着各地送来的珍贵的鸟兽；修建鹿台，用来存放无数的珍宝财物；他把酒倒进池中，把肉挂在树上。他还是个残暴的君主，用各种残酷的刑罚对付反对他的人。他发明一种刑罚叫

武王伐纣路线图
Sketch Map of King Wu's Route of the Campaign against King Zhou

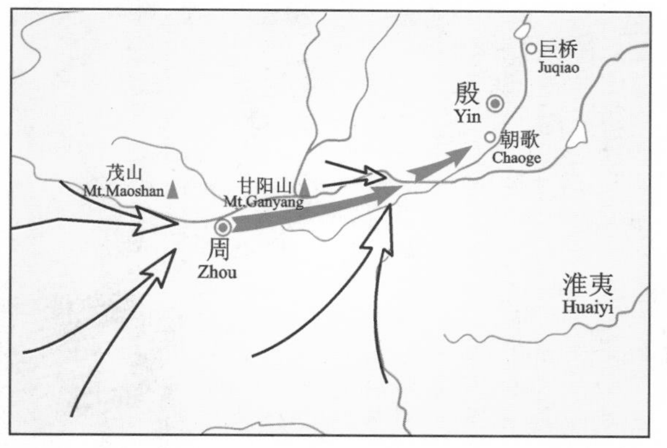

“炮烙（páoluō）之刑”，就是把涂满膏脂的铜柱放在燃烧的炭火上，强迫犯人在上面行走，犯人站不住，就掉在炭火中活活烧死。

商纣王的残暴加速了商朝的灭亡。这时，渭水流域的周部落一天天地强大起来了。周原来是商的属国。周文王一心要治理好自己的国家，重视农业生产，待人宽厚，重用人才。在姜太公的辅佐下，周文王和周武王整顿政治和军事，对内发展生产，使人民安居乐业；对外征服各部族，不断扩大疆土。

公元前11世纪中期，周武王联合西方和南方的部落，进攻商纣王。双方在牧野（今河南省境内）展开大战。商朝的军队中大部分是奴隶，他们平时恨透了纣王，不但不抵抗，还纷纷起义，引导周军攻入商朝首都。商纣王自焚而死，商朝终于灭亡。周武王得到了很多部落和小国家的拥护，于公元前1046年建立了周朝，定都镐京（Hàojīng，今陕西西安西南），历史上称为西周。

1 | 2

1. 陕西岐山周公庙
Duke Zhou's Temple, Qishan, Shaanxi Province
2. 商纣王像
A portrait of King Zhou

King Wu
Attacks King Zhou

The Shang was an ancient tribe along the lower reaches of the Yellow River. It is believed that the Shang's ancestry can be traced back to Qi, whose mother gave birth to him after swallowing an egg of a swallow. The Shang's tribe in its early period often moved about: its capital had been changed five times during its reign of 300 years. After Emperor Pangeng chose Yin (in the northwest part of today's Anyang, Henan Province) as its capital, the Shang Dynasty experienced a period of prosperity. During Wuding's 50 years rule, the Shang Dynasty reached its heyday.

The last monarch of the Shang Dynasty, King Zhou, is said to have been a cruel despot who neglected state affairs and abandoned himself to sensuous pleasures. Rare birds and animals dedicated to him were raised, flat platforms were built for storing numerous amount of money and valuables, wine was pored into the pool and meat was hung up on the trees. As an extremely cruel king, he invented various kinds of instruments of torture to punish his opponents. "The punishment of Pao Luo" (torture with hot pillar) was one of them. The bronze pillar covered with ointment was heated on the burning fire of charcoal. His prisoners were forced to walk on the pillar. They fell down and burned to death.

King Zhou's tyranny and atrocities accelerated the speed and downfall of the Shang Dynasty. A vassal kingdom of the Shang Dynasty called Zhou was growing powerful in the Weishui River Valley. The king of Zhou, named Wen, was an able and enlightened administrator who valued agriculture and made good use of talented people. Assisted by his able prime minister Jiang Taigong, King Wen and his son King Wu made his realm rich and powerful.

In the mid-11th century BC, the new ruler, King Wu, led an alliance of the western and southern tribes, toppled the tottering Shang Dynasty by defeating King Zhou at the Battle of Muye (in today's Henan Province). The victory was aided by a revolt in the Shang army, which consisted mostly of conscripted slaves. Seething of hatred, they led the Zhou army into the capital instead of fighting back. King Zhou burnt himself to death, and his throne was taken by King Wu. Supported by small states and tribes, King Wu founded the Zhou Dynasty in 1046 BC, and located his capital in Hao (in southwest of today's Xi'an, Shaanxi Province). This era is known as that of the Western Zhou Dynasty.

1 | 2

1. 姜太公像
   A portrait of Jiang Taigong
2. 河南洛阳周公庙
   Duke Zhou's Temple, Luoyang, Henan Province

小资料 Data

姜太公钓鱼，愿者上钩

姜太公，姜姓，吕氏，名尚，字子牙，又称太公望。传说他曾经在渭水边钓鱼，希望看到从这里经过的周文王。他的鱼钩是直的，上面没有鱼饵，而且离水面很高。他一边钓鱼，一边说："快上钩呀，愿意的就快上钩。"有一天周文王发现了他，于是就高兴地邀请他帮助自己治理国家。以后人们就用"姜太公钓鱼，愿者上钩"来比喻做一件事情是心甘情愿的。

Jiang Taigong Has His Own Way of Fishing

Jiang Taigong was surnamed Jiang and his given name was Shang. He styled himself Ziya but was also called "Taigong Wang". According to the legend, he used to sit by the Weishui River at a spot where King Wen often passed by, holding a fishing rod high above the water. His fishhook was straight with no bait on it. He would say "Those who are willing, please rise to the hook." One day King Wen passed by and invited him to help administer the country. Today the phrase "Jiang Taigong has his own way of fishing" has got a new meaning: someone does something of his own accord.

周公东征

Duke Zhou's Conquest of the East

1. 司母戊鼎
The Simuwu Square Ding cauldron
2. 四羊方尊
A zun wine vessel with the heads of four goats
3. 毛公鼎
Maogong Ding (bronze tripod of Duke Mao)

武王伐纣虽然推翻了商王朝的统治，但是商的残余势力还相当顽强。周武王和周公制定了以殷治殷的政策，封商纣王的儿子武庚（Wǔgēng）为殷侯，继续统治原来殷都附近的地区。为了便于对武庚的控制和监视，周武王派自己的弟弟管叔、蔡叔、霍叔为“三监”，率领周人居住在殷都以及附近地区，以便监视武庚及商朝的遗民。

周灭商两年后，武王病逝，临终时，武王把自己的儿子诵和军国大事托付给弟弟周公（名姬旦，Jīdàn）。太子诵（Sòng）即位为成王。由于成王只有13岁，不能处理朝政，周公就代替成王行使权利，处理国家大事。管叔、蔡叔对此非常不满，散布流言，说周公想要窃取王位。商的残余势力趁机与管、蔡串通起来，发动了叛乱，叛乱势力遍及今河南、河北、山东、安徽等地，使新生的周王朝处于危机之中。

面对不利形势，周公一方面向召公等人恳切解释，使周成王和王公大臣消除了对他的怀疑，使王室内部重新团结起来。另一方面，他联络和调集各地诸侯，亲自率领军队东征叛军。经过3年的苦战，诛灭了以武庚为首的商朝贵族叛乱势力，杀了武庚和管叔，流放了蔡叔，平定了参与反叛的东方小国。

Duke Zhou's Conquest of the East

Although the Shang Dynasty was overthrown by King Wu, the remaining forces of King Zhou were determined to be loyal to the old king. King Wu and Duke Zhou formulated a policy that made good use of the Yin to conquer itself. They put Wugeng, the son of King Zhou, as the Duke of Yin. And they ordered him to continue to rule the vicinity of the original Yin. In order to control Wugeng and place the people from the former Shang Dynasty under surveillance, King Wu sent his brothers Guan, Tsai and Huo as "three supervisors" to Yin. They led some Zhou people to live in the surrounding areas of Yin.

After two years, King Wu died of illness. Before his death, King Wu entrusted his son (named Song) and the state to his brother, Duke Zhou (named Jidan). His son came to the throne as King Cheng. As King Cheng was too young as a 13-year-old boy to handle the affairs of state, Duke Zhou exercised authority for him. This aroused the grievance of Guan and Tsai. They spread rumors that Duke Zhou intended to usurp the throne. The remnant forces of King Zhou, colluding with Guan and Tsai, launched a rebellion. Their forces extended far over to today's Hebei, Henan, Shandong and Anhui provinces. The new-born Zhou Dynasty was in a crisis.

Facing this unfavorable situation, Duke Zhou sincerely explained the truth to Duke Zhao and the other dukes as well, to get rid of their suspicion so as to keep the internal unity of the royal family. On the other hand, he assembled dukes from all the states, and led the army himself to the east to conquer the rebels. After three years, Wugeng, Guan and their followers were killed, Tsai was banished. Some small states involved in the rebellion were suppressed.

小资料 Data

灿烂的青铜文明

商朝和西周时期，青铜器制造业很发达，商朝后期制造的司母戊鼎，高1.33米，长1.1米，宽0.78米，重875千克，是现今世界上发现的最大的青铜器。另一件四羊方尊，造型雄奇，工艺高超，是商朝青铜器中的精品。

Brilliant Bronze Civilization

The manufacture of bronze wares reached its zenith during the Shang Dynasty and the Western Zhou Dynasty. The Simuwu square *ding* cauldron, made in the late Shang Dynasty, with 1.33 meters high, 1.1 meters long, 0.78 meters wide and 875 kilograms in weight, is the biggest item of bronze ware existing in the world. A *zun* wine vessel with the heads of four goats carved on it, also dating from the Shang Dynasty was grandly shaped with ingenious craftsmanship, and it is one of the finest examples of bronze ware known.

春秋五霸

The Five Hegemons of the Spring and Autumn Period

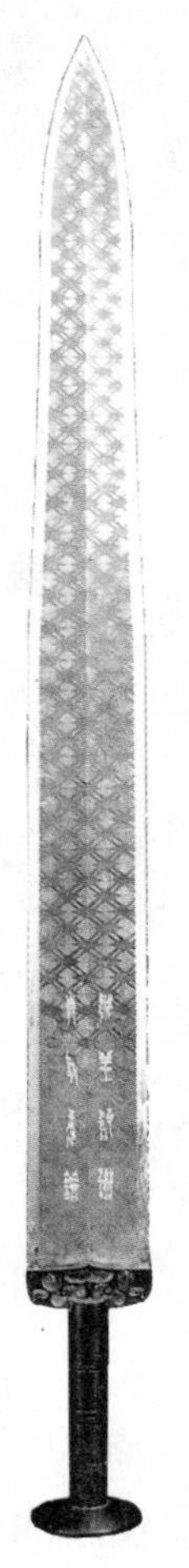

春秋初年诸侯国有100多个。各诸侯国为了争夺土地和人口，发生混战。力量强大的诸侯国一面不断吞并弱小的国家，一面争夺霸权。春秋时期先后起来争当霸主的有齐桓（huán）公、宋襄（xiāng）公、晋文公、秦穆（mù）公、楚庄王，历史上称为“春秋五霸”。还有一种说法，“春秋五霸”指齐桓公、晋文公、楚庄王、吴王阖闾（Hélǘ）、越王勾践（Gōujiàn）。

齐国是春秋时期东方一个富裕的国家。齐桓公在大政治家管仲的辅佐下，在政治上和经济上进行了一系列改革，发展生产，使齐国强大起来。齐桓公率兵击退山戎（Shānróng）等少数民族的进攻，又率领齐、鲁、宋等八国的军队讨伐中原的楚国，阻止了楚军的北进，威信大增。公元前651年，齐桓公召集各诸侯国订立盟约，周天子也派人参加，齐国称霸中原的时代开始了。

齐桓公之后，宋襄公一心想接替齐桓公做霸主，但没有成功。晋文公做了国君以后很快使晋国成为北方一大强国。当时南方的楚国也想称霸。公元前632年，晋国和楚国进行了一场大战，楚军大败，晋国从此成为中原的一大霸主。晋楚之间的争霸持续了100多年，后来楚庄王打败晋军，做了中原的霸主。秦穆公本来也打算向东发展，到中原去做霸主，没能成功，转而向西扩大地盘，将西戎12国并入秦土，得以称霸西方。

吴国和越国都是长江下游的国家。这两个国家都不大，但也加入了争霸战争。晋楚争霸时，吴国在晋国的支持下曾经攻破楚国的都城。后来吴越两国进行了多次战争，各有胜负。公元前494年，吴王夫差大败越国，越国成为吴国的属国。越王勾践经过10年的艰苦准备，终于灭掉了吴国。后来勾践又率军北上，成为春秋时期最后一个霸主。

这一时期在欧洲的希腊普遍出现了城邦国家，与春秋时代的诸侯国具有本质不同的是，在城邦的公民政治获得了较为充分的发展，王权逐渐衰落，绝大多数城邦甚至废弃君主而实行共和，并且限制贵族的权力，有些城邦甚至推翻了贵族统治，建立了古代公民权利最发达的民主政治。

1

1. 越王勾践剑
The sword of Goujian, ruler of the State of Yue

小资料 Data

越王勾践卧薪尝胆

公元前494年，吴王夫差打败了越国，越王勾践只得向吴屈辱求和，同意到吴国做吴王的奴仆。两年后勾践被释放回国，他立志报仇雪耻，他撤掉席子睡在硬硬的柴草上，每次吃饭之前都要先尝一尝苦胆，还要问自己"你忘了会稽（Kuàijī）的耻辱吗？"他时刻不忘国家破亡的痛苦，带领越国人发愤图强，终于灭掉了吴国，完成了霸业。后来人们经常用"卧薪尝胆"一语，来表达刻苦自励、奋发向上的决心。

King Goujian of Yue Underwent Self-imposed Hardships to Wipe out a National Humiliation

In 494 BC, defeated by the King of Wu, Goujian was forced to make a humiliating surrender to the King of Wu by relegating himself to become a servant. After two years' extreme servility, Goujian was finally released to his homeland. Determined to avenge himself, he removed the mat of his bed and rest on the rough brushwood. Each time before eating his meal he must have a taste of the gall bladder, and remind himself of his past by keeping asking the question "Would you ever forget the shame of Kuaiji?" He never forgot the suffering of the state for a moment. He led the Yue people to work hard so as to make their state stronger. Finally he overthrew the Wu, and accomplished his ambition to revenge. Later, people often use the phrase "sleep on brushwood and taste gall" (undergo self-imposed hardships) to express one's determination to make great progress in the future in order to get all his sufferings rewarded.

The Five Hegemons

of the Spring and Autumn Period

春秋列国形势图

Sketch Map of the Main Powers during the Spring and Autumn Period

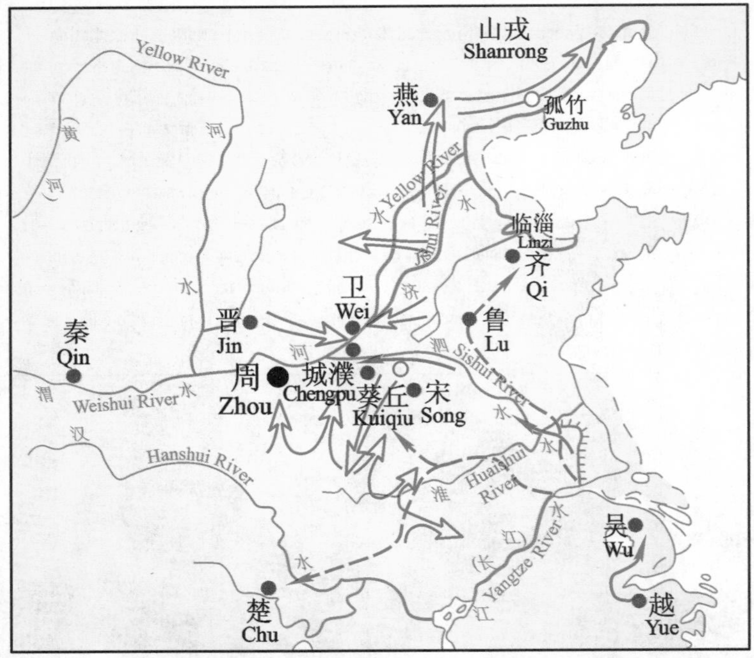

● 周王城 Capital of the Zhou Dynasty

● 各国都城 Capital of the vassal states

- - -> 吴国进军路线 Wu's route of advance

——> 越国进军路线 Yue's route of advance

⇒ 齐、楚扩张路线 Qi and Chu's route of expansion

In the early Spring and Autumn Period (770—476 BC) the Zhou Kingdom was divided into over 100 vassal states, all squabbling over land and population. Strong states annexed weak ones and contended for hegemony over all the others. During this period, Duke Huan of Qi, Duke Xiang of Song, Duke Wen of Jin, Duke Mu of Qin and King Zhuang of Chu became the hegemons in succession, and were called the Five Powers of the Spring and Autumn Period. Some historians rank the five powers as Duke Huan of Qi, Duke Wen of Jin, King Zhuang of Chu, King Helu of Wu and King Goujian of Yue.

Qi was a rich state in the eastern part of China. With the aid of the able statesman Guan Zhong, Duke Huan of Qi carried out a series of political and economic reforms, which helped the state to flourish and greatly enhanced its military power. Duke Huan defeated ethnic tribes such as Shanrong, and led the armies of Qi, Lu and Song to suppress the State of Chu in the Central Plains. All of this gave Duke Huan high prestige. In 651 BC, Duke Huan convened a meeting of the rulers of all the states, at which envoys from the Son of Heaven of Zhou (the Son of Heaven was the titular sovereign, having little real power) were present. A treaty of alliance was concluded, and the period of Qi hegemony commenced.

Following Duke Huan of Qi, Duke Xiang of Song tried to take his place but failed in the end. Duke Wen of Jin made his state a big power in the north and the State of Chu also had ambitions to be a hegemon. In 632 BC, the State of Jin defeated the State of Chu to rule the rest in the Central Plains. However, the fight for hegemony went on between the two states for 100 years, until King Zhuang of Chu smashed the Jin army and made himself the hegemon. In the meantime, Duke Mu of Qin was expanding his territory to the west after the failure of expansion to the east, and made himself a hegemon.

The States of Wu and Yue were both located in the lower reaches of the Yangtze River. They were not large, but they joined the war for hegemony. When the states of Chu and Jin made war for hegemony, the State of Wu captured the capital of the State of Chu with the support of Jin. Later, the two countries conducted several wars, each having its own victories. In 494 BC, the King of Wu defeated the King of Yue, the State of Yue came under the state of Wu's dominion. After 10 years of painstaking preparation, King Goujian of Yue finally destroyed the State of Wu. Later, he led his soldiers to the north and he became the last hegemon of the Spring and Autumn Period.

During this period in Greece, city-states appeared. The essential difference between the city-states and the states in the Spring and Autumn Period is that politics were more fully development in the former one, with a gradual decline of monarchical power. The overwhelming majority of city-states abandoned the monarchy and implemented direct rule by the people, and limited the power of aristocracy. Some city-states even overthrew aristocratic rule and founded the most developed democracy of the ancient world.

1 | 2

1. 管仲像
A portrait of Guan Zhong
2. 齐国的殉马坑（今山东省境内，殉马约有600匹，是齐国国力强大的一个证明）
Horses sacrificed upon the burial of a noble of the State of Qi in modern Shandong Province (A total of 600 immolated steeds indicate the wealth and power of Qi.)

战国七雄

The Seven Powers of the Warring States Period

春秋时期的兼并战争使诸侯国的数量大大减少。到战国时期，七个实力最强的诸侯国是齐、楚、燕（Yān）、韩、赵、魏、秦，被称作“战国七雄”。

战国初期，韩、赵、魏三家结成联盟，打败了齐、秦、楚等大国，成为较强盛的国家。后来这个联盟破裂，齐国、秦国却逐渐兴盛起来。

战国中期，魏国军队攻打赵国，赵国向齐国求救。大军事家孙膑（Sūn Bìn）以魏国精锐在赵国，内部空虚，便带领齐国的军队攻打魏国的首都。魏国军队本已攻破赵国首都，听见自己的国家情况危急，便急忙从赵国撤军回去救援，刚走到半路，就中了齐国军队的埋伏，齐军打了个大胜仗。这就是中国历史上著名的战例——“围魏救赵”。

11年后魏国进攻韩国，齐国的军队在孙膑的指挥下围魏救韩。齐军假装后退。第一天撤出后营地留下的炉灶足够做10万人的饭；第二天留下的炉灶只够做5万人的饭；第三天留下的炉灶减少到仅够做3万人的饭。魏军从炉灶的数量变化推测，以为齐军大量逃亡，于是挑选了精锐的士兵，追赶齐军，一直追到险要的马陵（今河南省境内）地区，结果被埋伏在这里的齐军彻底打败。这就是著名的“马陵之战”。两次战役后齐国取代了魏国称霸中原。

战国形势图

Sketch Map of the Warring States

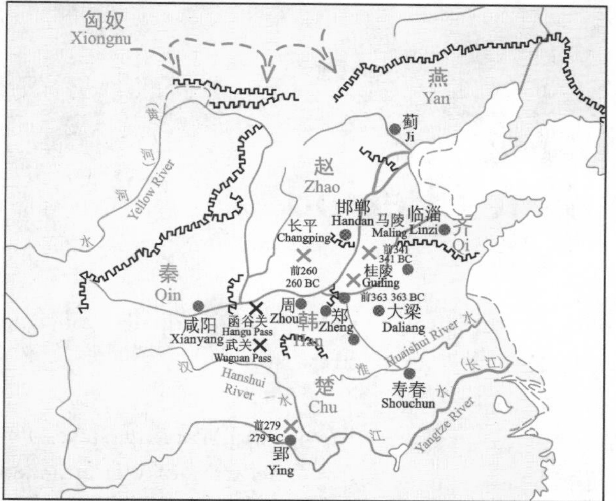

战国后期，秦国越来越强盛，其他六个国家都不能单独抵抗秦国，于是就想联合起来，共同抵抗秦国。秦国为了打败其余的六国，挑拨六国之间的关系，促使他们都和秦国亲近。各国为了自身的利益，一到关键时刻常常不能齐心合力，结果给了秦国机会。秦国先后征服了其他国家，并灭了周王室，统一了中国。

1 | 2
--- | 3

1、2. 战国时期青铜器

Bronze wares of the Warring States Period

3. 出土的战国兵器

Excavated weapons of the Warring States Period

小资料 Data

商鞅南门立木

公元前356年，秦孝公为了强兵富国，任用商鞅（Shāng Yāng）改革旧的制度，变法图强。

商鞅起草了一个改革的法令，但又怕老百姓不相信他，就叫人在都城的南门立了一根很高的木头，并说，谁能把木头搬到北门，就赏谁十金。很多人都以为这是开玩笑。商鞅知道老百姓不相信他，就把赏金提高到五十金。人们在木头旁议论纷纷，终于有一个人站出来，把木头扛到了北门，结果商鞅真的赏给那人五十金。这件事在秦国引起了轰动。商鞅说到做到，在老百姓中有了威信，于是商鞅就把新法令公布了出去。经过商鞅变法，秦国增强了国力，成为战国后期最强大的国家。

Shang Yang Erects Wood Pillar at the Southern Gate

In 356 BC, in order to make the Qin strong and powerful, Duke Xiao of Qin appointed Shang Yang to initiate new policies. Shang Yang drafted a new reform plan, but he was afraid that people would not accept him and the plan. He had a long wood pillar placed near the southern gate of the capital of Qin, and announced that he would give 10 pieces of gold to anyone who carried the log to the northern gate. A lot of people just took the offer as a joke. When nobody took up the log, Shang Yang raised the reward to 50 pieces of gold. Finally a man shouldered the log, and carried it to the northern gate. Shang Yang was as good as his word, and handed over 50 gold pieces to the man. This made a great stir in the whole state. And in this way, Shang Yang built up his prestige in people's minds which contributed much to the final success of his reforms. As a result of his successful efforts, the reforms made Qin the most powerful state in the late Warring States Period.

The Seven Powers

of the Warring States Period

The number of states was greatly reduced by the numerous wars. By the time of the Warring States Period (475—221 BC), only seven vassal states remained. The rest of the states were absorbed by the Qi, Chu, Yan, Han, Zhao, Wei and Qin. These seven states were called the Seven Powers of the Warring States Period.

In the early Warring States Period, the Han, Zhao and Wei formed an alliance, and defeated the Qi, Qin and Chu, séparately. Later the alliance broke up, while Qi and Qin gradually gained in strength.

In the mid-Warring States Period, the army of Wei attacked Zhao. Zhao asked the State of Qi for help. Seeing that the picked troops of Wei were in the State of Zhao and there was no army force inside Wei, the great military strategist Sun Bin led the Qi army against the Wei capital. Alarmed at the threat to their own lightly-defended state, the Wei troops, who had already occupied the Zhao capital, withdrew, and Zhao was saved. On their way back to Wei, the Wei forces were ambushed by

the Qi army, and were crushingly defeated. This was a famous battle in Chinese history, and gave rise to the saying "besieging Wei and saving Zhao".

Eleven years later, Wei launched an attack against the State of Han. The Qi army, again under the command of Sun Bin, took the strategy of besieging Wei to save Han. The Qi army pretended to retreat. On the first day they left behind enough camp fire sites to cook food for 100 000 soldiers, the second day enough for 50 000 soldiers, and the third day only enough for 30 000 soldiers. The Wei commander speculated that the Qi soldiers were deserting in great numbers. He chose an elite troop to chase the Qi army to Maling (in today's Henan Province). When the Wei forces caught up with what they thought was a small force of the Qi army, they were ambushed and defeated by the full strength of the Qi troops. This is the famous War of Maling. After these two victories, Qi later replaced Wei as the hegemon of the Central Plains.

In the late Warring States Period, Qin became stronger and stronger. The other six states allied against the growing power in the west, but Qin cleverly sowed discord among them, and they could never form a united front against it. Qin vanquished the other states one by one, abolished the Zhou's ruling, and united China under the Qin Dynasty.

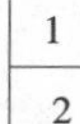

1. 战国水陆攻战铜壶拓片
   A rubbing of the pattern on the bronze pot
2. 战国水陆攻战铜壶
   The bronze pot incised with scenes of a battle on water and land (Warring States Period)

大教育家孔子

Confucius, the Great Educator

1. 孔子讲学图
   Confucius Giving a Lecture
2. 《诗经》是中国最早的一部诗歌总集，传为孔子所编，收集了从西周初到春秋中叶约500年间的诗歌305篇
   The Book of Songs was said to be edited by Confucius. It contains 305 songs — some of the oldest pieces of Chinese literature — which were collected during the 500 years dated from the early Western Zhou Dynasty through the Spring and Autumn Period.
3. 孔子像
   A portrait of Confucius

孔子是世界公认的世界十大思想家之一，他的思想在中国、在东亚都有广泛的影响。

孔子（公元前551—公元前479年），名丘，字仲尼，春秋末期鲁国陬邑（Zōuyì，今山东曲阜东南）人，是儒（rú）家学派的创始人。

孔子是个大思想家。首先，他提出“仁”的学说，即要求统治者能够体贴民情，爱惜民力，不要过度压迫剥削人民。其次，他主张以德治民，反对暴政。

孔子又是个大教育家。在那个时代，只有贵族子弟才能够受教育。孔子提倡“有教无类”，他收学生，不论他们地位贵贱，都一律平等地进行教育。孔子兴办私学，打破了官府对文化教育的垄断。据说孔子教过的学生有三千多人，其中著名的有72人。孔子主张“因材施教”，对不同的学生，进行不同的教育。他教育学生：“温故而知新”（学习知识要经常复习），“知之为知之，不知为不知”（学习态度要老实），还要求把学习和思考结合起来。

后来，孔子的学生们将孔子的思想言行记录下来，汇编成《论语》一书，《论语》成为儒家经典之一。孔子的学说成为中国两千多年封建文化的正统。

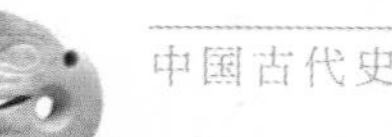

Confucius, the Great Educator

Confucius is one of the 10 internationally recognized thinkers, and his thoughts have had a wide-ranging influence in China and East Asia.

Confucius (551—479 BC) was surnamed Kong and his given name was Qiu. He styled himself Zhongni. He was born in Zouyi in the State of Lu (in the southeast of today's Qufu, Shandong Province) in the late Spring and Autumn Period. He was the founder of Confucianism.

He put forward the ideology of benevolence (*ren*) on the part of rulers toward their people, stressing that the political rule should be based on virtue not on force. He was against exploitation of the oppressed people. Additionally, he advocated the rule of the people by morality, not by tyranny.

Confucius was also a great educator. In his time, only children from aristocratic families could receive education. Confucius advocated that everyone was equal in education. He taught his disciples without discrimination, no matter what their social status was. Confucius established private schools and broke the government's monopoly over education. It is said that Confucius taught as many as 3 000 disciples, among whom 72 became very famous. Confucius proposed teaching students according to their aptitude. He said one should be honest in learning and not pretend to know what one did not know. He told his pupils to review what they had learned regularly during their study, because new knowledge can be gained by reviewing old knowledge. He also told his disciples to combine study with thinking.

The disciples of Confucius recorded his words and deeds in the *Analects of Confucius*, which is one of the classics of the Confucian school. Confucius's theories formed the orthodox ruling ideology in China for over 2 000 years.

小资料 Data

六经

即儒家的六部经典:《易》、《诗》、《礼》、《乐》、《书》、《春秋》,它们是由孔子亲自整理编订的,是孔子对中国古代文化发展作出的不朽贡献。

The Six Classics

The Six Classics are six ancient works considered central to the Confucian canon, namely, *The Book of Changes*, *The Book of Songs*, *The Book of Rites*, *The Book of Music*, *The Book of History* and *The Spring and Autumn Annals*. These works are said to have been compiled and edited by Confucius himself. They are immortal contributions Confucius made to the development of ancient Chinese culture.

诸子百家

The "Hundred Schools of Thought" and Their Exponents

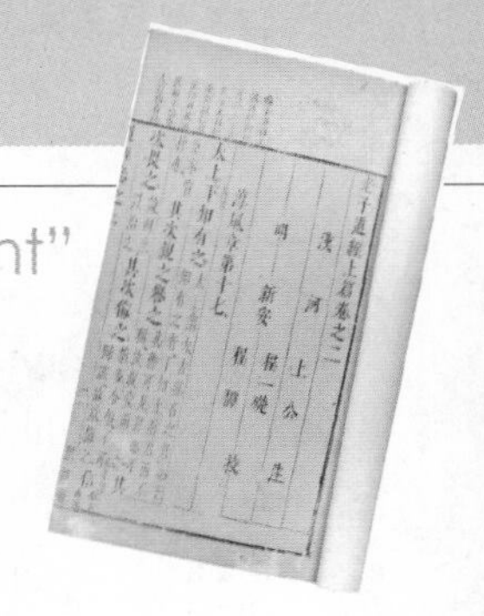

春秋战国时期，是中国历史上大变革的时代。社会大变革促进了文化的繁荣。

这一时期，出现了孔子、老子、庄子、孟子、荀子（Xūnzǐ）、墨子（Mòzǐ）、韩非子等大思想家，他们从不同的立场和角度出发，对当时的社会发表自己的意见，并逐步形成以道家、儒家、墨家和法家等为主的众多派别，在中国历史上被称为“诸子百家”。

老子是道家学派的创始人，著有《道德经》一书，他认为，各种事物都有对立面，如祸和福、有和无、生和灭、贵和贱、上和下、强和弱等都是对立的双方，它们之间会相互转化。道家学派还有一位著

名的人物——庄周，也叫庄子。他著有《庄子》一书，书中有很多有意思的故事，庄子借这些故事来表明他崇尚自然的主张。

墨子开创了墨家学派，主张节约，反对浪费，主张选用品德高尚、有才能的人来做官，并要求人们相互友爱，反对战争。

法家最重要的代表人物是韩非，著有《韩非子》一书，他主张“法治”，认为法律应当向全国公布，臣民应该严格遵守；强调用严厉的刑罚来镇压人民的反抗。他提倡改革，提出建立君主专制的中央集权的国家。他的思想后来被秦始皇采用。

1. 老子像
A portrait of Laozi
2. 山东崂山石刻《道德经》（上篇）
Stone Inscriptions of Laozi's *Tao Te Ching* (*The Classic of the Way and Virtue*) Part 1, in Laoshan, Shandong Province
3. 老子著作《道德经》
Laozi's *Tao Te Ching* (*The Classic of the Way and Virtue*)
4. 墨子像
A portrait of Mozi

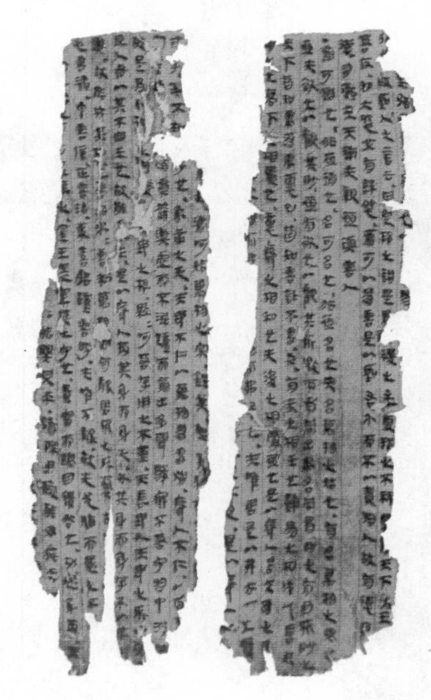

The "Hundred Schools of Thought" and Their Exponents

Great social changes took place during the Spring-Autumn and the Warring States periods. This spurred great cultural development. In these periods, there appeared many great thinkers, such as Laozi, Zhuangzi, Confucius, Mencius, Xunzi, Mozi and Hanfeizi. They stated their views on society from different standpoints and angles,

and gradually formed schools of philosophy represented mainly by the Taoist, Confucianist, Mohist and Legalist schools. These numerous schools and their representatives came to be known as the "Hundred Schools of Thought and their exponents".

Laozi was the founder of the Taoist School, and wrote *Tao Te Ching* (*The Classic of the Way and Virtue*). He deemed that all things have their opposites; for example, fortune and misfortune, existence and non-existence, life and death, nobility and baseness, high and low, strong and weak are all pairs of opposite aspects of a unity and can be transformed into each other. Zhuang Zhou is another famous figure of the Taoist School, and he is also called Zhuangzi. In his book (titled *The Book of Zhuangzi*) there are many interesting stories. Using these stories, Zhuangzi expressed his love of nature.

Mozi initiated the Mohist School. He encouraged frugality and combated waste. He advocated choosing noble-minded and talented people to be officials to govern the people. And he called on people to love each other and eschew war.

The most important representative of the Legalist School was Hanfeizi, who wrote *The Book of Hanfeizi*. He advocated ruling the country by means of strictly enforced laws. He deemed that the law should be promulgated to the whole state and the people should abide by the law in a very strict way. He emphasized the use of severe punishment for rebellious people. He advocated reforms and was in favor of a centralized autocratic monarchy. His theories were later adopted by Emperor Qinshihuang, China's first unifier.

1 | 3
2 |

1. 荀子像
   A portrait of Xunzi
2. 山东崂山石刻《道德经》（下篇）
   Stone Inscriptions of Laozi's *Tao Te Ching*, Part 2
3. 庄子像
   A portrait of Zhuangzi

世界第一部兵书——《孙子兵法》

The Art of War — The World First Treatise on Military Science

1. 孙武像
A portrait of Sun Wu
2. 清代版本《孙子兵法》
The Qing Dynasty edition of *The Art of War*

《孙子兵法》又称《孙子》，是中国古代著名的兵书，也是世界上现存最早的兵书。它的作者是春秋末期杰出的军事家孙武。孙武是齐国人，后来迁到吴国。那时候，各诸侯国为了争夺霸主的地位，不断地发动战争，社会动荡不安。孙武居住在吴国时，接连不断的战争吸引他去思考并总结战争的规律。经过艰苦的努力，终于完成了兵书的写作。

孙武将兵书献给了吴王阖闾。吴王任命孙武为大将，让他训练吴国军队。他军纪严明，练兵认真，曾率吴军攻破楚国，使吴国成为春秋时期的军事强国。

《孙子兵法》现存13篇，共6 000多字。在这不长的篇幅中，孙武全面论述了对战争的看法。他强调战争中要对敌我双方的情况调查清楚，提出了“知彼知己，百战不殆（dài）”（了解敌人，了解自己，无论打多少仗都不会受损），“攻其无备，出其不意”（在敌人没有防备时进攻，在敌人意想不到的地方下手），以及集中优势兵力打败敌人等思想。孙武特别强调“非危不战”（不到危急的时候，不要发动战争），因为打仗会大大加重人民的负担。战国时的军事家孙膑，是孙武的后代，他继承、发展了孙武的军事思想，写有《孙膑兵法》。

《孙子兵法》已被译为英、法、日、德、俄、捷等多种文字，这本书虽然讲的是战争规律，但对其他行业也有启示意义，因此在世界上享有很高的声誉。

The Art of War –

The World First Treatise on Military Science

The Art of War is the earliest work of military science existing in the world. Its author, Sun Wu (whose respected name was Sunzi), was an outstanding strategist in the late Spring and Autumn Period. Sun Wu was born in the State of Qi, later moving to the State of Wu. The endemic wars between the various states at that time caused Sun Wu to think deeply about military strategy through a lot of effort. He wrote *The Art of War*, and presented it to the ruler of Wu, who put him in command of his army. He imposed strict discipline on the army and he was very conscientious in training troops. In consequence, Wu soon became a major military power in the Spring and Autumn Period.

The Art of War consists of 13 chapters, amounting to some 6 000 characters. In this limited space, Sun Wu expounds his wide-ranging views on war. He emphasizes the importance of knowing yourself and knowing your enemy, attacking the enemy unexpectedly, and concentrating a superior force to thoroughly defeat the enemy. Sun Wu especially stressed the importance of using war only as a last resort, because war was a grievous burden on the people. Some 100 years later, during the Warring States Period, Sun Bin, an offspring of Su Wu, inherited and developed Sun Wu's military theory, and wrote *Sun Bin's Art of War*.

The Art of War has been translated into English, French, Japanese, German, Russian, Czech and other languages. Because it is deemed applicable to many areas, not just war, it enjoys high international prestige.

小资料 Data

三十六计

在《孙子兵法》一书中，孙子共列出了36条计谋，教人们如何去应对战争。他当时提出的“用间”，就是采用间谍战，至今还广为沿用。在这“三十六计”中，有一条最有名的计谋，那就是“走”。“三十六计，走为上计”早已成了成语，意思是：如果你没有获胜的希望，那最好的办法就是赶紧逃吧。

The 36 Stratagems

In *The Art of War*, Sun Wu lists 36 stratagems to teach people the rules of war. He recommends the use of spies, which is widely used by today's people. Of *the Art of War* the most famous is when you are hopeless of victory, the best strategy is to run away. "Of the 36 stratagems, running away is thought the best" was already used as a set phrase in China.

封建大一统时期——秦、汉

The Period of Great Feudal Unity — The Qin and Han Dynasties

概述

Introduction

秦汉时期，开始于公元前221年，结束于公元220年。秦朝是中国历史上第一个封建大一统的时代，也是统一的多民族国家的奠基时期。秦汉王朝开创的许多制度，为以后历代封建统治者所沿用。

秦朝建立于公元前221年，秦始皇采取了一系列巩固统一的措施，建立了一整套的统治制度，中国成为第一个统一的中央集权的多民族国家。但是，秦始皇和他的继承者对农民空前残暴的压迫和剥削，导致秦的统治在公元前206年被农民起义推翻。

汉朝包括西汉与东汉两个朝代，公元前202年，汉高祖刘邦建立汉朝，定都长安（今西安），历史上称之为西汉。西汉末年，王莽夺取西汉政权建立新朝。公元25年，西汉贵族刘秀借农民起义之机，恢复汉朝，定都于今天的洛阳，历史上称之为东汉。东汉末年，政权被农民大起义瓦解，最后结束于220年。两汉时期长达400多年，这个时期社会发展有很多成就，有些成就具有深远的历史影响。今天的汉族、汉字、汉语、汉文化等名称都与汉朝有关。秦汉时期，生产发展迅速，经济繁荣，国防巩固，科技文化事业发达，在医学、天文学、地质学等方面都取得了突出的成就，还涌现出许多著名的政治家、思想家、军事家、科学家、史学家、文学家。特别是造纸术的发明和改进，对世界文化事业的发展作出了巨大的贡献。

秦汉时期，从地中海、西亚到太平洋西岸，雄踞着四个帝国，其中汉朝与罗马的历史地位尤其重要。随着丝绸之路的开辟，中国辉煌灿烂的文化开始影响世界，当时世界上优秀的文明成就也逐渐融入中国的传统文化之中。

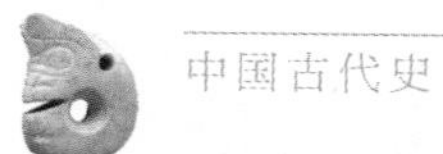

The Period of Great Feudal Unity —

The Qin and Han Dynasties

The period of the Qin and Han dynasties began in 221 BC and ended in 220 AD. The Qin Dynasty was the first feudal dynasty to rule all of China. It laid the foundation of a united multi-ethnic country. Many institutions initiated in the Qin and Han dynasties were inherited continuously by later dynasties.

The Qin Empire was established in 221 BC by Emperor Qinshihuang, who adopted a series of reforms bringing the whole system under his rule. He made the Qin Empire the first united multi-ethnic country with a centralized autocratic monarchy. However, the heavy-handed methods of Qinshihuang and his successor led to the overthrow of the Qin Dynasty in 206 BC by a peasant uprising.

The Han Dynasty includes two periods: the Western Han and the Eastern Han. In 202 BC, Liu Bang established the Han Dynasty, choosing Chang'an (today's Xi'an) as his capital. In 9 AD, Wang Mang staged a coup, and set up the Xin Dynasty. The Han Dynasty was restored in 25 AD by Liu Xiu, who moved the capital to the city known today as Luoyang. Subsequently, this period became known to historians as the Eastern Han Dynasty, and the previous one as the Western Han Dynasty. In 220, the Eastern Han Dynasty was overthrown by a peasant uprising. In its over 400 years of existence, the Han Dynasty had a profound influence upon the subsequent dynasties. The names of the Han nationality, Chinese characters, the Chinese language and Chinese culture today are all in relation with the Han Dynasty. In the Qin and the Han dynasties, the production grew, economy prospered, national defense was consolidate, technology and culture developed, and lots of outstanding achievements were made in medical science, astronomy, geology, etc. And there also appeared many great statesmen, thinkers, strategists, scientists, historians, and writers during this period. Notable among these achievements was the invention of the technique of papermaking, which was a great contribution to world civilization.

During the period of the Qin and Han dynasties, the Silk Road started to connect China with the Roman Empire and the Western world as a whole. With the opening up of the Silk Road, the brilliant Chinese culture began to influence the whole world, and the splendid cultural accomplishments of other countries gradually merged into traditional Chinese culture.

中国的第一位皇帝——秦始皇

Qinshihuang — The First Emperor in Chinese History

秦在公元前770年才被封为中国西部一个诸侯国，疆域较小，国力不盛，始终被中原诸侯看不起。但自从实行了商鞅变法后，国力日盛，很快成为战国七雄中的强国。秦王嬴政（Yíng Zhěng）当政以后，发动了大规模的战争。从公元前230年开始，历时10年，先后灭了韩、赵、魏、楚、燕、齐，于公元前221年统一了六国。

嬴政幻想秦的统治能永远继续下去，自称“始皇帝”，好让他的后代称二世、三世，以至千万世。因此，历史上称嬴政为秦始皇（公元前259—公元前210年）。

秦始皇统一后，采取了许多巩固统一的措施。

在中央，设置了丞相、御史大夫、太尉等职。丞相帮助皇帝处理全国的政务，御史大夫负责监察百官，太尉管理军事，都由皇帝任免。在地方，废除了商周以来的分封制，实行郡（jūn）县制度，全国划分为36个郡（后来增到40多个郡），郡下设县。长官称郡守和县令，也都由皇帝直接任免，负责管理人民。这样，皇帝把统治全国各地的权力牢牢控制在自己手里。秦始皇统一以后，把秦国原有的法律、法令推行到全国各地，使全国的法制统一到秦国法制上来。

战国时期，各国的度量衡都不一样，秦始皇统一了度量衡，使长度、容量、重量，都有了统一的标准，促进了经济的发展。秦朝还统一了货币。秦政府规定，把秦国的圆形方孔钱作为统一的货币，通行全国。这对促进各民族各地区的经济交流，十分有用。后来各个朝代的铜钱都基本上仿照秦朝的样式。

秦始皇还下令统一文字，把简化了的字体小篆（zhuàn）作为标准字体，通令全国使用。后来又出现了一种比小篆书写更简便的字体——隶书（lìshū）。现在的楷书（kǎishū），就是从隶书演化来的。文字的统一，促进了文化的交流。

公元前213年，丞相李斯认为，人们读了《诗》、《书》等古书之后，会用书中的观点批评时事，不利于朝廷的统治。他建议，民间藏书除了医药、种植等书以外，其余的书，尤其是各国史书及诸子书籍应全部烧掉。秦始皇采纳了他的建议。第二年，一些读书人背后议论秦始皇专横武断，滥施刑罚。秦始皇加以追查，最后活埋了460多人。这两件事，史称“焚书坑儒”。

秦始皇派蒙恬（Méng Tián）率军击败匈奴，为了防止匈奴再次侵犯边境，秦始皇还下令修筑长城。在南方，使越族归顺，扩大了民族交往。

秦始皇完成了统一大业，结束了长期以来诸侯割据称雄的局面，建立了中国历史上第一个统一的多民族的封建国家。秦朝的疆域，东到大海，西到陇西，北到长城一带，南到南海，人口达到2 000多万。

1 | 2

1. 秦始皇像
   A statue of Qinshihuang
2. 陕西秦始皇陵兵马俑坑
   Terra-cotta Warriors and Horses of Emperor Qinshihuang in Xi'an, Shaanxi Province

小资料 Data

兵马俑

1974年3月的一天，几位农民在秦始皇陵东打井时，意外地发现了许多碎陶人，至此被誉为“世界第八大奇迹”的秦代兵马俑才在沉睡千年之后展现在世人面前。

这是一支秦始皇陵从葬的庞大的地下军队。仅一号坑中与真人真马一样大小的武士俑和陶马就有6 000多个，排成方阵。秦兵马俑是以现实生活为基础而创作的，每尊陶俑的装束和神态都不一样，光是头发的式样就有许多种，手势也各不相同，脸部的表情也非常丰富。从它们的装束、表情和手势就可以判断出是官还是兵，是步兵还是骑兵。兵马俑具有鲜明的个性和强烈的时代特征。

秦兵马俑发现后，震惊世界，1987年被联合国教科文组织列入世界文化遗产名录。

Terra-cotta Warriors and Horses

In 1974, east of the Mausoleum of Emperor Qinshihuang in Lintong, near Xi'an, capital of Shaanxi Province, three pits filled with row after row of life-sized clay figures of warriors and horses were discovered by some well-digging peasants. Pit No. 1, the largest, contains more than 6 000 such figures in different lines and rows. This terracotta army, which guards the tomb of Emperor Qinshihuang has been called the Eighth Wonder of the World. The creation of these figures was based upon real people. Each figure has a different dress and appearance. Their hairstyles differ, gestures vary and facial expressions are abundant. Whether they are officers, cavalry, infantry or archers can be decided from their dresses, facial expressions and hands gestures. The Terra-cotta Warriors and Horses have the strong specific properties and embody the characteristics of that time.

The discovery of the Terra-cotta astonished the world. In 1987, they were included in the World Cultural Heritage List by the UNESCO.

Qinshihuang—

The First Emperor in Chinese History

1 | 2 / 3

1. 陕西西安秦始皇陵兵马俑
Terra-cotta Warriors and Horses of Emperor Qinshihuang in Xi'an, Shaanxi Province
2. 秦统一六国货币简图
The common currency of the Qin Dynasty
3. 秦统一六国文字简图
The common character of the Qin Dynasty

It was not until 770 BC that the State of Qin came into existence as one of the vassal states in western China. Later, it emerged as one of the seven most powerful states in China, assisted by Shang Yang's reform. King Ying Zheng (259—210 BC) embarked on a campaign of expansion. In the space of only ten years, Qin vanquished the Han, Zhao, Wei, Chu, Yan and Qi one after another, and united the whole of China in 221 BC.

Ying Zheng dreamed his power would be continuous and unbroken. He called himself the First Emperor of the Qin Dynasty (Qinshihuang), and his successors would be the second, third and so forth. Therefore, he is known historically as Qinshihuang.

Qinshihuang enacted a sweeping series of reforms to consolidate his power. The government was presided over by a prime minister. The Yushidafu supervised the bureaucracy, and the Taiwei was commander-in-chief of the army. They were all appointed and removed by the emperor himself. The whole country was divided into 36 prefectures (later increased to more than 40), which were in turn divided into counties. The magistrates of the prefectures and counties were also directly appointed and removed by the emperor. In this way, the emperor could grasp the power to control all of the state. After the unification, Qinshihuang expanded the original Qin's laws and orders to the whole country resulting in a system of unified law.

In the Warring States Period, linear measures differed from state to state. Qinshihuang set fixed standards for length, volume and weight, which propelled the development of the economy. The Qin Dynasty also issued a uniform currency. Round coins with a square hole in the middle were used all over China, and it promoted the economic communication among different nationalities and areas, and set the pattern for the coins of later dynasties.

Qinshihuang also promulgated order to unify the characters. The first reform of the characters resulted in the seal script (*xiaozhuan*). Then, the official script (*lishu*), a simplified version of the seal script, was devised. Today's regular script (*kaishu*) developed from the official script. The standardization of Chinese characters promoted communication and the culture.

In 213 BC, Qinshihuang adopted his prime minister, Li Si's advice that, all books, except for those on medicine and agriculture should be burned, in order to strengthen the regime's ideological control of the people. To further guard against dissent, the Emperor had 460 Confucian scholars buried alive in the second year. These two matters were called "burning the books and burying the Confucian scholars".

秦疆域图
Sketch Map of Qin Territory

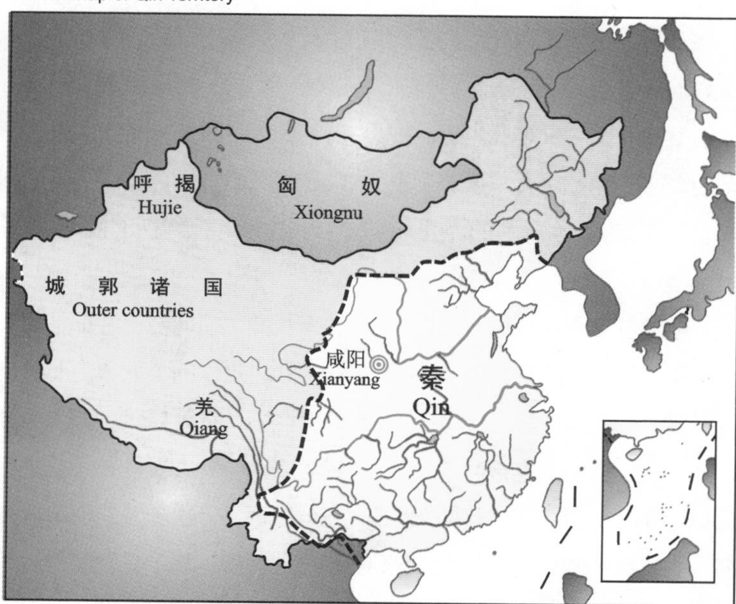

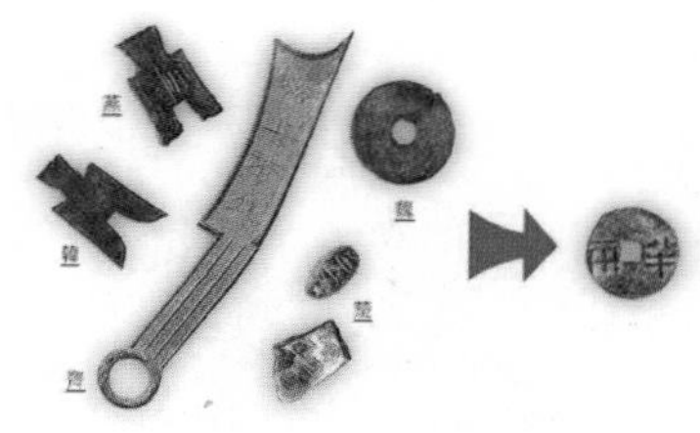

Qinshihuang sent General Meng Tian to defeat the Huns (*Xiongnu*). To curb the incessant invasions of the Hun nomads in the north, the Qin Dynasty set about building the Great Wall by linking up already existing defensive walls that had been built by various states. In the south, Qinshihuang subdued the Yue people and expanded the communication between different nationalities.

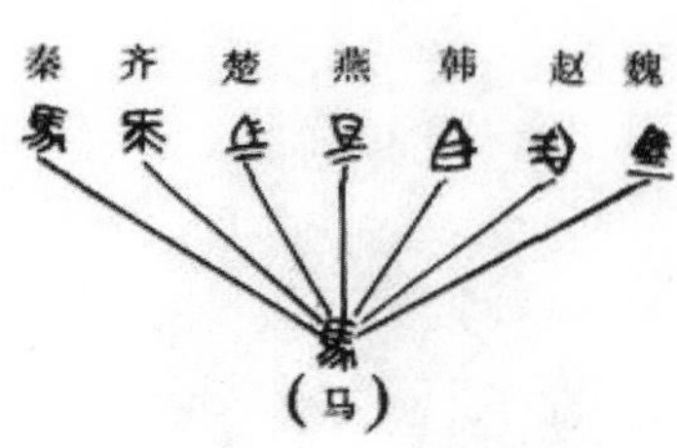

Qinshihuang ended the long divided situation, and established the first united multi-ethnic feudal country on Chinese soil. Qin's territory, embracing over 20 million people, reached the Pacific in the east, Longxi (west of the Longshan Mountains) in the west, the Great Wall in the north and the South China Sea in the south.

万里长城

The Great Wall

长城始建于公元前7世纪前后的春秋战国时期。秦始皇统一六国后，将原来秦、赵、燕等国修建的防御性长城扩建修葺，连结成东起辽东，西到临洮（Líntáo，今甘肃境内），绵延5 000多千米的巨大军事防御工事。这就是举世闻名的万里长城。此后许多朝代都进行过修整。明朝初年大规模修筑长城，约200年后完成，东部主要为砖石结构。

历史上的长城东起鸭绿江，西到嘉峪关，横穿中国北方8个省、自治区和直辖市（辽宁、河北、北京、山西、内蒙古、宁夏、陕西、甘肃），全长6 700多千米（约13 000华里）的长城，成为世界的著名奇迹之一。

长城由千百座关隘、城堡、堞楼和高大的城墙组成。遇有敌情，士兵会在长城北侧沿线的烽火台上点燃烟火，将情报传递到附近的城市直至皇帝的都城。

位于北京的八达岭长城、慕田峪长城、司马台长城都是明代修筑的。这里的长城依山而建，高大坚固，绵延起伏，城顶的通道可以容纳五六匹马并排前进，充分展现了万里长城的建筑风格和雄伟气魄。现今是著名的旅游胜地。

1. 孟姜女塑像
   A statue of Meng Jiangnu
2. 雄伟壮观的万里长城
   The magnificent Great Wall
3. 长城西端的嘉峪关
   Jiayu Pass is the western end of the Great Wall.
4. 长城东端的山海关
   Shanhai Pass is located at the eastern Great Wall.
5. 云海中的金山岭长城
   Jinshanling Great Wall in a sea of clouds

The Great Wall

The origin of the Great Wall can be traced to defensive walls erected by various states during the Spring and Autumn and the Warring States periods (around the seventh century BC). After Qinshihuang united the country, he repaired, linked up and extended the walls built by the former states of Qin, Zhao, Yan and others into a huge military defense works which started from Liaodong Peninsula in the east and ended at Lintao (in today's Gansu Province) in the west, a distance of more than 5 000 km. This is the world-famous Great Wall. The Wall was repaired and maintained over the course of many dynasties, especially during the Ming Dynasty, when the work continued for some 200 years. The eastern part of the wall was mostly of bricks and stones.

Historically, the Great Wall started from Yalu River in the east to Jiayu Pass in the west. Today, the Great Wall crosses five provinces (Liaoning, Hebei, Shanxi, Shaanxi and Gansu), two autonomous regions (Inner Mongolia and Ningxia) and one municipality (Beijing) in North China, with a total length of over 6 700 km. It is one of the foremost wonders of the world.

The Great Wall is composed of hundreds of passes, fortresses, towers and stretches of wall. Beacon towers are situated at suitable intervals to give the alarm if an enemy approached.

The parts of the Great Wall located at Badaling, Mutianyu and Simatai in Beijing were all constructed during the Ming Dynasty. These parts of the wall were built along mountain ridges. On many parts of the wall five or six horsemen could ride side by side. Parts of the wall renovated in modern times are popular tourist attractions.

小资料 Data

孟姜女哭长城

千百年来，中国民间流传着这样一个动人的故事：秦朝时候，一个叫孟姜女的姑娘，刚刚结婚，丈夫就被抓去修筑长城了。孟姜女在家日日夜夜地等待，丈夫一直没有回来。冬天到了，天气冷了，孟姜女做好了棉衣，给丈夫送去。她走了很长的路，终于到了长城，却得知丈夫已经死了。孟姜女跪在长城边，哭了几天几夜，竟把一段城墙哭倒了。最后，孟姜女悲痛地投水自杀了。

Meng Jiangnu Weeps Beside the Great Wall

A touching story has been circulating in China for many centuries. It tells how, during the Qin Dynasty, the husband of a woman named Meng Jiangnu was conscripted for forced labor on the Great Wall immediately after their marriage. When winter came, Meng Jiangnu made padded clothes for her husband, and started off on a journey to the Great Wall to deliver them to him. When she finally reached her destination, she learned that her husband had already died. Meng Jiangnu knelt by the Great Wall, and cried for several days. As a result of her wailing, part of the Great Wall collapsed. Finally, Meng Jiangnu drowned herself.

大泽乡起义

The Dazexiang Uprising

公元前210年，秦始皇在一次巡游中去世。他的二儿子胡亥（Húhài）即位，称为二世皇帝。秦二世十分残暴，百姓非常怨恨他，社会局势动荡不安。

公元前209年，900多名贫苦农民被迫前往边境驻守，途中遇雨，困在大泽乡（今安徽宿州东南），不能按期赶到边境。按照秦朝法律，误期都得处死。农民们被迫死里求生。陈胜、吴广合谋杀死押送的军官，举行起义。

为了使人们相信起义是上天的旨意，陈胜和吴广派人将写有“陈胜王”三字的帛（bó）书放到鱼肚子里，戍卒（shùzú）买鱼发现了帛书，惊奇得不得了。吴广还派人模仿动物，发出“大楚兴，陈胜王”的叫声，人们听到后更是感到神奇。陈胜慷慨激昂地说：“王侯将相，宁有种乎！”（那些王侯将相，难道都是天生的贵种吗？）中国历史上第一次大规模的农民起义在大泽乡爆发了。起义军很快攻克了附近的几个县城，不到一个月，队伍就壮大到几万人。陈胜在陈地（今河南淮阳）称王，国号“张楚”。然后，起义军的主力西进，这年9月攻入函谷关，打到秦都城咸阳附近，队伍发展到几十万人。

秦二世得知起义军入关，非常害怕。来不及调集军队，只好派章邯（Zhāng Hán）率领正在建造骊山（Líshān）陵墓的几十万人应战，击溃了起义军的主力。不久，吴广被部将所杀，陈胜也被叛徒刺死，起义军虽进行了将近半年的艰苦奋斗，最终被秦军镇压。

1. 陈胜、吴广起义图
   A portrait of the Uprising of Chen Sheng and Wu Guang
2. 河南商丘陈胜墓
   Chen Sheng Mausoleum, Shangqiu, Henan Province
3. 陈胜揭竿起义曾攻入函谷关，直逼秦都咸阳
   Chen Sheng once led the peasants to capture Hanguguan Pass and threatened to attack the capital Xianyang.

The Dazexiang Uprising

In 210 BC, Qinshihuang died during an inspection tour. His second son, Huhai, succeeded to the throne. He was so cruel that the people were in enmity and the society was in a turmoil.

In 209 BC, over 900 poor peasants drafted to guard the boundaries were delayed by rain in Dazexiang (southeast of today's Suzhou in Anhui Province) on their way to their posts. According to the harsh Qin laws, they faced the death penalty, and in desperation, led by Chen Sheng and Wu Guang, they killed the officers escorting them, and rose in revolt. This was the beginning of the first great peasant uprising in the unified China.

In order to convince the people of heavenly determination on their rebellion, they had a piece of silk, on which three characters "King Chen Sheng" were written, put into the belly of a fish. A frontier guard bought the fish, discovering the silk and was greatly surprised. They also had people imitate animals to cry "Da Chu flourishes, King Chen Sheng" to make people more astounded. Chen Sheng impassioned with the remark "Are all the kings and nobles born naturally?" The first great peasant uprising broke out in Dazexiang. The peasants army soon conquered several nearby counties, in no more than a month, the army expanded into tens of thousands. Chen Sheng proclaimed himself emperor in Chendi (today's Huaiyang, Henan Province), and the name of the state "Zhang Chu". The army marched westward, and moved in Hanguguan Pass in September. When approached the capital of Qin, Xianyang, the army expanded several hundred thousand.

The Second Emperor was afraid of their revolt when he learned the army was almost at the gate. It was so urgent that he had to dispatch Zhang Han to defeat the main force by leading several hundred thousands of people who were constructing the Lishan Tombs at the moment. Soon, Wu Guang was killed by one of his soldiers, Chen Sheng was also assassinated by treachery. Although the rebel army was in war for almost half a year, it was finally surpressed.

小资料 Data

揭竿而起

揭：高举；竿：竹竿，代表旗帜；起：起义。这个成语描述的是陈胜、吴广起义时，人们"斩木为兵，揭竿为旗"（砍树木做兵器，举竹竿当旗帜）的情形。后来指不愿受压迫的人民自己组织起来，举行起义。

Hold Up a Stick and Rise

This is a set phrase in Chinese. It refers to the time when Chen Sheng and Wu Guang started the uprising. The rebels felled trees to make weapons and held up sticks as flags. Later, it signified revolt against oppression by desperate people.

刘邦与项羽

Liu Bang and Xiang Yu

陈胜、吴广起义失败以后，刘邦和项羽继续领导农民反抗秦朝统治。公元前207年，项羽以少胜多，在巨鹿（今河北平乡西南）大败秦军主力。同时，刘邦带兵直逼咸阳。秦朝统治者向刘邦投降，秦朝灭亡。

秦朝灭亡以后，项羽自称为西楚霸王，封刘邦为汉王。自公元前206年开始，项羽和刘邦为争做皇帝，进行了将近4年的战争，历史上称为“楚汉战争”。战争初期，项羽实力雄厚，有40万大军；刘邦只有10万人。但是刘邦关注百姓的疾苦，进驻咸阳时，宣布废除秦朝的严酷法令，向老百姓“约法三章”——杀人的要被处死，打伤人以及偷盗都有罪；刘邦还很重视人才，得到萧何、张良、韩信等人帮助。另外，刘邦有富饶的关中作为根据地，因此，刘邦率领的汉军逐渐由弱变强。相反，项羽骄傲自大，不听取他人的意见，放任士兵烧杀抢掠，使老百姓深感失望。

1 | 2

1. 刘邦像
   A portrait of Liu Bang
2. 项羽像
   A portrait of Xiang Yu

公元前202年，刘邦率大军攻打项羽，在垓下（Gāixià）（今安徽省境内）把项羽的楚军重重包围。夜里，项羽听到汉军军营中的楚歌从四面八方传来，十分吃惊，以为楚的地方全都被汉军占领了。项羽悲痛地与宠姬虞姬（Yújī）诀别，率领800多名骑兵突围逃走。汉军紧追不舍，形势十分危急，项羽被迫在乌江（今安徽和县东北）自杀。项羽虽然失败了，但是他的英雄气概仍然为后人赞叹，李清照的“生当作人杰，死亦为鬼雄，至今思项羽，不肯过江东”的诗句就是诗人对这位盖世英雄的深切追念。

刘邦战胜项羽后，建立汉朝，定都长安（今西安西北），国号“汉”，历史上称为西汉（公元前202—公元8年）。刘邦就是汉高祖。

小资料 Data

楚河汉界

西楚霸王项羽和汉王刘邦之间长达4年之久的“楚汉战争”，给后人留下了深刻的影响和教训。人们把这段历史融入了象棋，在象棋的棋盘上，双方棋子之间的空白地带称为“楚河汉界”。它形象地提醒下棋的人，他们之间也是在进行一场智力上的“楚汉战争”。

The Chu River and the Han Boundary

The four-year war between Xiang Yu and Liu Bang had a great impact on later generations. It even finds an echo in Chinese chess. On the chessboard, the blank area between the positions of the opponents is called the Chu River and the Han Boundary, which reminds people who play chess that they are engaging in a kind of war between Chu and Han.

Liu Bang and Xiang Yu

1 | 2

1. 中国象棋上的楚河汉界
Chu and Han borders on the Chinese chessboard
2. 鸿门宴图
A portrait of the Hongmen Banquet

After the uprising led by Chen Sheng and Wu Guang failed, Liu Bang and Xiang Yu continued to lead peasants against the Qin Dynasty. In 207 BC, Xiang Yu with a small force routed the main body of the Qin army at Julu (southwest of today's Pingxiang in Hebei Province). At the same time, Liu Bang's peasant army pressed on toward Xianyang, and forced the abdication of the second Qin emperor.

Xiang Yu then proclaimed himself the King of Western Chu, and made Liu Bang the King of Han. From 206 BC, Xiang Yu and Liu Bang fought for rule of the empire for nearly four years, in what historians call "the War between Chu and Han". At the beginning of the war, Xiang Yu had an army of 400 000, whereas Liu Bang's forces numbered only 100 000. But Liu Bang won the support of the common people by abolishing the draconian laws and decrees of the Qin Dynasty, and enforcing strict discipline on his troops. In addition, he had the assistance of able officials like Xiao He, Zhang Liang and Han Xin. Occupying the rich and fertile central Shaanxi plain, the Han army led by Liu Bang gradually grew stronger. Xiang Yu, in contrast, was arrogant, and his army was lawless. Wherever they went they lost the support of the people.

In 202 BC, the Han army besieged the Chu army in Gaixia (in today's Anhui Province). At a night, Xiang Yu heard the Chu songs from the Han army's camps on all sides. Greatly astonished, he thought that the Chu regions had already been occupied by the Han army. He sadly bid farewell to his favorite Concubine Yuji and escaped the encirclement with a small force, but was trapped at the Wujiang River (in the northeast of today's Hexian County, Anhui Province), and committed suicide.

Liu Bang then established the Han Dynasty, with Chang'an (in the northwest of today's Xi'an) as the capital. It is historically called the Western Han Dynasty, and Liu Bang is known as Hangaozu.

小资料 Data

鸿门宴

公元前206年，刘邦攻占秦都咸阳，不久，项羽率40万大军攻来，进驻鸿门（今陕西临潼(Líntóng)东），准备消灭刘邦。在项羽叔父项伯的调解下，刘邦亲自到鸿门会见项羽。宴会上，项羽的军师范增命令大将项庄舞剑，表面上说是给大家饮酒助兴，其实是要找机会杀掉刘邦。项伯看出了项庄的意图，也拔剑起舞，保护刘邦。正在情况危急之时，刘邦手下大将樊哙（Fán Kuài）赶到，刘邦趁机脱逃。现在人们常用“鸿门宴”一词形容用邀请对方吃饭的形式，预设陷阱，引诱对方上钩，以达到自己的目的。

The Hongmen Banquet

In 206 BC, Liu Bang conquered the capital of Qin, Xianyang, soon Xiang Yu's army of 400 000 soldiers were stationed at Hongmen (east of today's Lintong, Shaanxi Province) and were going to attack Liu Bang. After the mediation of Xiang Bo, Xiang Yu's uncle, Liu Bang met Xiang Yu at Hongmen in person. In the banquet, Fan Zeng, Xiang Yu's military advisor, commanded Xiang Zhuang to practice his sword as entertainments, but indeed, he would kill Liu Bang unexpectedly. Xiang Bo learned the intention of Xiang Zhuang, then joined the sword practice and protected Liu Bang. At the critical moment, a general of Xiang Yu, Fan Kuai appeared and helped Liu Bang to escape. Nowadays, people used this set phrase *hongmenyan* (the Hongmen Banquet) to indicate a banquet given with ill purposes, teasing the opponents to be cheated and to achieve his own goal.

汉武大帝

Emperor Wudi the Great of the Han Dynasty

汉武帝刘彻，公元前140—公元前87年在位。他的雄才大略，文治武功使汉朝进入了鼎盛时期，成为当时世界上最强大的帝国之一。

汉初，刘邦分封一些同姓的子弟到全国各地做王，想借此永保刘家的天下。受封的诸侯王的权力很大，他们可以在辖区内拥有军队，征收租税，铸造钱币，任免官吏。后来诸侯王的势力过大，严重削弱了中央的统治。汉武帝当政后，准许诸侯王把自己的封地再分给子弟，建立侯国，这就是“推恩令”，一个王国分出许多小侯国，直属的领地就小了，再没有力量对抗中央。后来，汉武帝又陆续夺去大批王、侯的爵位。这样，经过长期斗争，王国对中央的威胁终于解除了，中央集权制度得到加强。

汉武帝时期，儒生董仲舒为了适应中央集权政治的需要，对儒家学说进行了发挥。第一，宣扬天是万物的主宰，皇帝是天的儿子，即天子，代表天统治人民。因此，全国人民都要服从皇帝的统治，诸侯王也要听命于皇帝，这叫做“大一统”。第二，提出了“罢黜（chù）百家，独尊儒术”的建议。主张只提倡儒家学说，禁止其他各家学说传播，以实行思想上的统一，从而巩固政治上的统一。

汉武帝采纳了董仲舒的学说，汉朝政府里就有许多信奉儒家思想的人做了大官。儒家思想逐渐成为中国封建社会两千年间的正统思想。

汉武帝加强了中央军权，设立了中央常备军。他还在北方边塞地区大规模移民屯田，加强城寨，巩固边防，使帝国的军事实力壮大起来。从公元前133年起，在名将李广、卫青和霍去病的率领下，汉军向经常来犯的匈奴发动了攻势，经过三次大规模的战役，取得了决定性的胜利。他多次向边境和亚洲腹地发动军事远征，使中华帝国的版图迅速扩大了。

汉武帝两次派张骞（Zhāng Qiān）出使西域，使汉朝和西域各国建立了联系。张骞回国后向汉武帝报告了西域见闻，也提到了中国丝绸出口的目的地——罗马帝国。

汉朝的强大，使中原人不再被称为“秦人”，而被通称“汉人”、“汉族”了。汉武帝成为秦始皇之后又一位建立丰功伟业的中华帝国君主。

1 | 2

1. 汉武帝像
A portrait of Emperor Wudi
2. 漠北之战图（公元前119年，汉武帝派兵战胜匈奴）
A painting of the battle at Mobei (In 119 BC, Emperor Wudi sent his army to fight the Huns and won.)

Emperor Wudi the Great

of the Han Dynasty

Reigned from 140 BC to 87 BC, Liu Che was known as Emperor Wudi of the Han Dynasty. He had a great talent, bold vision, outstanding statecraft and brilliant military exploits, which made China enter into a time of great prosperity and one of the most powerful empires in the world.

Soon after Liu Bang founded the Han Dynasty, he granted territories in strategic parts of the country to nobles of his clan, with the title of king. The kings had their own armies, levied their own taxes, issued currency, and appointed and removed officials within their own jurisdictions. When Emperor Wudi came to the throne, fearing that the kings were too powerful, he instituted a system whereby the descendants of the kings inherited parts of the kingdoms as marquisates. Thus the kingdoms quickly became divided into smaller and weaker territories, and came under the direct control of the imperial court. Later, Emperor Wudi went even further, depriving many nobles of their titles, and strengthening central rule.

It was during the reign of Emperor Wudi that the Confucian scholar Dong Zhongshu adapted Confucian theory to the needs of centralized politics. First, he stressed that Heaven dominated everything in the world. The emperor was the Son of Heaven, and he ruled over the people on behalf of Heaven. Therefore, all people, including kings, should abide by the will of the emperor, a concept which was called grand unification. Second, Dong Zhongshu advocated suppressing the hundred Schools of Thought and making Confucianism the state ideology. This, he argued, would unify the people's minds, which in turn would consolidate political unity.

Emperor Wudi was impressed by Dong Zhongshu's theories, and filled his administration with Confucian scholars. Confucianism thereby gained a foothold as the dominant ideology in China's feudal society.

Wudi enforced the central military power, set forth a central standing army. He also moved a large number of people to the northern border areas to open up wastelands, enforced the frontier fortress and strengthen the defense so that the empire's military force was empowered. From 133 BC, under the lead of famous generals Li Guang, Wei Qing and Huo Qubing, the Han army attacked the frequently intruding Huns, and after three great battles, they achieved a decisive victory. He also endeavored an expedition toward the boundary and the hinterland of Asia, and expanded the territory of China.

Zhang Qian was sent on diplomatic missions twice by Wudi, connecting communication among the countries in the Western Regions and the Han Dynasty. Zhang Qian reported his experiences to Wudi and mentioned the destination of Silk Road — the Roman Empire.

With the increasing power, the people of the Central Plains began to be called "Han people" or "Han nationality" instead of "Qin people". Wudi became the second great emperor who made great achievements to the country.

张骞出使西域

Zhang Qian's Mission to the Western Regions

1

1. 张骞出使西域图
Zhang Qian's diplomatic mission to the Western Regions

汉代，在“丝绸之路”上的悠长驼铃声中，中国与域外各民族建立了广泛的交往，中西文明开始碰撞和交融。汉武帝时，北方匈奴常常袭扰汉朝边境，还控制了当时西域的几十个小国。公元前138年，汉武帝派张骞带100多人出使西域，联络大月氏（Dàyuèzhī），准备左右夹攻匈奴。没想到刚出边境，张骞就被匈奴抓住了。在被扣留期间，他学会了匈奴语，掌握了匈奴的地形。10多年后，张骞逃了出来，找到了已经西迁的大月氏。张骞在当地呆了一年，熟悉了西域的环境。后来，见大月氏国王不想报仇，他只好回国。当年与他同去的100多人，回到长安时只剩下两人。

公元前119年，汉武帝再次派张骞出使西域，这次随行的有300多人，带去了上万头牛羊和货物。他们访问了许多国家，这些国家也派了使臣带了礼物回访。从此以后，汉朝和西域的往来越来越多。后来，汉朝还在今天新疆地区设了西域都护府，归中央政府管理。

张骞出使西域后，中西交流的“丝绸之路”开辟了。“丝绸之路”东起长安，向西到地中海东岸，转至罗马帝国。汉朝的商队，用大量的丝织品同波斯人、印度人、罗马人进行商品交换，同时带回了外国的核桃、葡萄、胡萝卜等。此后的许多世纪，以丝绸贸易为主的中西交流大多经过“丝绸之路”进行。

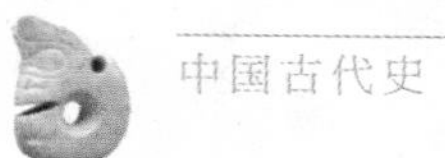

Zhang Qian's

Mission to the Western Regions

With the jingle of the camel bell in the Han Dynasty, China established contact with other nations outside in the Western Regions. Since then, Chinese and foreign cultures have clashed and mixed. In the time of Emperor Wudi, the Huns in the north often harassed the boundary of Han. Meanwhile, they also controlled several small nations in the Western Regions. In 138 BC, Emperor Wudi sent Zhang Qian with a delegation of over 100 people on a diplomatic mission to the Western Regions to seek allies, preparing for an attack of the Huns in two sides. Unexpectedly, Zhang Qian was captured by the Huns just as he left the Han territory, and was held prisoner for a dozen years. During this period, he learned the Hun language, and got to know well the geography of their territory. Ten years later, Zhang Qian escaped and found the west-moved Dayuezhi. He lived there for a year and got familiar with the circumstances of the Western Regions. Later, when he learned Dayuezhi had no intention to seek revenge, Zhang Qian made his way back to Chang'an, with only one companion left of the 100 who had set out.

In 119 BC, Emperor Wudi sent Zhang Qian on a second diplomatic mission to the Western Regions. This time, he had an entourage of 300, with thousands of head of cattle and sheep and a large amount of gifts. They visited many countries, and these countries sent envoys with tribute to the Han court. From then on, the Han Dynasty had frequent contacts with the countries in the Western Regions, later setting up a Western Regions Frontier Command in today's Xinjiang Uygur Autonomous Region, which was under the administration of the central government.

The Silk Road was another outcome of Zhang Qian's journeys. The Silk Road started from Chang'an in the east and stretched westward to reach the eastern shore of the Mediterranean Sea and the Roman Empire. Trade caravans from China carrying large amounts of silk fabrics exchanged merchandise with traders from Persia, India and Rome, and brought home walnuts, grapes and carrots from abroad. In the following several centuries, Sino-Western exchanges mainly characterized by the silk trade were mostly carried on through the Silk Road.

张骞通西域及丝绸之路图

Sketch Map of Zhang Qian's Journeys to the Western Regions and the Overland Silk Road

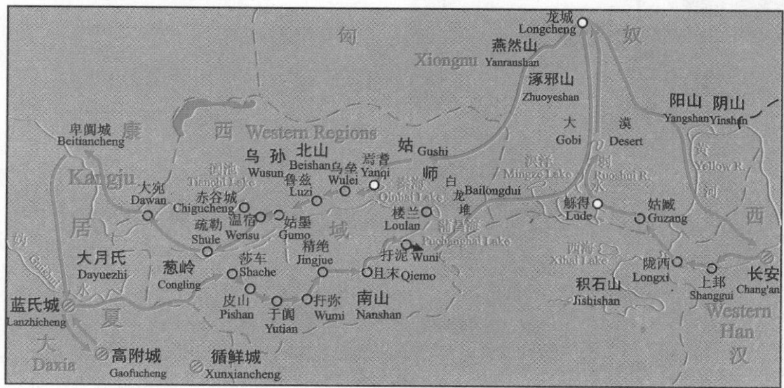

小资料 Data

海上"丝绸之路"

汉代，海上也有一条"丝绸之路"。它从今天广东沿海港口出发，经10个多月的航行，到达泰国和印度。汉代使者带去丝绸、黄金，换回那儿著名的蓝宝石。东汉时，中国的远洋帆船甚至可到达非洲，并与罗马帝国建立了直接的交往。

The Maritime Silk Road

There was also a Silk Road on the sea during the Han Dynasty. It started from coastal ports in today's Guangdong Province, and ended in India by way of Thailand after a 10-month voyage. The Han merchants took with them silk and gold, and exchanged them for sapphires. In the Eastern Han Dynasty, Chinese sailing ships reached as far as Africa, and established trade contact with the Empire of Rome.

昭君出塞

Zhaojun Goes Beyond the Great Wall as a Bride

秦汉之际，中国北方古老的游牧民族匈奴势力强大，多次南下威胁中原。汉初国力不强，无法与匈奴对抗，便采取了和亲政策，求得相对的和平。随着汉朝经济、军事力量的增强，反击匈奴的条件成熟了。到汉武帝时，便放弃了和亲政策，对匈奴采取了攻势。从此，西汉与匈奴80年没有和亲。

汉宣帝时，匈奴的势力衰落了。此时，匈奴内部出现了两个单于（chányú，匈奴君主的称号）对抗的局面。其中呼韩邪（Hūhányé）单于想借助汉朝的支持，统一整个匈奴，于是决心归依汉朝。他两次到长安见汉朝皇帝，受到隆重的欢迎，他也表示愿协助汉朝政府保护边境。公元前36年，汉朝派兵攻打了另一个单于，呼韩邪统一匈奴。公元前33年，他第三次到长安，向当时的汉元帝提出，愿意当汉家的女婿，再恢复和亲。汉元帝立即答应，并在宫女中进行选拔。有一个叫王昭君的宫女主动提出要去和亲。王昭君又美丽又聪明，很受呼韩邪的喜爱，被封为“宁胡阏氏（yānzhī）”，意思是将与汉朝建立和平友好的关系。

王昭君出塞以后，生活在匈奴游牧地区几十年。在她的影响下，她的子女及周围的人，都努力维护匈奴与汉的友好关系，使汉朝北方边境出现了少有的安定和谐的景象。

1 | 2

1. 湖北兴山县昭君故里的昭君塑像
   The sculpture of Zhaojun, Xingshan County, Hubei Province
2. 昭君出塞图
   A portrait of Zhaojun leaving hometown to marry the chief of the Huns

Zhaojun

Goes Beyond the Great Wall as a Bride

During the Qin and Han dynasties, the Hun nomads became a threat to the people of the Central Plains, launching numerous southward invasions. In its early years, the Han Dy-

nasty was not strong enough to repel the Huns, so the Han rulers resorted to the policy of *heqin* (peace through marriage ties) to pacify the borders. With the strengthening of the economic and military forces of the Han Dynasty, the policy of appeasement was replaced by one of military pacification. By the end of the reign of Emperor Wudi, the Han Dynasty had not intermarried with the Huns for 80 years.

During the reign of Emperor Xuandi (74—49 BC), the power of the Huns had declined drastically. At that time, two men contended for the title of khan, or paramount chief, of the Huns. One of them, Huhanye by name, sought the help of the Han Dynasty. He visited Chang'an twice, and pledged his allegiance to the emperor. He also expressed his willingness to help the Han Dynasty guard the border areas. In 36 BC, Emperor Yuandi, Emperor Xuandi's successor, dispatched troops, which ensured Hu-hanye's victory. In 33 BC, Huhanye went to Chang'an for the third time, and offered to restore the *heqin* system by marrying a Han princess. Emperor Yuandi agreed immediately, and set about selecting a woman from his palace to marry Huhanye. A palace maid named Wang Zhaojun volunteered to marry Huhanye. The latter gave her the title Ninghuyanzhi, which signified that the Huns would build peaceful and friendly relations with the Han Dynasty.

Wang Zhaojun lived in the Huns' encampments for many years. Under her influence, her children and the people around her all did their best to maintain the good relations between the Huns and the Han Dynasty, which brought a rare period of stability to the northern border areas.

司马迁与《史记》

Sima Qian and His *Records of the Historian*

《史记》的作者司马迁（公元前145年—？），生于陕西。受父亲影响，他少年时就阅读古人的书籍。20岁时，他到各处去游历，搜集了很多古代名人的资料。后来，他被任命为郎中，可以常随皇帝出游。这些游历，为他以后写《史记》作了准备。

父亲死后，司马迁接替他的职务做了太史令，有机会翻阅了很多图书，做了大量笔记。公元前104年，他正式开始写作《史记》。他在写作过程中，因为得罪了皇帝，被判重刑。司马迁因此想到了自杀，但想到自己的书还没有写完，就忍受着痛苦，发愤编写，终于完成了《史记》。

《史记》全书130篇，从传说中的黄帝，一直写到汉武帝时代，跨越了3 000年的历史。这是中国第一部纪传体通史，内容涉及到了政治、经济、文化、军事等各个方面。它的文字简洁通俗、生动传神，既是一部有价值的史学著作，也是一部杰出的文学著作。

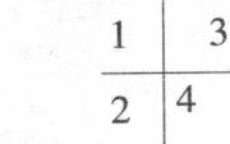

1. 《史记》明初抄本
   Hand-written copy of the *Records of the Historian* in the early Ming Dynasty
2. 陕西韩城司马迁墓
   Mausoleum of Sima Qian, Hancheng, Shaanxi Province
3. 《史记》是中国第一部纪传体通史
   Records of the Historian was the first comprehensive biographical history book in China.
4. 司马迁像
   A portrait of Sima Qian

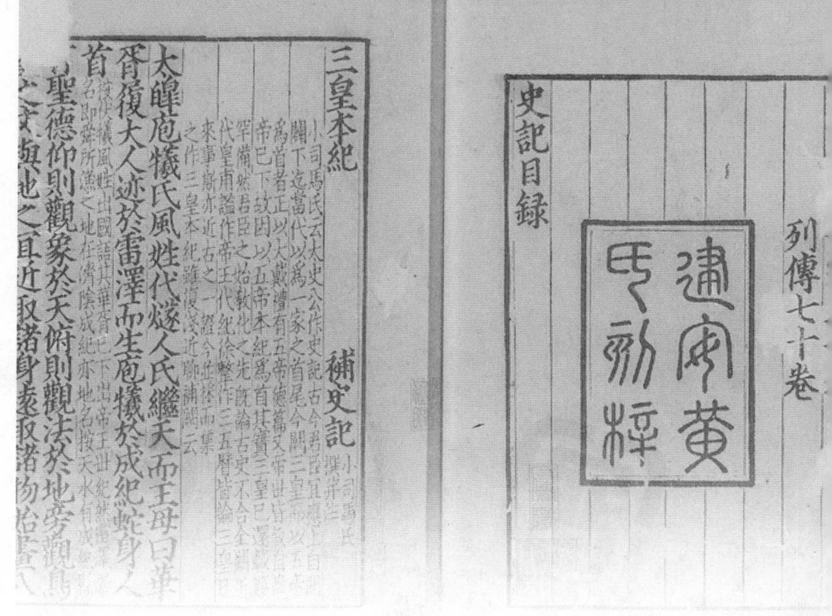

Sima Qian and His *Records of the Historian*

The author of *Records of the Historian*, Sima Qian (145 BC—?), was born in what is now Shaanxi Province. Encouraged by his father, he began to read ancient books when he was still very young. At the age of 20 he started to travel extensively, and gathered a great deal of material on ancient celebrities. Later, he was appointed to an official post, and often went on tours with the emperor.

Not long after his father's death, Sima Qian succeeded to his position as the official in charge of historical records. Thus he had the opportunity to read many books and made a great many notes. In 104 BC, Sima Qian commenced his *Records of the Historian*. Falling foul of the emperor, he was castrated and dismissed from office. From that time on, he devoted all his time to his life's work.

Records of the Historian is composed of 130 chapters. It starts from the legendary Emperor Huangdi, and ends with the reign of Emperor Wudi of the Han Dynasty, spanning 3 000 years. It was the first comprehensive biographical history book to appear in China. It covers a wide range of subjects: political, economic, cultural, military, etc. Its language is terse and lively, and easy to understand. *Records of the Historian* is not only a valuable historical work, but also an outstanding work of literature.

科学家张衡

Zhang Heng, a Pioneering Scientist

张衡（78—139年），河南南阳人，东汉杰出的科学家，也是世界上最早的天文学家之一。他特别爱好数学和天文学。朝廷听说他有学问，就让他担任了太史令，掌管历史和历法，负责观察天文。

经过多年的观察，他研制了一架“浑天仪”。凡是知道的重要天文现象，都刻在“浑天仪”上。

东汉时期，地震很活跃。当时的人们不懂科学，以为地震是鬼神发怒。张衡认为地震是一种自然灾害，他根据自己对于地震现象的观测，在132年发明了“候风地动仪”，这台仪器成为世界上第一台观测地震方向的仪器。地动仪制好后，放在洛阳的灵台。138年2月的一天，地动仪朝西的龙嘴吐出铜球，掉到了蛤蟆嘴里，这说明西北方向发生了地震。但是洛阳一点也没有地震的感觉，因此，大伙都说张衡的地动仪是骗人的。过了几天甘肃东南部有人来报告说，那里前几天发生了大地震，人们这才相信。

这是人类历史上第一次用仪器来观测地震方向。中国以外，直到13世纪，才有类似的仪器出现。

Zhang Heng,
a Pioneering Scientist

Zhang Heng (78 — 139) was born in Nanyang, Henan Province. He was one of the world's first astronomers. He was also a learned mathematician. He was appointed as an official with historiographic duties, and was also in charge of drawing up the calendar and observing astronomical phenomena.

He developed an armillary sphere, on which were carved all the astronomical phenomena known at that time.

Contrary to the popular belief at that time, Zhang Heng maintained that earthquakes were not signs of Heaven's anger but natural disasters. As a result of careful observations of earthquakes, he invented a seismograph in 132, which was the world's first instrument to identify and ascertain the direction of earthquakes. When an earthquake occurred in February, 138, a bronze ball fell from the mouth of the carved dragon's head westward on the instrument facing the direction of the epicenter of the earthquake into the mouth of a bronze toad below. Since it could not be felt in Luoyang, the capital, it was believed deceitful. It was not believed until several days later when it was reported that an earthquake occurred in the southeastern Gansu Province.

It was the first instrument to observe earthquakes in human history. It was not until the 13th century that similar instruments appeared outside China.

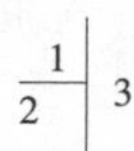

1. 北京古观象台
   Beijing Ancient Observatory
2. 张衡像
   A portrait of Zhang Heng
3. 地动仪模型（地动仪是世界上第一部测定地震方向的仪器，由张衡创制）
   A model of Zhang Heng's seismograph (the world's first instrument to identify and ascertain the direction of earthquakes)

"医圣"张仲景与"外科鼻祖"华佗

Zhang Zhongjing, the Saint of Medicine, and Hua Tuo, the Founder of Surgery

汉代有两位名医，一位是被尊称为"医圣"的张仲景，另一位是被尊称为"外科鼻祖"的华佗。

张仲景（约150—219年）是东汉末年河南南阳人。那时瘟疫流行，他的家人在不到10年间因患伤寒死了三分之二。他精心研究古代医学，广泛收集民间秘方，写成了《伤寒杂病论》16卷。在他的书里，不仅有大量内服药方，还介绍了中医理论，奠定了中医治疗学的基础。

华佗（约141—208年）安徽亳州（Bózhōu）人，生活在东汉末年。他在内科、外科、妇科、小儿科方面都很精通。华佗的外科技术很高超，他制成了一种麻醉药，叫做"麻沸散"。他曾让患了阑尾（lánwěi）炎的病人用酒服"麻沸散"，等病人全身麻醉后，他便开始动手术，最后在伤口上敷上有消毒作用的膏药，一个月以后，病人完全恢复了健康。华佗是世界上第一个应用全身麻醉技术的医生。

此外，华佗还精通针灸（zhēnjiǔ）技术。当时丞相曹操得了神经性头痛，就派人请华佗来为自己治病。华佗给曹操针灸，一针下去，曹操的头就不疼了。

华佗重视治疗，更重视疾病的预防。他模仿虎、鹿、熊、猿、鸟五种动物，独创了一套名为"五禽戏"的体操，用来增强体魄。

Zhang Zhongjing, the Saint of Medicine and Hua Tuo, the Founder of Surgery

Zhang Zhongjing (c.150—219) was born in Nanyang, Henan Province. He devoted himself to the study of medicine after typhoid fever decimated most of his family. He gathered folk remedies, and compiled a work titled *Febrile and Other Diseases* in 16 volumes. This medical classic not only recorded many Chinese medicine prescriptions, but also expounds the theories of traditional Chinese medicine.

Hua Tuo (c.141—208) was born in Bozhou, Anhui Province. He was proficient in internal medicine, surgery, gynecology and pediatrics. He is credited with being the first surgeon in the world to use the technique of general anesthesia, using a concoction called *mafeisan* to operate on an appendicitis patient with some disinfecting plasters. One month later, the patient made a good recovery. He was also an expert acupuncturist, and once cured Cao Cao, the renowned prime minister at the end of the Eastern Han Dynasty, of a neural headache using this technique.

Hua Tuo attached importance to therapy. He also emphasized prevention. He devised a set of exercises, known as the Five-Animal Exercises, to strengthen the physique, imitating the actions of the tiger, deer, bear, ape and bird.

傷寒論卷第一

漢 張仲景述 仲景全書第一

晉 王叔和撰次

宋 林億校正

明 趙開美校刻

沈琳仝校

辨脉法第一

平脉法第二

辨脉法第一

問曰脉有陰陽何謂也答曰凡脉大浮數動滑此名陽也脉沈濇弱弦微此名陰也凡陰病見陽脉者生陽病見陰脉者死

	3
1	4
2	5

1. 张仲景像
   A portrait of Zhang Zhongjing
2. 华佗独创的"五禽戏"体操
   Hua Tuo devised the Five-Animal Exercises
3. 华佗像
   A portrait of Hua Tuo
4. 刮骨疗伤图（据说东汉末年蜀将关羽被毒箭射中，华佗为他刮骨疗伤）
   A portrait of Hua Tuo treating General Guan Yu for an arrow wound
5. 张仲景所著的《伤寒杂病论》
   Zhang Zhongjing's *Febrile and Other Diseases*

封建国家的分裂和民族大融合时期——三国、两晋、南北朝

The Division of China Once More and the Intermingling of Ethnic Groups — The Three Kingdoms, the Two Jin Dynasties and the Southern and Northern Dynasties

概述

Introduction

三国、两晋、南北朝，又称魏晋南北朝，从220年曹丕（Cáo Pī）称帝开始，到589年隋灭陈统一全国结束，共经历了360多年。

220年曹丕建立魏国，221年刘备建立蜀国，222年孙权建立吴国，形成了魏、蜀、吴三国鼎立的局面。三国的都城分别在今天的洛阳、成都、南京。

263年，魏国灭蜀国，265年魏国大臣司马炎夺取魏的政权

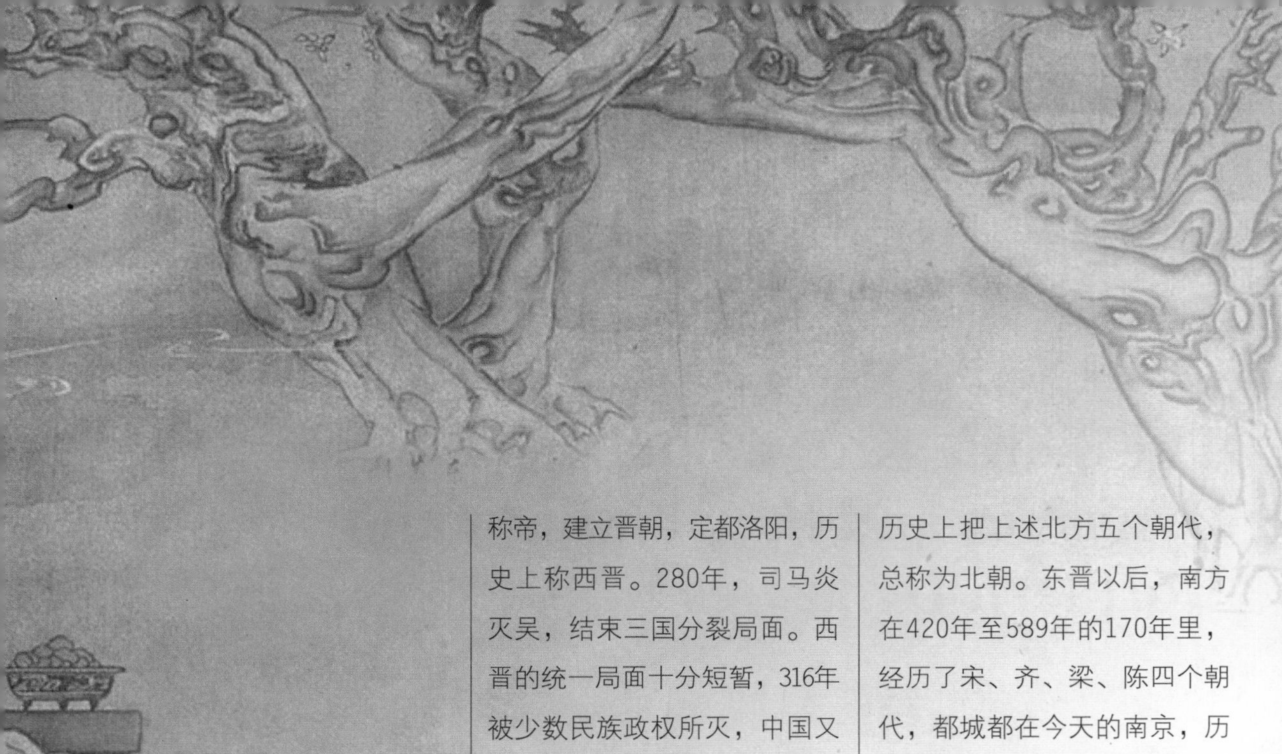

称帝，建立晋朝，定都洛阳，历史上称西晋。280年，司马炎灭吴，结束三国分裂局面。西晋的统一局面十分短暂，316年被少数民族政权所灭，中国又陷入分裂割据局面。

317年，晋王室的司马睿（Sīmǎ Ruì）称帝，建立了东晋王朝，都城在今天的南京。同时，迁居到黄河流域的几个少数民族，先后建立了许多国家。北方处于长达130多年的分裂割据时期，历史上称为“十六国”时期。

439年，少数民族建立的北魏政权统一了北方。后来，北魏孝文帝进行改革，规定少数民族学习汉族的制度、语言、服饰，促进了北方民族的大融合。后来北魏政权分裂为东魏和西魏，接着北齐取代东魏，北周取代西魏。历史上把上述北方五个朝代，总称为北朝。东晋以后，南方在420年至589年的170年里，经历了宋、齐、梁、陈四个朝代，都城都在今天的南京，历史上称之为南朝。南朝和北朝并存时期，史称南北朝时期。

三国鼎立时期，政治、经济、外交各具特色，充满生机，涌现出曹操、诸葛亮等一批杰出的政治家。三国两晋南北朝时期，出现了许多著名的思想家、军事家、科学家、文学家、画家、书法家，还有许多对社会科学和自然科学产生积极影响的名著。这些科学、文化成就，至今仍是中国文化遗产中的瑰宝。

三国两晋南北朝时期，欧洲强大的罗马帝国分裂，西罗马帝国灭亡，日耳曼人的王国在西欧建立，欧洲开始进入封建社会。

The Division of China Once More and the Intermingling of Ethnic Groups —

The Three Kingdoms, the Two Jin Dynasties and the Southern and Northern Dynasties

Introduction

The period of the Three Kingdoms, the Western and Eastern Jin Dynasties and the Southern and Northern Dynasties is also called the period of Wei, Jin and the Southern and Northern Dynasties. It started in the year of 220, when Cao Pi claimed himself emperor of the Kingdom of Wei, and ended in 589, when the Sui Dynasty wiped out Chen and united the whole country once more, and it was prolonged more than 360 years.

In 221, the year after the setting up of the Kingdom of Wei by Cao Pi, Liu Bei established the Kingdom of Shu, and in 222 Sun Quan founded the Kingdom of Wu, which formed a situation of tripartite confrontation. The capitals of these three kingdoms were located in today's Luoyang, Chengdu and Nanjing, respectively.

In 263, Wei wiped out Shu. In 265, Sima Yan, a Wei minister, seized the throne of Wei, declared founding of the Jin Dynasty and chose Luoyang as his capital. This is known as the Western Jin Dynasty. In 280, Sima Yan conquered Wu, ending the Three Kingdoms Period, but the Jin Dynasty itself was overrun by nomadic people in 316. China fell into disruption again.

In 317, Sima Rui, a descendant of the royal family of the Jin Dynasty, proclaimed himself emperor of the Eastern Jin Dynasty, whose capital was today's Nanjing. At the same time, several minority ethnic groups in the Yellow River basin also established many states. For more than

130 years, northern China was chaotically divided, this period is called the period of the Sixteen States.

In 439, the Northern Wei, established by a minority people, united the north. Emperor Xiaowen of the Northern Wei conducted reforms, decreeing the adoption of native Chinese institutions, language and costume. This resulted in a great intermixing of different ethnic groups in the north. Later, the Northern Wei split into the Eastern and Western Wei, and then the Northern Qi replaced the Eastern Wei, and the Northern Zhou replaced the Western Wei. The above five northern dynasties are known as the Northern Dynasties. During the 170 years from 420 to 589, following the fall of the Eastern Jin, there appeared four dynasties in succession, namely, the Song, Qi, Liang and Chen, whose capitals were all situated in today's Nanjing. These four dynasties are called the Southern Dynasties. The period when the Southern Dynasties and the Northern Dynasties co-existed is called the Southern and Northern Dynasties.

During the Three Kingdoms Period, the social politics, economy and diplomacy all achieved its unique style, and there emerged a great number of outstanding statesmen and generals, the foremost of whom were Cao Cao and Zhuge Liang. The Three Kingdoms Period, the two Jin dynasties and the Northern and Southern Dynasties, produced many famous thinkers, strategists, scientists, literary figures, painters and calligraphers. Also, a large number of famous works were produced which had a positive influence on the development of the social and natural sciences. These scientific and cultural achievements are gems of the Chinese cultural heritage.

During the Three Kingdoms Period, the two Jin dynasties and the Northern and Southern Dynasties, the powerful European Rome Empire fell into parts and the Western Rome Empire drew its last breath as well. The Teutons established their Kingdom in the Western Europe, and since then Europe stepped into the feudal society.

曹操

Cao Cao

曹操是东汉末年一位杰出的政治家、军事家、文学家。

曹操（155—220年），字孟德，安徽人。东汉末年，曹操在镇压农民起义的过程中，建立起一支强大的军队。

作为一个军事家，他喜爱研究兵书，认为打仗要随机应变。在官渡之战中，曹操仅有二万军队，他正确分析了敌我形势，以少胜多，打败了袁绍的十万大军，壮大了自己的军队。军队壮大了，就需要更多的粮食。曹操便让士兵们在不打仗的时候进行耕作，这种“屯田”的办法，不仅解决了军粮的问题，而且使北方社会的经济逐步好转。

在政治上，曹操看到豪强地主势力的发展，造成了东汉末年的分裂局面，因此，他很注意控制豪强地主的势力。他曾在官府门前设立一些大棒，专门打击那些以强欺弱的人，还让敢打击豪强地主的人做官。这些做法，有利于巩固统治。

在用人方面，曹操提出“唯才是举”的方针，也就是只要有真才实学，不管出身怎样，都被录用。因此，在他当权的时候，很多有才华的人都受到了重用。这些人为曹操统一北方出了不少力。

由于这些优势，再加上他控制了汉献帝，所以从200年官渡之战后，曹操先后消灭了北方各种军阀势力，结束了北方分裂状态。这不仅有利于中原地区社会经济的恢复，也为后来西晋统一全国打下基础。

当时的名士许劭（Xǔ Shào）评价曹操是：“治世之能臣，

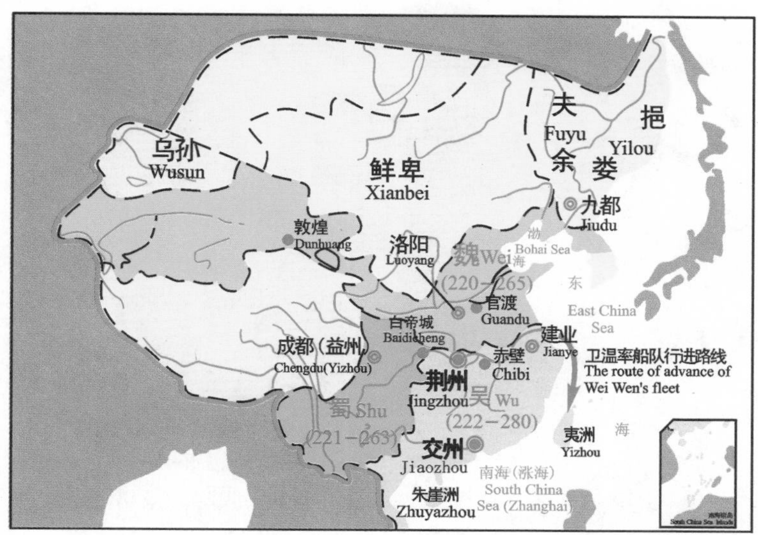

三国鼎立形势图

Sketch Map of The Triangular Balance of Power between the Three Kingdoms

乱世之奸雄”。在传统戏曲中，曹操一直都是以奸臣的形象出现在舞台上。曹操曾说过有一句话：“在这个混乱的时代，如果没有我，还不知道有多少人会称霸，会当皇帝呢！”

曹操还很重视文化，他多才多艺，曾写下了《蒿里行》、《观沧海》、《短歌行》和《龟虽寿》等许多不朽的诗篇。他的两个儿子曹丕、曹植也都是有名的文学家。

小资料 Data

挟天子以令诸侯

挟（xié），挟持；天子，即皇帝；诸侯，即割据各地的军阀势力。汉朝末年，皇室力量衰弱。196年，曹操将汉献帝迎往许都（今河南许昌）。曹操凭借自己强大的军事势力，控制了朝政大权，常用皇帝的名义向其他割据势力发号施令，以获得政治上的主动权，被当时的人称为“挟天子以令诸侯”。

Controlling the Emperor and Commanding the Nobles

Xie means “to control”, *Tianzi* refers to “the emperor” and *Zhuhou* refers to “dukes” or “nobles”. Toward the end of the Han Dynasty, the imperial family was very weak. In 196, Cao Cao invited Emperor Xiandi to his headquarters at Xudu (today’s Xuchang, Henan Province), where he was put under the protection of Cao Cao’s army. From then on, Cao Cao effectively controlled the state power, and issued orders to the other nobles in the name of the emperor. This was what people called “controlling the emperor and commanding the nobles”.

1 | 2

1. 曹操像
   A portrait of Cao Cao
2. 邺城遗址（曹操所建，在今河北省境内）
   Remains of Yecheng (built by Cao Cao, in today’s Hebei Province)

Cao Cao

Cao Cao (155—220), who named himself Mengde, was an outstanding statesman, strategist and man of letters of the late Eastern Han Dynasty.

He was born in today's Anhui Province. He built up a powerful army in the course of suppressing peasant uprisings.

As a strategist, Cao Cao found great interest in studying military works and believed that one should act according to changing conditions in wars. Devoted to the theory of military strategy, Cao Cao had some resounding

successes in warfare. At the Battle of Guandu, he properly analyzed the situation between the enemy and his own forces, thus, with only 20 000 men, he soundly defeated Yuan Shao's force of 100 000 and strengthened his troops. A strong army needed more food. Between campaigns, Cao Cao made his soldiers cultivate the land to supply themselves with food. This policy of "garrison fields" not only solved the army's food supply problem, it also improved the economy in the north.

On the political stage, Cao Cao saw the rise of powerful landlords in the late Eastern Han Dynasty as a threat to the unity of the country. Therefore, he paid much attention to the control of the powerful landlords. He once made the local authorities put some big rods in front of the government office and encouraged them to punish magnates who bullied the weak and gave government posts to anti-landlord elements. This was proved to be effective for strengthening his dominion.

In the placement of personnel, Cao Cao held the principle of "employing whoever is a talent". In fact, Cao Cao insisted on promoting any person of talent, no matter what his background was. Therefore, under his domination, a lot of talented people found their positions in the government. Those people contributed a lot to Cao Cao's unity of North China.

Because of these advantages, added to the fact that he had the Han emperor Xiandi under his control, Cao Cao put down all the warlords one after another in the north after the Battle of Guandu in 200 and ended the fissioning condition in North China. This not only was advantageous to the social economy restoration in the Central Plains, also built the foundation for the subsequent Western Jin Dynasty as a unified nation.

Then famous litterateur Xu Shao appraised Cao Cao as an able official in governing the country and an insidious hero in the tumultuous times. In traditional drama, Cao Cao continuously appeared as a disloyal image on the stage. Cao Cao once said, "In this chaotic time, without me, who knows how many people would want to dominate and claim to be the emperor!"

Cao Cao also attached importance to culture. As a multitalented man, he wrote the "*The Burial Ground*", "*Gazing at the Ocean*", "*Short Songs*" and "*Despite the Tortoise's Longevity*", and many other immortal epics. His two sons Cao Pi and Cao Zhi were well-known writers as well.

1

1. 甘肃民间制作的曹操木偶
Wooden image of Cao Cao carved by folks of Gansu Province

诸葛亮

Zhuge Liang

诸葛亮（181—234年）是一位杰出的政治家、军事家。

诸葛亮，字孔明，号卧龙，琅邪（Lángyá）阳都（今山东沂南）人。后来定居在隆中，在那儿，他阅读了大量书籍。诸葛亮读书与当时大多数人不一样，不是拘泥于一章一句，而是掌握文章的主旨。通过潜心钻研，他不但熟知天文地理，而且精通战术兵法。他志向远大，希望能为天下统一尽自己的力量。诸葛亮还十分注意观察和分析当时的社会，积累了丰富的治国用兵的知识。

曹操统一北方后，准备南下统一中国。当时孙权占据长江中下游。刘备借驻荆州（Jīngzhōu），他的势力最弱。他三顾茅庐，请当时年仅27岁的诸葛亮帮助他。诸葛亮为刘备详细分析了天下的形势，提出了联合孙权抗击曹操的办法。刘备听了诸葛亮这一番精辟透彻的分析，顿时豁然开朗。他觉得诸葛亮人才难得，于是恳切地请诸葛亮出山，帮助他完成兴复汉室的大业。

后来，刘备采取了诸葛亮的建议，在赤壁之战中获胜，势力由弱转强。

刘备称帝后不久，病死在白帝城，临死前将蜀国的大权都交给了诸葛亮。诸葛亮一心帮助刘备的儿子新国君刘禅。此时西南少数民族乘机起兵，225年，诸葛亮亲自带军南下，用计谋和平地解决了矛盾，并获得了当地少数民族首领孟获的信任。此后，诸葛亮就任用少数民族首领管理当地人，蜀政权与少数民族关系大大改善。同时，他还大力进行了内部的改革，任用有才能的人，注意农业生产和水利建设，加强部队纪律，使蜀国很快摆脱了危机。

后来，为了国家的统一，他六次北上攻打曹魏，但都失败了。在最后一次北伐中，他由于过度劳累，病死在五丈原军营中。

在中国人的心目中，诸葛亮是智慧的化身，他的传奇故事被广为传颂。

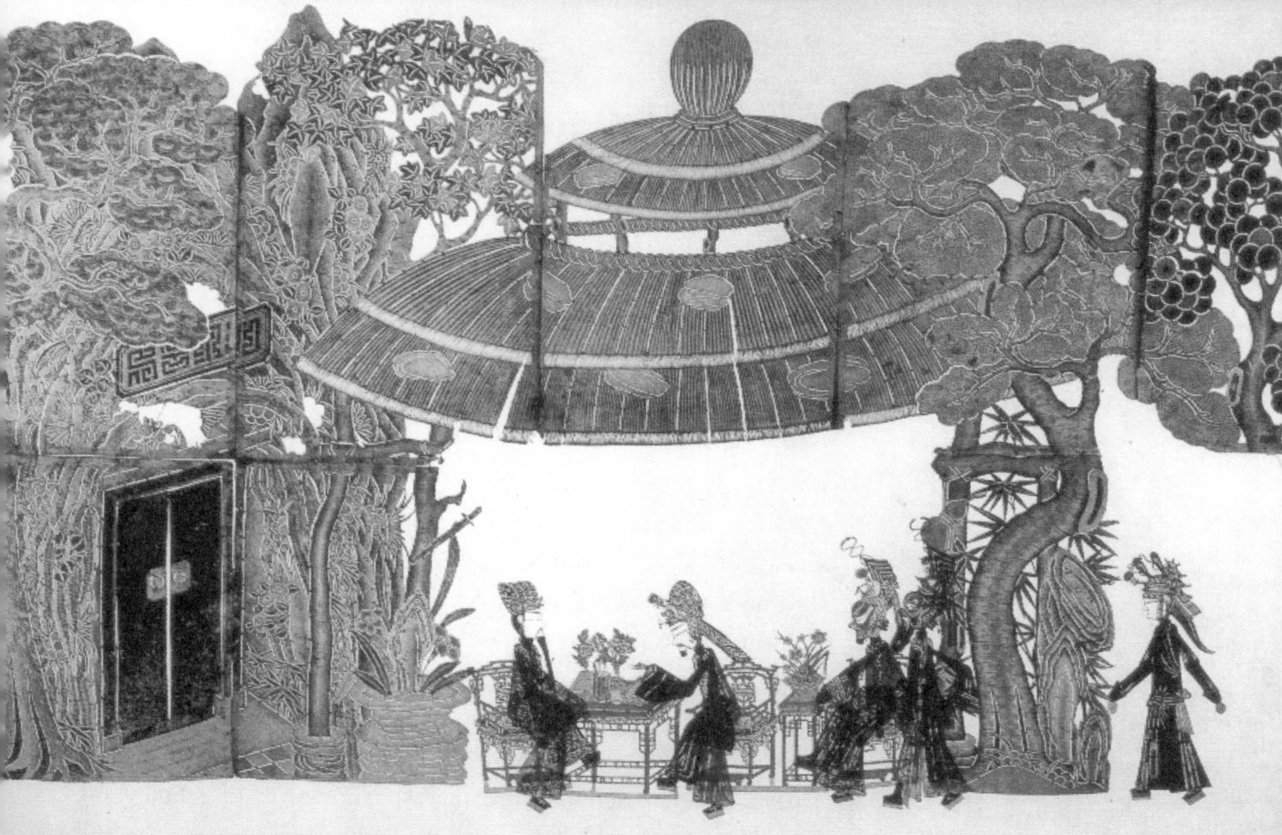

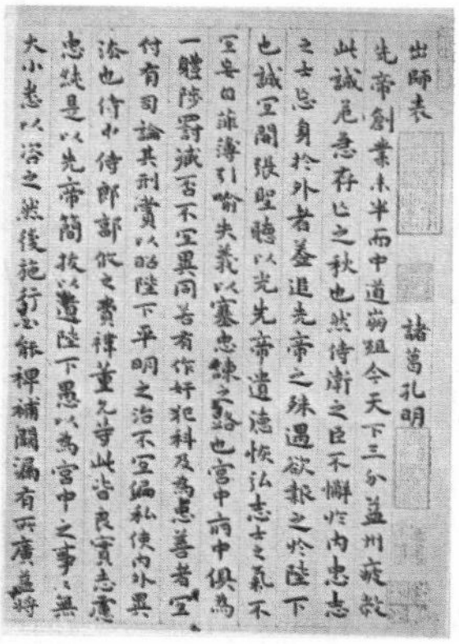
出師表 諸葛孔明
先帝創業未半而中道崩殂今天下三分益州疲敝此誠危急存亡之秋也然侍衛之臣不懈於內忠志之士忘身於外者蓋追先帝之殊遇欲報之於陛下也誠宜開張聖聽以光先帝遺德恢弘志士之氣不宜妄自菲薄引喻失義以塞忠諫之路也宮中府中俱為一體陟罰臧否不宜異同若有作奸犯科及為忠善者宜付有司論其刑賞以昭陛下平明之治不宜偏私使內外異法也侍中侍郎郭攸之費禕董允等此皆良實志慮忠純是以先帝簡拔以遺陛下愚以為宮中之事事無大小悉以咨之然後施行必能裨補闕漏有所廣益

1 | 2 / 3

1. 诸葛亮像
   A portrait of Zhuge Liang
2. 三顾茅庐皮影
   Shadow play displaying Liu Bei's paying three visits to Zhuge Liang's thatched cottage
3. 诸葛亮所著的《出师表》
   Memorial to the Emperor for a Northern Expedition by Zhuge Liang

小资料 Data

三顾茅庐

刘备与关羽、张飞二人结为兄弟，拥有一个不大的军事集团，依附荆州的刘表。为扩大自己的势力，他开始网罗人才。他曾听说过诸葛亮，知道他很有谋略，便带着关、张二将，到隆中诸葛亮的草庐去拜访。一连两次，诸葛亮都避而不见。第三次，诸葛亮被刘备的诚心感动，才出来会见。刘备终于找到了一位有才能的军师。

Three Visits to the Thatched Cottage

Liu Bei, Guan Yu and Zhang Fei swore to be brothers and with a small military bloc, they attached themselves to Liu Biao, the governor of Jingzhou. To expand his influence, Liu Bei began his quest for talents. Liu Bei had heard about Zhuge Liang, knowing he was an outstanding talent, so, together with his sworn brothers, Guan Yu and Zhang Fei, Liu Bei visited the thatched cottage in Longzhong where Zhuge Liang was living in obscurity. Zhuge Liang refused to meet Liu Bei the first two times he called, but on the third occasion he was touched by Liu Bei's sincerity, and agreed to meet him. Finally, Liu Bei found a talented adviser.

Zhuge Liang

Zhuge Liang (181—234), who named himself Kong Ming and Wo Long, was an outstanding statesman and strategist.

He was born in Yangdu, Langya (today's Yinan, Shandong Province), and later settled in Longzhong where he devoted himself to acquiring knowledge, and his reputation for wisdom spread far and wide. Zhuge Liang did not concern himself with doing textual research into every sentence or chapter like most people did at that time, but to grasp the gist of the articles. Through great efforts, he was familiar with astronomy, geography, and well-versed in the tactical arts. He ambitiously hoped to reunify the nation with his own strength. Zhuge Liang also paid great attention to social observation and analysis, and accumulated a wealth of experience in running the country.

Meanwhile, after uniting the north, Cao Cao prepared to march south for the dream of a completely united China. At that time, Sun Quan controlled the middle and lower reaches of the Yangtze River, and Liu Bei, the weakest of the three antagonists, was stationed in Jingzhou. Liu Bei went to visit the twenty-seven year-old Zhuge Liang three times to ask for the latter's assistance. Zhuge Liang analyzed the situation in the country in detail for Liu Bei, and recommended that he ally with Sun Quan against Cao Cao. By listening to Zhuge Liang's incisive analysis, Liu Bei became suddenly enlightened. He thought that Zhuge Liang was a talent hard to come across, and therefore, he earnestly requested Zhuge Liang to go with him, helping him to complete the great cause of vitalizing the Han Dynasty.

Later, Liu Bei adopted Zhuge Liang's suggestion and defeated Cao Cao in the Battle of the Red

Cliff, his forces emerging as a much stronger power.

Not long after he proclaimed himself the emperor, Liu Bei died of illness in Baidicheng. Before he died, he handed over the state power of Shu to Zhuge Liang, to be wielded on behalf of Liu Bei's son, Liu Chan, the new emperor. The southwestern minorities exploited the situation to start an armed revolt. In 225, Zhuge Liang led an army south, and pacified the rebellious tribes there peacefully with his outstanding wit. The leader of the local tribes thus had faith in him. His strategy was to govern through the local chieftains, which greatly improved relations between the Shu government and the minority peoples. Meanwhile, he also carried out far-reaching internal reforms employing people with ability, stressing agricultural production and the construction of irrigation works, and strengthening discipline in the army, which helped Shu quickly overcome a series of crises.

Later, Zhuge Liang launched six expeditions northward in an attempt to overthrow Wei and unify the country, but failed. On his last northern expedition, he died of overworking in the Wuzhangyuan military camps (in today's Qishan County, Shaanxi Province).

In the eyes of the Chinese people, Zhuge Liang is the incarnation of wit, and his stories are wide spread.

1 | 2 / 3

1. 湖北襄樊三顾堂是刘备三顾茅庐的纪念堂
In need of a brilliant military strategist, Liu Bei paid three visits to Zhuge Liang's thatched cottage to seek his assistance.
2. 诸葛亮采用攻心战术，七擒叛军首领孟获
Zhuge Liang captured Meng Huo — the head of rebels seven times by psychological tactics.
3. 纪念诸葛亮的四川成都武侯祠
Wuhou Temple, Chengdu, Sichuan Province (in memorial of Zhuge Liang)

赤壁之战

The Battle of the Red Cliff

曹操统一了北方之后，剩下能与他对抗的，就只有在长江一带的孙权和在湖北一带的刘备了。

208年，曹操带了20万大军（号称80万）南下。刘备退守湖北武昌，此时他只有军士2万多人。在军师诸葛亮的建议下，他决定与孙权共同抗曹。诸葛亮向孙权指出，曹操虽然人多，但其中有七八万是刚投降的荆州士兵，这些人主要是水军，是作战的主力，但他们不一定真心服从曹操。而曹操的北方士兵，不善于水战，长途而来生病的也很多。这些分析使孙权看清了形势，同意派大将周瑜带领3万军士与刘备一起作战。

曹军驻扎在赤壁（今湖北赤壁市，又一说在今湖北嘉鱼县东北），曹操下令用铁索把战船锁在一起，以便北方士兵在船上行走。诸葛亮和周瑜都决定用“火攻”的方法进攻曹操。一天夜里，刮起了东南风。周瑜派部下黄盖假装投降曹操，带着10艘战船，船上装满浇了油的柴草，向曹军驶去。接近曹军时，他们同时点火，火船顺风向曹操的战舰驶去，曹军战舰因为锁在一起，一时无法解开，不一会便成了一片火海。火又烧到了岸上，曹军死伤很多，大败而逃。

赤壁之战后，全国形势发生了变化。曹操退回北方。曹操死后，220年，他的儿子曹丕废掉汉献帝自立，国号为“魏”，

都城为洛阳。刘备乘机占据了荆州大部分地方，又向西发展，在221年，也自立为帝，国号为“蜀”，建都成都。孙权则巩固了长江中下游的势力，222年称王，国号为“吴”，都城为建业（今南京）。三国鼎立的局面，直至280年西晋灭吴才结束。

1. 周瑜塑像
A statue of Zhou Yu
2. 江西九江甘棠湖（相传为三国时期东吴都督周瑜的点将台旧址）
Gantang Lake, Jiujiang, Jiangxi Province (Legend has it that this was where the military governor Zhou Yu of the Kingdom of Wu appointed commanders for war during the Three Kingdoms Period.)

小资料 Data

孙权称霸江东

孙权（约182—252年），字仲谋，今浙江人。他在哥哥孙策死后，接管了长江中下游的军政大权。当时有人很轻视他，公开反叛，孙权迅速调来军队，把反叛的人杀了。大家见他这样有胆量，都很佩服他。后来，曹操要孙权送一个儿子去做人质，保证双方友好。孙权听从了周瑜的意见，决定不服从曹操，利用江东的地理优势，自己开创霸业，于是才有后来三国鼎立的出现。

Sun Quan Rules the Roost in Jiangdong

Sun Quan (c.182 — 252) was born in today's Zhejiang Province and named himself Zhongmou. After his elder brother Sun Ce's death, he took over his rule over the middle and lower reaches of the Yangtze River area. At that time, there were people who looked down on him and rebelled publicly against him. Sun Quan dispatched troops quickly and killed the rebels. Seeing he was so courageous and resourceful, people all admired him very much. Later, Cao Cao proposed that as long as Sun Quan sent one of his sons to Cao Cao as hostage, Cao Cao would promise to keep good relations with Sun Quan. Adopting Zhou Yu's advice, Sun Quan did not listen to Cao Cao's proposal. Instead, he developed and expanded his own power relying on the geographical advantages in Jiangdong (roughly the areas south of the Yangtze River), which finally led to the situation of tripartite confrontation.

The Battle of the Red Cliff

1 | 2

1. 孙权像
A portrait of Sun Quan
2. 湖北赤壁山
The site of the Battle of the Red Cliff, Hubei Province

After Cao Cao united North China, he had only two rivals, Sun Quan in the middle and lower reaches of the Yangtze River and Liu Bei in what is now the area of Hubei Province.

In 208, Cao Cao led an army of 200 000 men (claimed to be 800 000 men) south. Liu Bei retreated to Wuchang, Hubei. At that time, he only had army of about 20 000 men. Based on the military strategist Zhuge Liang's suggestion, he decided to make an alliance with Sun Quan to fight together against Cao Cao. Zhuge Liang argued before Sun Quan that, although Cao Cao outstripped them in the quantity of the army, about 70 000 to 80 000 of his men were soldiers surrendered from Jingzhou. These people were mainly navy soldiers and were the operational main force, and they had no certain loyalty to Cao Cao. Furthermore, the northern soldiers were not good at battle on the water, and many fell into a bad illness after their long-distance advance. This analysis caused Sun Quan to clearly see the situation, and he agreed to send his senior general Zhou Yu to lead 30 000 sergeants to fight against Cao Cao together with Liu Bei.

Cao Cao anchored at a place called the Red Cliff (in today's Chibi City, Hubei Province, although it has been alternately located in the northeast of today's Jiayu County in Hubei). He chained his ships together so that the northern soldiers could walk steadily on them. Both Zhuge Liang and Zhou Yu decided to attack Cao Cao with fire. One night, when there was a favorable southeastern wind, Zhou Yu dispatched the general Huang Gai with 10 ships to sail toward the enemy, pretending to be surrendering. The ships were loaded with firewood soaked in oil. When they were near enough to Cao Cao's fleet, they set their

ships on fire and left them to drift into the enemy ships. Because Cao Cao's ships were chained together and were hard to untie in such a short time, Cao Cao's fleet was immediately caught in a sea of fire. Later, the fire expanded to the land, and Cao Cao's troops were severely destroyed.

After the Battle of the Red Cliff, the situation of China changed. Cao Cao retreated back to the north. In 220, after Cao Cao's death, his son Cao Pi dethroned Emperor Xiandi of the Han Dynasty and proclaimed himself emperor, renaming his territory Wei, with Luoyang as its capital. Following his victory in the Battle of the Red Cliff, Liu Bei occupied most of Jingzhou, and then spread his power to the west. In 221, he also proclaimed himself emperor, and named his state Shu, with the capital in Chengdu, Sichuan Province. Sun Quan consolidated his power in the middle and lower reaches of the Yangtze River, and proclaimed himself emperor in 222. He named his state Wu, and made Jianye (today's Nanjing) his capital. The situation of tripartite confrontation lasted until 280, when the Western Jin Dynasty wiped out Wu.

赤壁之战示意图

Sketch Map of the Battle of the Red Cliff

西晋八王之乱

Eight Kings' Insurrection in the Western Jin Dynasty

1

1. 司马炎像
A portrait of Sima Yan

265年，司马炎逼迫魏帝退位，自立为帝，他就是晋武帝，国号为“晋”，史称西晋，定都洛阳，西晋出兵灭吴，重新实现了全国的统一。西晋初年，政府实施了一系列政策，鼓励农民种田养蚕，开垦荒地，增加生产。在两年多的时间里，全国户口数比两年前增加了130余万，出现了短暂的繁荣局面。

晋武帝司马炎为了保住司马氏的天下，恢复了古代的分封制，把司马宗室的27人封为王驻守各地。不久，司马氏家族就发生了内讧（nèihòng），赵王伦、楚王玮等8个王为了争夺皇权刀兵相见，在291至306年间，演出了一场长达16年之久的“八王之乱”。争战中的诸王为了加强自身的力量，利用北方少数民族势力参战，使匈奴、鲜卑（Xiānbēi）、羯（Jié）等军队长驱直入中原，北方地区出现了空前的大动荡。

304年，匈奴首领刘渊起兵并逐步控制了并州的大部分土地。308年，刘渊在平阳（今山西临汾）称帝，并派兵攻打洛阳。316年，匈奴军队攻入长安，俘虏了晋愍（mǐn）帝。西晋在不到40年的短暂统一之后灭亡了。

Eight Kings' Insurrection

in the Western Jin Dynasty

In 265, Sima Yan forced Emperor Weidi to give up the throne, and proclaimed himself the emperor. Sima Yan was the Emperor Wudi of the Jin dynasty. The state was called "Jin", which is known as the Western Jin Dynasty in history with its capital at Luoyang. The Western Jin Dynasty's troops wiped out Wu and reunified the country. In the early years of the Western Jin Dynasty, the government implemented a series of policies to encourage farmers' enthusiasm in farming, raising silkworm, reclamation of wasteland, and increasing production. Over a period of more than two years, the number of households and the total population increased by more than 1 300 000 over two years, and a brief prosperity occurred.

In order to keep the world of Sima family, Emperor Wudi of the Jin dynasty reinstated the ancient system of enfoeffment, and 27 kings from the Sima family were stationed around. Shortly, internal strife arose among the Sima family. The eight kings including Lun (King of Zhao), Wei (King of Chu) and others were fighting for imperial power from 291 to 306, which lasted as long as 16 years. In order to strengthen their own power, the eight kings made use of the northern minority forces. Thus, the Huns, the Xianbei, the Jies and other military forces pushed deep into the Central Plains, and the northern regions experienced unprecedented upheaval.

In 304, Liu Yuan, leader of the Huns, started a war and gradually took control of most of the land of Bingzhou. In 308, Liu Yuan proclaimed himself emperor in Pingyang (today's Linfen, Shanxi Province), and sent troops to attack Luoyang. In 316, the Hun army overran Chang'an, captured emperor Mindi of the Jin Dynasty. In less than 40 years, the Western Jin Dynasty perished after a brief reunification.

淝水之战

The Battle of Feishui

1. 司马睿像
A portrait of Sima Rui

317年，晋朝皇族司马睿在王导等人的拥戴下即位，定都建康（今南京），史称东晋。在北方，内迁的各族和汉族在黄河流域先后建立了16个政权，史称“十六国”。

4世纪下半期，前秦皇帝苻坚（Fú Jiān）统一了北方。383年，苻坚发兵南下，打算一举消灭东晋。战前有人劝阻苻坚，东晋有长江作为屏障，很难攻打。苻坚不听，他说：“我们人多势众，只要我们一人扔一根鞭子，长江水都会断流的！”

面对前秦的进攻，东晋上下决心同心协力抗敌。当时，晋军将领是谢石、谢玄和刘牢之，总数只有8万人。10月，前秦军队攻占寿阳（今安徽寿县），苻坚派被俘的东晋将军朱序到晋军中去劝降。朱序到了晋营，趁机告诉谢石，前秦军队到达前线的只有25万军士，建议晋军率先发起进攻。

11月，刘牢之带精兵5 000人进攻，消灭了前秦军5万人。谢石等随后乘胜前进，在淝水与前秦军隔水对阵。一天，谢玄以隔水不方便打仗为理由，请秦军后退。苻坚想乘晋军渡河时用骑兵猛冲，消灭晋军，于是命令秦军后退。可是，前秦士兵不明白后退的意思，以为秦军已经战败了。此时，朱序又乘机大喊，“秦军败了！秦军败了！”，前秦军队顿时大乱。晋军乘机渡过了淝水，秦兵拼命逃跑，苻坚被箭射伤，只带了10多万人逃回长安。

这是历史上有名的以少胜多的战役。淝水之战后，前秦瓦解，北方又重新分裂。而东晋则保证了南方的稳定。后来东晋

东晋和十六国形势图
Sketch Map of Eastern Jin and the Sixteen States of North China

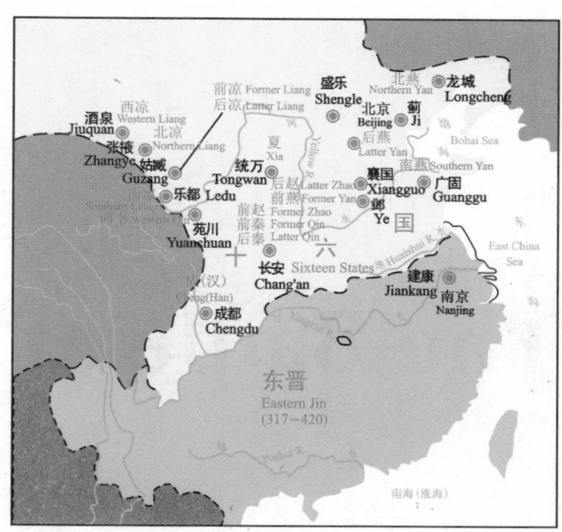

政权被大将刘裕夺取，建立了宋。420年至589年的170年里，南方先后经历了宋、齐、梁、陈四个朝代，历史上称之为南朝。439年北魏政权统一北方，与南朝形成对峙的局面，历史进入了南北朝时期。

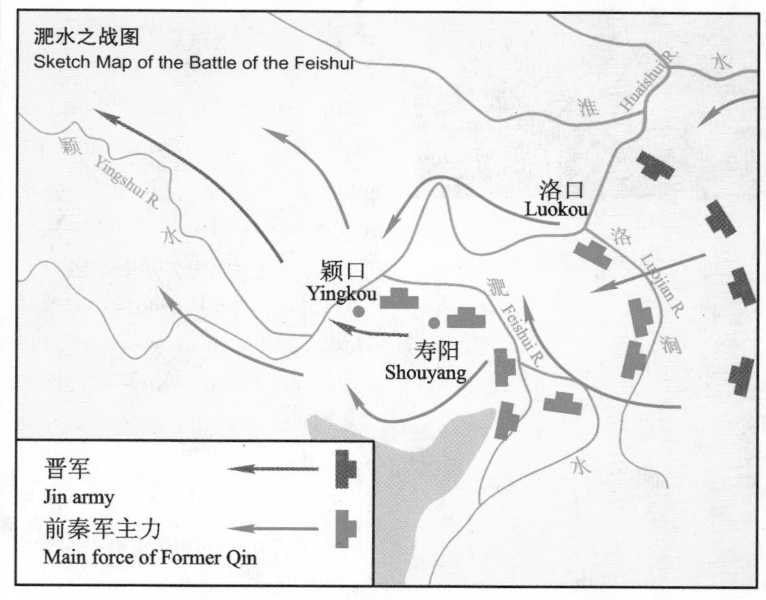

淝水之战图
Sketch Map of the Battle of the Feishui

小资料 Data

“草木皆兵”的来历

淝水之战时，前秦军队与晋军隔着淝水对阵，准备决战。一天，苻坚登上寿阳城头观察对岸晋军的形势，他一眼望去，只见晋军的营帐排列得整整齐齐，又往远处看，对面八公山上草木摇动，不知部署了多少晋兵。他对身旁的弟弟说道，这是很厉害的敌人，怎么能说他们很弱呢。说完脸上露出害怕的神情，命令秦兵严加防守。这就是成语“草木皆兵”的来历，用来形容人在非常害怕的时候，听到一点点动静，就很紧张。

The Origin of “Every Bush and Tree Looks like an Enemy”

During the Feishui campaign, the Former Qin army and the Jin army paddled across the Feishui river, preparing for a decisive battle. One day, Fu Jian boarded the defense wall of Shouyang city to observe the situation of the Jin army. Glancing afar, he found that the Jin army's tents were arranged in an orderly fashion, studying further, the bushes and trees on opposite Bagong Mountain were shaking, which did not allow one to know how many Jin soldiers were hidden there. He said to his brother, who was just beside him, that this was a powerful enemy, how could people say they were weak. After saying that, his face showed an expression of fear, and he ordered the Qin army to keep a close watch. This is the origin of the Chinese idiom of “Every bush and tree looks like an enemy”, which is a metaphor for extreme timidity when one is in extreme fear.

The Battle of Feishui

In 317, Sima Rui, a member of the royal clan, was proclaimed emperor under the support of Wang Dao and set up his capital in Jiankang (today's Nanjing, Jiangsu Pronvince). This is known as the Eastern Jin Dynasty in history. In the north, the minorities who had moved inward and the Han set 16 authorities in the Yellow River basin, which is called the "16 States".

In the latter half of the fourth century, Fu Jian, the ruler of the Former Qin Dynasty, united the north. In 383, Fu Jian led an army south hoping to wipe out the Eastern Jin in one attack. Before the war, some people firmly advised against Fu Jian doing so, arguing that the Eastern Jin Dynasty, with the Yangtze River as a natural barrier, was very difficult to attack. Fu Jian insisted and said, "We will overwhelm with numerical strength, so long as every one of us throws a whip into the Yangtze River, its water can not keep flowing!"

Facing the attack from the Former Qin Dynasty's army, the Eastern Jin Dynasty decided to make concerted efforts to fight against the enemy. At that time, the leaders of the Jin army were Xie Shi, Xie Xuan and Liu Laozhi. They had an army of only 80 000 men. In the 10th lunar month Fu Jian's army captured Shouyang (today's Shouxian County, Anhui Province). Fu Jian sent Zhu Xu, a Jin general captured by the Former Qin army, to the Jin army to induce them to capitulate. Seizing the chance of going to the Jin camp, Zhu Xu told Xie Shi that there were only 250 000 Former Qin soldiers in the front line, and he suggested the Jin army launch an attack first.

In the 11th month, Liu Laozhi

attacked the Former Qin army with 5 000 crack soldiers and wiped out 50 000 Former Qin soldiers. Xie Shi and other generals advanced on the crest of the victory and confronted the Former Qin army with each army on one side of the Feishui River. One day, Xie Xuan proposed that it was not convenient for the two belligerent parties to fight on different sides of the river, and asked the Former Qin army to draw back. Fu Jian had planned to attack the Jin army with his cavalry when they crossed the river, so he ordered his army to retreat. However, his soldiers did not know the real meaning of the retreat, and many of them thought that they had lost the battle. Just at that time, Zhu Xu shouted loudly, "The Qin's army has lost the battle! The Qin's army has lost the battle!" This threw the Former Qin's soldiers into great confusion at once. The Jin army took advantage of the occasion and crossed the Feishui River. Fu Jian's soldiers fled desperately and Fu Jian himself got wounded by an arrow. At last, Fu Jian returned to Chang'an with only a little more than 100 000 soldiers.

This was the famous Battle of Feishui in history, in which a small army defeated a big one. After the Battle of Feishui, the Former Qin Dynasty fell, and North China was again rent by independent regimes. The Eastern Jin ensured stability in the south. Later, Jin's authority was taken by the general Liu Yu who founded the Song Dynasty. During the 170 years from 420 to 589, the south went through four dynasties, namely, the Song, Qi, Liang and Chen, historically known as the Southern Dynasties. In 439, the Northern Wei Dynasty unified the northern regime, and entered into a confrontational situation with the Southern Dynasties. Thus, the history entered a period known as the Northern and Southern Dynasties.

1 | 2

1. 淝水之战主战场
Battlefield of the Battle of Feishui
2. 淝水之战图
A portrait of the Battle of Feishui

孝文帝改革

The Reforms of Emperor Xiaowen

1 | 2 | 3

1. 孝文帝像
A portrait of Emperor Xiaowen
2. 敦煌北魏时期壁画
Dunhuang Murals created in the Northern Wei Period
3. 北魏石刻
A sculpture of the Northern Wei

建立北魏、统一北方的拓跋（Tuōbá）氏是鲜卑族杰出的一部。拓跋部早期没有房屋、文字和法律，魏晋之际，他们游牧到阴山以南草原，成为36个鲜卑部族的首领，并开始定居，从事农业生产，逐渐强大起来。386年拓跋珪（Guī）即王位，改国号魏。439年太武帝拓跋焘（Tāo）统一了北方，结束了100多年分裂混战的局面，但是，北魏前期的统治一直处于不稳定状态，能否巩固统治的关键就在于改革鲜卑旧的习俗和加速汉化上。

孝文帝拓跋宏是北魏杰出的政治家，他认为要巩固统治一定要吸收中原文化，改革鲜卑族落后的习俗。490年孝文帝亲政，他继续推行文明太后的改革措施，加快了改革鲜卑旧俗、全面汉化的步伐。

494年，孝文帝把都城从平城(今山西大同)，迁到了洛阳。

孝文帝迁都后，推行了一系列改革措施。改革的主要内容有：改革官制；要求鲜卑官民穿汉族的服装；三十岁以下在朝廷做官的鲜卑人一律说汉语；改用汉族姓氏；鼓励鲜卑人与汉族通婚等等。

孝文帝喜欢读书，主张用儒家思想来治理国家。孝文帝并封孔氏宗子为崇圣侯。他曾亲自到曲阜祭孔庙，提倡儒学，建立学校，得到了汉族士人的拥护。

孝文帝推行汉化政策是非常坚决的，他坚决镇压反对改革的叛乱，对改革措施也实施严格督察。一次，他在街上看见一个妇女坐在车中，一身鲜卑打扮，就在朝廷上责备任城王拓跋澄（Chéng）督察不严，并让史官记载下来。

孝文帝的改革，加速了鲜卑和北方的汉化过程，促进了北方民族的大融合，洛阳附近的许多荒地得到了开垦，北魏的政治和经济有了很大的发展，北魏政权也得到了巩固。

The Reforms of Emperor Xiaowen

The Tuoba tribe, who had established the Northern Wei Dynasty and reunified the north, was an outstanding Xianbei ethnic group. The early Touba tribe lacked housing, language and the law. During the period of the Wei and Jin Dynasties they traveled to the nomadic grassland south of the Yinshan Mountain and became the leader of 36 Xianbei tribes, and began to settle in agricultural production and grow up. In 386, Tuoba Gui inherited the crown and changed the name of the country to Wei. In 439, Emperor Taiwu Tuoba Tao unified the north and ended the state of separation that had existed for over 100 years. However, the early Northern Wei Dynasty's reign was in an unstable condition and the key to consolidating their ruling was to accelerate the reform of the Xianbei's customs and learn from the Han people.

Emperor Xiaowen Touba Hong of the Northern Wei was a prominent statesman. He realized that it was necessary to absorb the advanced culture of the Central Plains and reform the Xianbei's backward customs in order to consolidate the reign. In 490, Emperor Xiaowen reigned. He continued the reform measures which were put forward by his mother, which speeded up the pace of changing the Xianbei's old customs and the comprehensive sinicization.

In 494, Emperor Xiaowen moved the capital from Pingcheng (today's Datong, Shanxi Province) to Luoyang.

After moving the capital city, Emperor Xiaowen implemented a series of reform measures. The main reform measures included: reforming the civil service system, requiring all the Xianbei people to wear Han clothing, requiring officials under 30 years of age to speak Chinese, requiring the Xianbei people to adopt Han surnames, and encouraging marriage between the Xianbei and the Han people.

Emperor Xiaowen liked reading and advocated the use of Confucian thought to govern the country. Emperor Xiaowen conferred the Confucian offspring and students as the St. Hugh Zonta. He went to the Confucius Temple in Qufu to offer sacrifices, promoted Confucianism and established schools, which won the support of the Han people.

Emperor Xiaowen was very firm in implementing the policy of sinicization, he resolutely suppressed the rebellion against the reform and strictly inspected the implementation of the reform measures. Once in the street, he saw a woman sitting in a coach wearing Xianbei dresses. He blamed the governor Touba Cheng of Rencheng for failure to fulfill his duty as an inspector, and let the historiographer document it.

Emperor Xiaowen's reform accelerated the localization process of the Xianbei, and promoted national integration in the north. Many wastelands near Luoyang were farmed and the political and economic situation of the Northern Wei Dynasty was greatly developed, and the Northern Wei regime was also consolidated.

花木兰代父从军

Hua Mulan Joined the Army in Place of Her Father

1 | 2

1. 河南商丘花木兰祠
Hua Mulan's Memorial Temple, Shangqiu, Henan Province
2. 民间剪纸花木兰
A paper cut figure displaying Hua Mulan

"唧唧复唧唧，木兰当户织，不闻机杼（zhù）声，唯闻女叹息……"这是一首流传很广的北方民歌《木兰辞》的开头，这首民歌的主角是一位英勇的北方女性，叫花木兰，这首长篇叙事诗讲述了花木兰女扮男装替父从军的传奇故事。

据说花木兰是北魏人，北方人喜欢练武。花木兰的父亲以前是一位军人，木兰十来岁时，他就常带木兰到村外小河边练武、骑马、射箭、舞刀、使棒。空余时间，木兰还喜欢看父亲的旧兵书。

北魏经过孝文帝的改革，社会经济得到了发展，人民生活较为安定。但是，当时北方的游牧民族柔然族不断南下骚扰，北魏政府规定每家出一名男子上前线。木兰的父亲年纪大了，哪能上战场呢？家里的弟弟年纪又小，于是木兰决定替父从军，从此开始了她长达12年的军队生活。去边关打仗，对于很多男人来说都是艰苦的事情，更不要说木兰是女子，既要隐瞒身份，又要与伙伴们一起杀敌。但是花木兰最后完成了自己的使命，12年后胜利还家。皇帝因为她的功劳，想请她做大官，被花木兰拒绝了。

千百年来，花木兰一直是受中国人尊敬的一位女性，因为她既勇敢又纯朴。1998年，迪士尼公司将花木兰的故事改编成了动画片，受到了全世界的欢迎。

Hua Mulan

Joined the Army in Place of Her Father

"Click, click, click. Mulan wove cloth in the house. Yet we could not hear the sound of the shuttle, but the sound of Mulan's sighs..." This is the opening of *The Ballad of Mulan*, a well-known folk song in north China. The heroine of this ballad was a heroic woman in the north named Hua Mulan. The song tells how Hua Mulan disguised herself as a man, and joined the army in place of her father.

It is said that Mulan lived in the Northern Wei Dynasty, and that people in the north were fond of practicing martial arts. When Mulan was about ten years old, her father, an ex-soldier, taught her military skills, including martial arts, horse riding, archery and swordsmanship. Hua Mulan also read her father's books on military science in her spare time.

After Emperor Xiaowen's reform, the Northern Wei Dynasty saw a picture of socio-economic development and more stable lives. To ward off incursions by the Rouran nomads, the ruler of the Northern Wei ordered that every household provide a man to join an expedition against them. Mulan's father was old then, and her younger brother was too young to go and fight. So Mulan decided to join the army instead of her father. Mulan spent 12 years in the army. Fighting at the border is even hard for many men, let alone a girl such as Mulan because she had to conceal her identity while fighting against the enemy together with her partners. But Hua Mulan finally completed her mission, and returned home with victory 12 years later. In view of her exploits on the battlefield, the ruler of the Northern Wei offered Mulan a high official position, but she refused it.

Hua Mulan, for her braveness and purity, has been highly respected as a filial daughter by the Chinese people for hundreds of years. In 1998, her story was adapted into an animated cartoon by Disney in the United States, to the acclaim of viewers young and old.

"书圣"王羲之与"画绝"顾恺之

Wang Xizhi, the Saint of Calligraphy, and Gu Kaizhi, the Matchless Painter

王羲之（Wáng Xīzhī）（约303—361年），山东人，东晋大书法家，后人尊称他为"书圣"。

王羲之年轻时跟卫夫人学习书法，后来又游历名山大川，观察、学习了前辈书法家们的碑刻。他练习书法十分刻苦，据说，他曾在浙江绍兴兰亭的池塘边日夜练习，竟使一池清水变成了黑色。最后，他终于形成了自己独特的风格。王羲之的行书和草书对后人影响很大，他有名的碑帖有《兰亭集序》、《快雪时晴帖》等。唐太宗对王羲之的书法非常重视，特别选取了他书法作品中的1 000个字，编成《古千字文》一书，让学生们学习。

顾恺之（Gù Kǎizhī）（约345—409年），东晋时期杰出的画家，后人把他和陆探微、张僧繇（Zhāng Sēngyáo）、吴道子并称为"画家四祖"。他曾游遍中国南方，为绘画创作积累了丰富的素材。

顾恺之的人物画特别出色，他强调"以形写神"，主张通过人物的眼睛看见心灵的秘密。他曾在一座寺庙里作壁画，画完人物后不点眼珠，等到参观的时候，他当场点画眼珠，人像顿时精神焕发，仿佛真人一样。顾恺之的绘画真迹早已失传，现在保存的有古人照原样绘制的《女史箴（zhēn）图卷》、《洛神赋图卷》、《列女仁智图卷》等。

小资料 Data

楷书的初创者

汉末魏初有一位书法名人叫钟繇（Zhōng Yáo），他擅长书法，特别精通楷书。他是中国书法史上第一位楷书大家，他的楷书，使得中国字由以前流行的隶书向楷书转变，对于汉字的定型作出了贡献。他的代表作有《宣示表》和《荐季直表》。

The Inventor of Regular Script

During the period from the end of the Han Dynasty to the beginning of the Wei Dynasty, there was a famous calligrapher named Zhong Yao who gained a full mastery of the regular script. He was the first master of regular script in Chinese history, and his calligraphy helped the transition from official script to regular script as the ordinary writing system. He also helped set the style of Chinese characters. His representative works include *Statement of Proclamation* and *Statement Recommending Jizhi*.

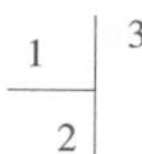

1. 王羲之像
   A portrait of Wang Xizhi
2. 王羲之《丧乱帖》
   Wang Xizhi's calligraphy
3. 顾恺之《洛神赋图卷》局部
   Part of Gu Kaizhi's *Picture Scroll of the Luoshui River Nymph*

Wang Xizhi, the Saint of Calligraphy, and Gu Kaizhi, the Matchless Painter

1 | 2 / 3

1. 浙江绍兴兰亭（传"鹅池"二字为王羲之所书）
It is said that the tablet inscription at the Orchid Pavilion in Shaoxing, Zhejiang Province, was written by Wang Xizhi
2. 王羲之《兰亭集序》
Wang Xizhi's most celebrated piece of calligraphy — *The Preface of the Orchid Pavilion*
3. 顾恺之《女史箴图卷》局部
Part of Gu Kaizhi's *Picture Scroll of Female Scholars*

Wang Xizhi (c.303—361) was born in today's Shandong Province. He was a great calligrapher of the Eastern Jin Dynasty, and was called by later generations the Saint of Calligraphy.

Wang Xizhi studied calligraphy under the calligraphy master Madame Wei in his youth. Then he traveled widely to study tablet inscriptions executed by famous calligraphers of older generations. It is said that he used to practice calligraphy by the pond beside Lan (Orchid) Pavilion in Shaoxing, in today's Zhejiang Province. He worked day and night, until the clear pond water turned black from his dipping his inky brush into it so many times. At last, He had finally formed his own unique style. Wang Xizhi's unique style in both the running hand and cursive script had a great influence on later generations of calligraphers. His famous rubbings of stone inscriptions include the *Preface to Orchid Pavilion* and the *Kuaixueshiqing Rubbing*. Emperor Taizong of the Tang Dynasty admired Wang Xizhi's calligraphy, and chose 1 000 characters written by Wang Xizhi, which he included in a book titled *Ancient 1 000-Character Text* to be used as a guide for students of calligraphy.

Gu Kaizhi (c.345—409) was an outstanding painter in the Eastern Jin Dynasty. Later generations grouped him together with Lu Tanwei, Zhang Sengyao and Wu Daozi, and called them the "Four Ancestors of Painting". Gu

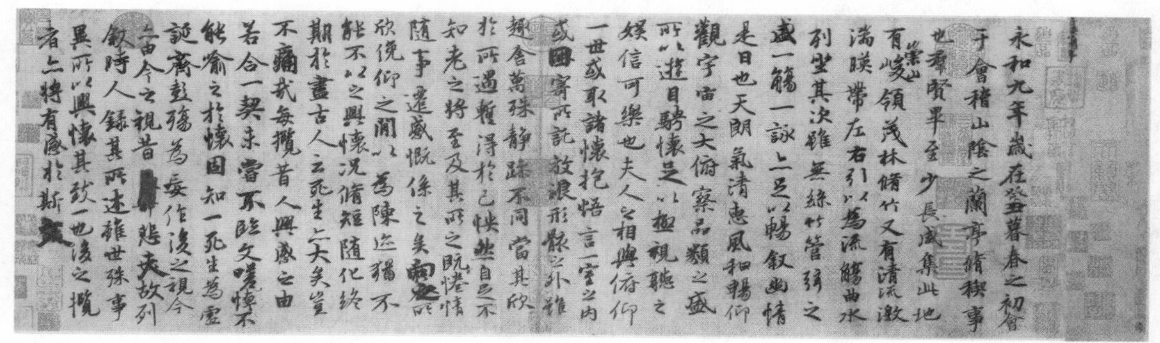

traveled all over south China accumulating rich materials for his paintings.

Gu Kaizhi was especially good at figure painting, and he stressed the "spirit by describing". He maintained that a subject's heart could be read through looking deep into his or her eyes. He once worked in a temple on a mural, but he did not finish the figure's eyes until visitors came. He painted the eyes, and viewers said that the figure's face suddenly filled with energy and seemed like a real person. Gu Kaizhi's works have long been lost. What remains today are only facsimiles of his *Picture Scroll of Female Scholars*, *Picture Scroll of the Luoshui River Nymph* and the *Picture Scroll of Virtuous Ladies*.

数学家祖冲之

Zu Chongzhi, the Remarkable Mathematician

祖冲之（429—500年），南朝宋齐时期人。他年轻时就学问渊博，喜爱数学，也喜欢研究天文历法。

祖冲之最大的成就还是在数学方面，他求出了比较精确的圆周率。圆周率是圆的周长和直径之间的比例，中国古代很早就知道这个概念，但不太准确。祖冲之总结前人经验，决定利用三国时候刘徽的“割圆术”来求圆周率。可是，那时运算的工具是竹棍，对于9位数的运算，要经过130次以上的反复计算，而且又容易出错。祖冲之每算一次，至少重复两遍，直到几次的结果完全相同才行。经过刻苦运算，终于得出圆周率大于3.1415926，小于3.1415927的结论。

祖冲之是世界上第一个把圆周率的准确数值算到小数点后7位数字的科学家，直到15世纪的阿拉伯数学家阿尔卡西（Al-Kashi）和16世纪法国数学家韦达（Viete）才推算到小数点后16位，超过了他。除此之外，祖冲之编写过一部《缀（zhuì）术》，收集了他研究数学的主要著作。唐朝时把《缀术》列为数学课的主要教科书。

Zu Chongzhi,

the Remarkable Mathematician

Zu Chongzhi (429—500) lived in the period of the Song and Qi of the Southern dynasties. He devoted himself to study in his youth, being especially fond of mathematics. He also liked ancient astronomical research.

Zu Chongzhi's greatest achievements lay in maths. He calculated a more precise ratio of the circumference of a circle. *Pi* is the ratio between the diameter and circumference of the circle. The ancient Chinese understood this concept very early, but not too accurately. Zu Chongzhi summed up the experience and decided to use the way of "Cut Circle" pioneered by Liu Hui, who lived in the period of the "Three Kingdoms", to seek *pi*. However, the computation tools at that time were bamboo sticks. For the nine-digit arithmetic, 130 times of computation were needed, which was prone to error. Zu Chongzhi repeated each count at least twice, until a few calculations got the same results. After working hard on the calculation, he finally reached the ratio of the circumference of a circle to its diameter at between 3.1415926 and 3.1415927.

Zu Chongzhi was the world's first scientist operator to put *pi* seven digits after the decimal point. And it was not until the 15th century that an Arab mathematician named Al-Kashi and a 16th century French mathematician Viete surpassed him by projecting it to 16 digits after the decimal point. In addition, Zu Chongzhi compiled his major achievements in mathematics into a book called *Zhuishu*, which became the main textbook on mathematics in China during the Tang Dynasty.

1

1. 祖冲之像
A portrait of Zu Chongzhi

封建社会的繁荣时期——隋、唐

The Heyday of Feudal Society — The Sui and Tang Dynasties

概述

Introduction

从东汉末年到隋朝初年近400年间，统一的势力一直在增长，这表明秦汉以来以汉族为核心的中华民族，已经形成了一个相对稳定的共同体，隋的统一是历史的趋势。

581年，杨坚夺取北周政权，建立隋朝。杨坚就是隋文帝。589年，隋灭陈，重新恢复了中国的统一。618年，隋炀（yáng）帝被起义军杀死，隋朝灭亡。在这场农民大起义中，隋朝大官僚李渊父子乘机起兵，建立唐朝。从唐太宗、武则天到唐玄宗前期，唐朝先后出现过“贞观之治”和“开元盛世”。唐朝的疆域空前辽阔，东到大海，南及南海诸岛，西越巴尔喀什湖，东北到外兴安岭一带，边疆少数民族地区逐步得到开发，国势十分强盛。

隋唐时期，经济空前繁荣，对外交往频繁，科技文化成就辉煌灿烂。唐代的书法、绘画、雕刻等成就都很高；唐诗在中国古代诗歌史上发展到了最高峰，李白、杜甫是唐朝最伟大的诗人；唐代散文也有很大成就，韩愈和柳宗元是杰出的代表。唐朝不仅是中国古代强大的王朝，也是当时世界上最繁荣富强的国家之一。

隋唐时期，西欧国家分裂，政局混乱，社会经济文化处于缓慢发展时期。与之相反，亚洲则生机勃勃。当时的亚洲，两大帝国都非常强盛，一是地跨欧、亚、非三洲的阿拉伯帝国，二是中国封建社会的隋、唐王朝。隋、唐王朝的兴盛也影响了周边国家，特别是日本、朝鲜等东亚国家。当时日本专门派人到中国来学习各种制度和文化。唐都长安（今陕西西安），不仅是当时的政治中心，而且是亚洲各国经济文化交流的中心之一。因为唐朝在国际上的影响巨大而深远，国外称中国人为“唐人”。直到现在，海外的华裔（huáyì）聚居的地方还被称为“唐人街”。

The Heyday of Feudal Society—

The Sui and Tang Dynasties

During the 400 years from the late Eastern Han Dynasty to the early Sui Dynasty, the reunification of the forces in China had been growing. This indicated that the Chinese nation, with the Han nationality at the core, had become a relatively stable community, thus, the Sui's reunification was a historical trend.

In 581, Yang Jian usurped the throne of the Northern Zhou, and established the Sui Dynasty. Yang Jian reigned as Emperor Wendi of Sui. In 589, the Sui conquered the Chen Dynasty, and reunified the northern and southern parts of the country. In 618, a peasant uprising brought about the end of Sui, with the death of Emperor Yangdi. During the peasant uprising, Li Yuan, a powerful Sui official, and his sons, seized the opportunity to revolt and established the Tang Dynasty. The period from the reign of Emperor Taizong, Wu Zetian, and to the early part of the reign of Emperor Xuanzong is called the time of the "Benign Administration of the Zhenguan Reign Period" and the "Flourishing Kaiyuan Reign Period". The territory ruled by the Tang Dynasty was broader than that of any of the previous dynasties. It reached the East China Sea in the east, extended to the islands in the South China Sea in the south, bordered Lake Balkhash in today's Kazakhstan in the west and extended as far as the Outer Hinggan Mountains in the northeast. The minority ethnic groups inhabiting the border were gradually developed, and the country was very powerful.

During the Sui and Tang dynasties, the economy of China prospered, exchanges with the outside world were frequent, and glorious scientific and cultural achievements appeared. Calligraphy, painting and sculpture flourished in the Tang Dynasty. In particular, Tang Dynasty poetry is regarded as the acme of this genre, represented by the greatest poets Li Bai and Du Fu. In the field of prose literature, Han Yu and Liu Zongyuan were outstanding. Tang was one of the richest and most powerful countries both in ancient China and in the world at that time.

During the period of Sui and Tang dynasties, Western countries were splitting and politics was in chaos. The economy and culture were in laggard development. In contrast, Asia was thriving. In Asia, two empires were very strong. One was the Arab Empire which crossed the European, Asian and African continents, and the other was the feudal societies of China's Sui and Tang dynasties. The burgeoning economy and culture of the Sui and Tang dynasties influenced the countries around China, especially the countries in East Asia such as Japan and Korea. At that time, Japan especially sent people to study the system and culture of China. Chang'an (today's Xi'an, Shaanxi Province), the capital city of the Tang Dynasty, was not only the political center of China at that time, it was also one of the centers for economic and cultural exchanges for the whole Asian region. Because of the Tang Dynasty's enormous international influence, Chinese people were called the "People of Tang" by their neighbors. Until now, the overseas place where Chinese community in a foreign land is still called "*Tangrenjie*"(Chinatown).

隋朝大运河

The Grand Canal of the Sui Dynasty

中国的大河如黄河、长江等，大多数是从西向东奔流入海。但是，有一条贯通南北的河流，它是一条人工河道，这就是著名的大运河。

605至610年，隋炀帝为了加强对全国的控制，使江南地区的物资能够更方便地运到北方来，动用了几百万民工，花费了约6年的时间，开凿了这条大运河。其中有些河段，是把以前挖好的运河修复、增宽、加深，中间也利用一些天然河、湖与运河相连接。

这条以洛阳为中心、贯通全国的大运河，全长2 000多千米，水面宽30到70米不等，北通涿郡（Zhuōjūn，今北京），南达余杭（今杭州），它沟通了海河、黄河、淮河、长江、钱塘江等大河流，经过今天的河北、山东、河南、安徽、江苏和浙江等广大地区。因此，大运河是我国历史上的伟大工程之一。

大运河的开通，使南方的粮食和物资源源不断运到北方，对于促进南北经济、文化的交流和发展，维护国家的统一，起到了非常重要的作用。

元朝在疏通旧河道的基础上又开凿了山东运河和通惠河，形成一条北起北京、南达杭州的京杭直通大运河，使它成为中国南北交通的重要水路。

中国今日又计划修复大运河，目的不仅是为方便南北的联系，更主要是使南水北调，解决北方缺水的问题。

1. 京杭大运河扬州段
   The Yangzhou section of the Beijing-Hangzhou Grand Canal
2. 隋炀帝像
   A portrait of Emperor Yangdi

The Grand Canal of the Sui Dynasty

China's major rivers, such as the Yellow River and the Yangtze River, all flow from west to east into the ocean. But there is a river which joins up the north and the south. It is a man-dug waterway, known as the famous Grand Canal.

From 605 to 610, in order to strengthen his control of the country and to transport the materials more accessibly from the area south of the Yangtze River to the north, Emperor Yangdi of the Sui Dynasty gathered several million workers to construct this Grand Canal. It took them about six years to complete. Some sections were the former canals which workers only repaired, broadened and deepened them, and some natural rivers and lakes were also included in the project.

The Grand Canal went throughout the country and took Luoyang as its center. It was originally some 2 000 km long, and the width of the water surface was from 30 to 70 m. The canal reached Zhuojun County (in today's Beijing) in the north, and extended to Yuhang (today's Hangzhou) in the south. It was connected to big rivers like the Haihe, the Yellow River, the Huaihe, the Yangtze River and the Qiantang River. The canal flows through today's Hebei, Shandong, Henan, Anhui, Jiangsu and Zhejiang provinces. Therefore, it is one of the greatest projects in China's history.

The opening of the Grand Canal helped to transport grains and materials from south to north continuously and thus played a very important role in promoting the economic and cultural development of the whole country and in maintaining political unity.

In the Yuan Dynasty, on the model of the old Grand Canal, people dug the Shandong Canal and the Tonghui River, which extended from Beijing in the north to Hangzhou in the south and became the main north-south communication waterway in China.

Today, China is planning to restore the Grand Canal, not only for the convenience of transportation between the north and the south, but also to transfer water from the south to the north to solve the problem of water shortage in the north.

小资料 Data

隋炀帝游江都

隋炀帝是个很有才干的政治家，也是一位追求奢侈享乐、滥用民力的暴君。

隋朝时的江都（今江苏扬州）是东南地区的政治、经济和文化中心。大运河刚刚修好，隋炀帝就乘坐4层龙舟，率一二十万人南下江都，开始大规模的巡游。随行的船有几千艘，在大运河中船头船尾相连，竟有100多千米。到了江都，每次出游的仪仗队就长达10千米，花费了大量人工和钱财，无休止的劳役使运河沿岸的老百姓怨声载道，不断起来反抗。618年隋炀帝在江都时，他的部下发动兵变，隋炀帝被处死。

Emperor Yangdi's Extravagant Trip to Jiangdu

Emperor Yangdi was a talented politician, but abandoned himself to sensuous pleasures without any mercy to his people. Jiangdu (Yangzhou City in Jiangsu Province) was the political, economic and cultural center in the southeastern region. The Grand Canal had hardly been completed when Emperor Yangdi boarded his four-floored dragon boat with thousands accompanying boats, and nearly 200 000 in his retinue, and sailed downwards to Jiangdu for his extravagant traveling. Excessively material and labor resources were splurged for his enjoyment. For instance, the honor guard had extended as long as 10 km. Endless forced labor aroused the resentment among the people along the banks of the canal. Continuous revolts had eventually overthrown the government of the Sui Dynasty. In 618, Emperor Yangdi was put to death in a mutiny launched by his subordinates.

贞观之治

The Benign Administration of the Zhenguan Reign Period

唐太宗李世民在年轻时辅佐父亲李渊创建唐朝，他很会打仗，也很善于用人，有很高的威望。唐太宗李世民当皇帝时，年号是贞观。贞观年间（627—649年），唐太宗吸取隋朝灭亡的教训，用心治理国家，实行了很多开明的政策和利国利民的措施，使唐朝政权得到巩固，社会经济得到恢复和发展，从而出现了一个比较安定祥和的社会环境。历史学家把这一时期称为“贞观之治”。

唐太宗知道要做到政治清明，就要善于用人，还要广泛听取意见。因此只要有才能的人，不管出身贵贱，都能够得到他的重用。丞相魏征敢向太宗直接提意见，即使太宗生气，也不退让。魏征病死时，太宗痛哭着说：“用铜作镜子，可以整理衣帽；用历史作镜子，可以了解兴亡；用人作镜子，可以明白对错，魏征死了，我失去了一面镜子。”

唐太宗采取了许多措施，如合并州县，节省开支；让农民拥有一定的土地；减轻劳役负担，让农民的生产时间得到保证等。这些措施很得民心，唐太宗引用古人的话说，皇帝是船，人民是水；水能载船，也能覆船。

唐太宗采用较为开明的民族政策，赢得各民族的拥护。北方各族尊称他为“天可汗（kèhán）”。唐太宗还将文成公主嫁给吐蕃（Tǔbō）的王，使汉藏民族关系更加友好亲密，对中国多民族国家的稳定作出了贡献。

The Benign Administration of the Zhenguan Reign Period

Emperor Taizong, Li Shimin, enjoys a prestige which is quite high. When he was young, he assisted his father in establishing the Tang Dynasty. Very talented as a general in war, he wisely employed capable persons to assist him in governing the country. He named the period of his reign "*Zhenguan*" (627—649). Drawing lessons from the downfall of the Sui Dynasty, Emperor Taizong carried out many enlightened policies and measures beneficial to the country and the people, which consolidated the state power of the Tang Dynasty, restored social stability and boosted the economy. Therefore, the reign was termed "the Benign Administration of the Zhenguan Reign Period" by historians.

Emperor Taizong knew that a well-ordered administration needed capable people and a wide range of expert opinions. So he made good use of capable people no matter what their backgrounds were. He once said that using a bronze mirror, one could tidy one's clothes; using history as a mirror, one could know the way of governing a country; using people as a mirror, one could tell right from wrong.

Emperor Taizong implemented many measures that enjoyed the support of the people, such as joining counties and prefectures together to reduce expenditure; letting peasants have a certain amount of land and reducing the burden of corvee labor to ensure that peasants had time to work on their land. Citing an ancient saying, Emperor Taizong said that the emperor was like a boat and the people were like water; water could carry the boat, but it could also capsize it.

Emperor Taizong won the support of all the minority peoples by adopting relatively enlightened policies toward them. The ethnic groups in the north called him "Great Khan". The emperor sent Princess Wencheng to the king of Tubo, in Tibet, which made the relations between the Han and Tibetan people closer, and contributed to the stability of China as a multi-ethnic country.

1 | 2
  | 3

1. 唐太宗像
   A portrait of Emperor Taizong
2. 唐三彩
   The Tang tricolor pottery models
3. 唐阎立本《步辇图》（唐太宗会见吐蕃王松赞干布派来求婚的使者）
   A portrait of the formal meeting between Emperor Taizong and the messengers (of King of Tubo — Songtsen Gampo) presenting a marriage proposal

女皇帝武则天

Wu Zetian, China's First Female Monarch

武则天（624—705年）是杰出的政治家，也是中国历史上唯一的女皇帝。

武则天从小聪明果断，通文史，长得又漂亮，14岁那年被唐太宗召进皇宫，成为才人。太宗死后，武则天被送进寺院做尼姑。太宗的儿子高宗当太子时就看中了武则天，他当上皇帝两年后，就把武则天从尼姑庵（ān）里接了出来。后来又废掉皇后，立武则天为皇后。

武则天当上皇后以后，帮高宗处理朝廷事务，并趁机除掉了一些反对她的大臣。唐高宗身体不好，他看武则天十分能干，有时就把朝政大事交给她去处理，武则天的权力因此越来越大。当时高宗与武则天被称为“二圣”，就是两个皇帝的意思。

683年，高宗死后，武则天就以太后的名义管理朝政。690年，武则天改国号为周，正式做了皇帝。此后，武则天继续推行唐太宗发展生产的政策，还破格提拔许多有才能的人。唐朝的政治经济在武则天时又得到发展。但是，她统治时期重用武氏家族、大建寺院、过分崇佛等，也给老百姓增加了负担。武则天去世前在大臣的逼迫下将皇位传给了儿子中宗，死后被封为“大圣则天皇后”，后称“武则天”。

Wu Zetian, China's First Female Monarch

Wu Zetian (624—705) was the first and the only female monarch in the history of China and an outstanding politician.

She was a smart, courageous, and beautiful girl; she knew literary history in her childhood. At the age of 14, she was taken into the imperial palace by Emperor Taizong as a concubine. After Emperor Taizong died, she was sent to a temple and became a nun. Emperor Gaozong, son of Emperor Taizong, was fond of Wu Zetian when he was crown prince. Two years after he succeeded to the throne, he had Wu Zetian brought back to the imperial palace. Then he demoted his consort, and made Wu Zetian his empress.

Wu Zetian soon became involved in affairs of state and palace intrigue, including getting rid of officials who opposed her. Emperor Gaozong, not being in good health, often let her handle his duties for him. At that time, Emperor Gaozong and Wu Zetian were called the "Two Saints" by the people, which meant they had two emperors.

When Emperor Gaozong died in 683, Wu Zetian administered the country as the Empress Dowager. In 690, Wu Zetian changed the name of the dynasty to Zhou, and became the empress herself. She carried on the policy of developing production initiated by Emperor Taizong. She also promoted many talented people in defiance of protocol, especially members of her own clan. She was a devout Buddhist, and spent money lavishly on the construction of temples. Eventually, Wu Zetian was forced by her senior ministers to hand over the power to her son, Zhongzong.

小资料 Data

宰相狄仁杰（630—700年）

武则天为了巩固自己的统治地位，十分重视选拔和任用有才能的人。她听说狄仁杰办事公道、执法严明，在百姓中间有着很高的威望，就破格提拔他为宰相（中国古代帮助皇帝治理国家的最高官员）。狄仁杰当上宰相后，也努力为朝廷举荐人才，他推荐的张柬之等几十人，后来都成为一代名臣。有人对狄仁杰说："天下桃李，都出自你狄公的门下了。"狄仁杰却回答："这实在算不上什么，推荐人才是为了国家，不是为了我个人的私利啊！"

Di Renjie, the Prime Minister

In order to reinforce her regime, Wu Zetian valued preeminent figures. Heard that Di Renjie (630—700) enjoyed great prestige for justly handling affairs, and strictly enforcing the law, she nominated him as the Prime Minister (the highest level of official in ancient China). Even when Di Renjie was the Prime Minister, he spared no efforts to recommend many standouts to the government. Those who were appreciated by him, such as Zhang Jianzhi, became a couple of well-known ministers later. Some one said to him, "The elitists in the country are all your honor's pupils." Di Renjie replied, "Nothing is more important than recommending the capable people for our country."

1 | 2

1. 四川广元皇泽寺（为纪念武则天而修建的寺院）
   The Huangze Temple, Guangyuan, Sichuan Province, was built in memorial of Wu Zetian.
2. 皇泽寺内的武则天像
   A statue of Wu Zetian in the Huangze Temple

开元盛世

The Flourishing Kaiyuan Reign Period

1 | 2

1. 唐玄宗像
   A portrait of Emperor Xuanzong
2. 唐开元通宝（唐代流行时间最长、最重要的货币）
   Kaiyuantongbao coins — the longest-lasting and most important form of currency used during the Tang Dynasty

“开元”是唐玄宗李隆基前期的年号。从唐太宗贞观初年到开元末年，经过100多年的积累，唐朝出现了全面繁荣的景象，历史上叫做“开元盛世”。

唐玄宗又称唐明皇，是武则天的孙子。他当上皇帝后，立志继承唐太宗的事业，任用有才能的人，接受大臣的正确意见，精心治理国家。有一年河南闹蝗灾，蝗虫飞过时，黑压压的一大片，连太阳都遮没了。田里的庄稼都被蝗虫吃光了。许多人都认为这是上天降给人们的灾难。但唐玄宗听从当时宰相的意见，认为蝗虫只不过是一种害虫，没有什么可怕的，应坚决消灭它。由于采取了有效的措施，各地的虫灾都得到了治理。

唐玄宗在位最初的20年里，唐朝出现了兴盛的景象。大诗人杜甫在《忆昔》诗中这样描述：“忆昔开元全盛日，小邑（yì）犹藏万家室。稻米流脂粟米白，公私仓廪（cānglǐn）俱丰实。”诗句的意思是：开元全盛时期，连小县城都有上万户人家；农业连年获得丰收，粮食装满了公家和私人的仓库，人民生活十分富裕。

开元年间，社会安定，天下太平，商业和交通也十分发达。扬州位于大运河和长江交汇处，中外商人汇集，城市特别繁华。唐都长安城里更是热闹非凡，世界上很多国家的使臣、商人、学者、工匠都争相前往唐朝进行友好交往，开展贸易、学习文化和技术。中国封建社会出现了前所未有的盛世景象，这就是历史上有名的“开元盛世”。

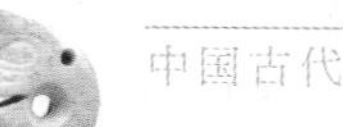

The Flourishing Kaiyuan Reign Period

Kaiyuan (713—741) was the earlier reign title of Li Longji, Emperor Xuanzong (712—756). Through over 100 years of development from the beginning of Zhenguan reign of Taizong to the end of Kaiyuan reign, the Tang Dynasty became unprecedentedly prosperous. So this period was referred to as the "Prosperous Kaiyuan Period".

Emperor Xuanzong was the grandson of Wu Zetian, but he modeled his rule on that of Emperor Taizong. He made use of capable people, listened to his ministers' advice and devoted himself to state affairs. He demonstrated his capability with prompt measures one year by combating a plague of locusts in northern China, and saved the people from starvation.

The renowned poet Du Fu described the prosperity of that time in his poem *Remembering the Past*: "Remember the good old Kaiyuan days/When even a small county had ten thousand households/The rice shone and the corn was white/And granaries of state and people burst with grain alike." During the Kaiyuan Period, the society was stable and peaceful, and commerce and transportation were highly developed. Yangzhou, located where the Grand Canal meets the Yangtze River, was a bustling city where merchants from all over China and abroad converged. Chang'an, the capital of the Tang Dynasty, was then one of the world's great metropolises. Envoys, merchants, scholars and artisans of many countries flocked to Chang'an to trade, and to study the advanced culture and technology of the Tang Dynasty.

小资料 Data

安史之乱

唐玄宗晚年宠爱杨贵妃，不专心治理国家，朝廷政治腐败，军队战斗力也大大减弱。他为了加强边防，在边境重要的地方设立了10个藩镇（fānzhèn），藩镇的长官叫节度使，是朝廷派出镇守边境的重要官员。

天宝年间，安禄山得到皇帝的信任，成为一身兼任三镇的、最有权势的节度使，控制了北部边境的大部地区。755年，安禄山和他的部将史思明在范阳发动叛乱，发兵15万，进攻长安，史称“安史之乱”。直到762年叛乱才最后平息。这场叛乱使北方经济遭受严重摧残，唐朝国力大大削弱，唐朝从此走向了衰落。

The Revolt of An Lushan and Shi Siming

In the second half of his reign, during the Tianbao Period (742—756), Emperor Xuanzong was obsessed by his favorite concubine, Lady Yang. He neglected his duties and the court was corrupt, and the army weak. An Lushan (703—757) wormed his way into Emperor Xuanzong's confidence, and took command of a great part of the armed forces. In the year of 755, An Lushan and Shi Siming staged a revolt in Fanyang with an army of 150 000, marching toward Chang'an. This was known historically as the Revolt of An Lushan and Shi Siming. It is until the year of 762 that the revolt was finally suppressed. This revolt did serious damage to the economy of north China, and marked the decline of the Tang Dynasty.

繁盛的长安城

The Heyday of Chang'an

唐代的都城长安（今名西安）建于隋代，叫大兴城，唐代改称长安城，经过近100年的建设，规模宏大的长安城才最后建成。唐代的长安城比现在的西安旧城大近10倍，是当时的国际性都市。

唐都长安，有雄伟的宫城，是皇帝居住和处理国家政务的地方。宫城南面的皇城里有政府的官署。城内街道和住宅设计得像棋盘，布局整齐，东西对称。城里的很多街道宽度都在100米以上，其中朱雀大街最宽。这充分体现出当时国力的强盛和经济的繁荣。明清时代的北京城就是仿照唐代长安城修建的。

长安城内有坊（fāng），有市。坊为住宅区，市为繁华的商业区，市坊分开。市里开设了许多店铺，叫做"行"，有"肉行"、"鱼行"、"药行"、"绢行"、"铁行"、"金银行"等，据说仅东市就有200多种行业。四面八方的奇珍异宝，在这里都有出售。

长安城还是当时的文化中心，娱乐活动丰富多彩，如音乐、舞蹈、斗鸡、拔河、荡秋千等。唐代最有名的画家、书法家和诗人经常聚集在长安城中，他们的创作活动给长安城增添了许多光彩。

长安城还是东西方文明的交汇点。当时和唐朝交往的国家有70多个，丝绸之路进入了全盛时期。日本、新罗（今朝鲜半岛）等许多国家都派人来长安留学，波斯（今伊朗一带）和大食（今中亚一带）的商人也纷纷前来长安城经商。当时，百万人口的长安，长期居住的外国人达万人以上。长安不仅是唐代中国的政治、经济、文化中心，而且已经成为了当时国际上著名的城市。

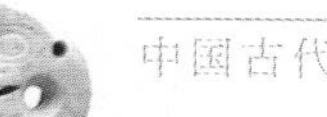

The Heyday of Chang'an

1 | 2

1. 今陕西西安市的明代城墙，部分建在唐长安皇城墙基上
The south gate and the embrasure watchtowers in today's Xi'an (The city wall of today's Xi'an was built on the base of the Imperial City of Chang'an in the Tang Dynasty.)
2. 唐玄宗李隆基的离宫——兴庆宫的拓片
A rubbing of the Tang Dynasty's Xingqing Palace (Emperor Xuanzong's detached palace)

Chang'an, the capital city of the Tang Dynasty, is now called Xi'an. The city of Chang'an was built in the Sui Dynasty, and called at that time Daxing. The city took nearly 100 years to build. During the Tang Dynasty, Chang'an was almost 11 times as big as today's Xi'an, and was a metropolis of international renown.

The emperor lived and ruled in the imperial palace in Chang'an. To the south of the palace there was the so-called Imperial City, where the government offices were located. The streets and residences of Chang'an were designed like a chessboard, with neat and symmetrical layout of the east and west. The width of many streets and avenues inside the city was over 100 m (Zhuque Avenue was the widest street). The city of Beijing in the Ming and Qing dynasties was modeled on the pattern of Chang'an.

The residential areas and commercial areas inside the city were located separately. In the commercial areas there were many shops: meat shops, fish shops, medicine shops, silk shops, iron shops, gold and silver shops, etc. There were said to be over 200 kinds of shops in the eastern commercial area. All kinds of precious and rare goods were available there.

Chang'an was also the cultural center of China at that time, with rich and colorful recreational activities, such as music, dancing, cock fighting, tug-of-war, swing-playing, etc. The most famous painters, calligraphers and poets of the Tang Dynasty usually gathered in Chang'an, and their creative activities added much glory to the city. Students came from Japan and Korea to study in Chang'an, and merchants flocked there from Central Asia. Among the population of around one million in Chang'an, there were over 10 000 foreign households.

松赞干布与文成公主

Songtsen Gampo and Princess Wencheng

吐蕃人是藏族的祖先，很早就生活在青藏高原一带，过着农耕和游牧的生活。7世纪前期，吐蕃杰出的首领松赞干布统一了那里的许多部落，定都逻些（Luóxiē，今西藏拉萨）。

松赞干布非常喜爱唐朝文化，也希望得到先进而强盛的唐朝的支持，他几次向唐求婚，于是，唐太宗把文成公主嫁给了他。

641年，文成公主在唐朝官员的护送下来到吐蕃，与松赞干布举行盛大的婚礼。吐蕃人民像过节一样，唱歌跳舞，欢迎文成公主入藏。吐蕃人原来住帐篷，据说为了迎接文成公主，特地修建了华丽的王宫，就是今天布达拉宫的前身。

文成公主读过许多书，很有才华。她入吐蕃时带去了许多医药、生产技术书籍和谷物、蔬菜的种子，还有唐朝精制的手工艺品。与她一起进藏的还有许多会养蚕、酿酒、造纸的工匠和会纺织、刺绣的侍女。文成公主信佛教，据说大昭寺的基址就是她选定的。先进的汉族文化传入吐蕃，对吐蕃生产和文化的发展起了很大的促进作用。

文成公主在吐蕃生活了40年。她为汉藏两族人民的友谊作出了贡献，一直受到藏族人民的怀念和爱戴。直到现在，在大昭寺和布达拉宫中，还保存着文成公主的塑像。在藏族人民中间，流传着许多关于文成公主的美好传说。

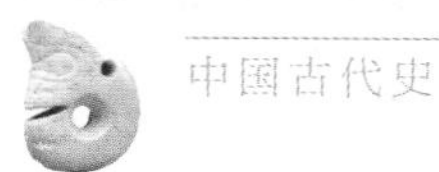

Songtsen Gampo and Princess Wencheng

The Tubo people were the ancestors of the Tibetan people. They appeared on the Qinghai-Tibet Plateau at a very early period. They were farmers and herders. In the early seventh century, Songtsen Gampo united the various Tubo tribes, and made Luoxie (today's Lhasa) the capital of the Tubo kingdom.

Songtsen Gampo admired the culture of the Tang Dynasty, and was eager to form an alliance with that powerful empire. In 641, Emperor Taizong sent Princess Wencheng to him as his bride.

The Tubo people used to live in tents. It is said that a gorgeous palace was built specially for her, which was the predecessor of today's Potala Palace.

Princess Wencheng took with her to Tubo medicines, books on science and technology, grain and vegetable seeds, and exquisite handicrafts of the Tang Dynasty. In addition, people who were proficient in raising silkworms, making wine and paper, and weaving and embroidering accompanied her, to teach these arts to the people of Tibet. Princess Wencheng was an ardent believer in Buddhism. It is said that the location of the Jokhang Temple was chosen by her.

Princess Wencheng lived in Tubo for 40 years, making great contributions to the friendship between the Han and Tibetan peoples. She is still remembered and loved by the Tibetans. Statues of Princess Wencheng are preserved in the Jokhang Temple and Potala Palace. There are many beautiful legends told about Princess Wencheng among the Tibetan people.

1 | 2 | 4
3

1. 松赞干布像
   A statue of Songtsen Gampo
2. 文成公主像
   A statue of Princess Wencheng
3. 文成公主入藏图
   Painting of Princess Wencheng going to Tubo
4. 西藏拉萨布达拉宫
   Potala Palace, Lhasa, Tibet

玄奘西游

Xuanzang's Journey to the West

《西游记》讲的是唐僧去西天（今印度半岛）取经的故事。故事中的唐僧带着他的3个徒弟——孙悟空、猪八戒、沙和尚，历尽艰辛、斩妖除魔，经过“九九八十一难”，终于到达西天，取到了真经。这虽然是个虚构的故事，但历史上，还真有这么一位去西天取经的僧人，他的法号叫玄奘（Xuánzàng）。

玄奘（602—664年）少年时就出家做了和尚，认真研究佛学，精通佛教经典。他发现翻译过来的佛经错误很多，于

玄奘西游行程略图
Sketch Map of Xuanzang's Journey to the West

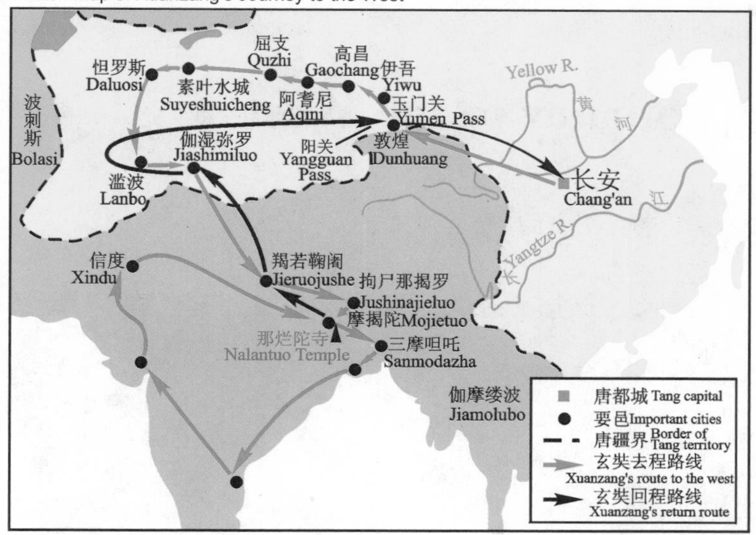

是决心到佛教发源地的天竺（Tiānzhú，今印度半岛）去取经求学。

627年，玄奘从长安出发，一路西行。他穿过大片沙漠，克服重重困难，整整走了一年，终于到达天竺。

玄奘在天竺先后拜访佛教六大圣地，留学天竺达15年之久。他的壮举感动了许多天竺人，有的国王还派人为他抄录经典，他也把当地失传的佛经介绍给他们。他还学会了天竺的语言，参加那里研究佛学的盛会，发表演讲。玄奘的博学，受到天竺人民的尊敬。

42岁时，玄奘带着657部佛经回到长安，受到热烈欢迎。回国后，玄奘立即开始大规模的翻译佛经工作，前后翻译佛经74部，约1 335卷。还培养出一大批出色的弟子。

作为一名高僧、一位大翻译家、中印人民的友好使者，玄奘为中国文化的发展，为中外尤其是中国和印度之间的文化交流作出了巨大的贡献。

小资料 Data

《大唐西域记》

玄奘西游回国后还写了《大唐西域记》一书，共12卷。书中详细记载了取经途中经过的100多个国家和地区不同的风土人情、物产、气候以及地理、历史、语言、宗教的情况，其中大多数是他西行的所见所闻，是今天研究中亚和南亚古代的地理和历史的重要资料。现此书已被译成多种外国文字，成为一部世界名著。

Records on the Western Regions of the Great Tang Empire

After he returned to China, Xuanzang wrote a book titled *Records on the Western Regions of the Great Tang Empire*. The book records in detail the different traditions and customs, products, climates, geographical conditions, histories, languages and religions of over 100 countries and areas in the Western Regions at that time. Most of the contents were what he saw and heard on his journey, which are very important materials for research into the geographical and historical conditions in ancient Central and South Asia. Now this book has been translated into many languages, and enjoys worldwide fame.

1

1. 西安大雁塔玄奘塑像
A sculpture of Xuanzang in the Greater Goose Pogoda of Xi'an

Xuanzang's Journey to the West

In the classic novel *Journey to the West*, a monk entitled the Tang Priest, goes on a pilgrimage to India to fetch the Buddhist scriptures back to China. Together with his disciples Monkey, Pig and Friar Sand, he overcomes 81 hardships and his mission is successful. The novel is a collection of legends, but in history there really was such a monk. His Buddhist name was Xuanzang.

Xuanzang (602—664) renounced the world and became a monk when he was young. He acquired a good command of the Buddhist classics, and he found that there were a great many errors in the translated Buddhist scriptures. Therefore, he decided to go to Tianzhu (today's Indian Peninsula), the birthplace of Buddhism, to study and bring back authentic scriptures.

Xuanzang started his journey to the west in 627. He crossed mountains and deserts, overcoming numerous hardships, and finally reached Tianzhu after a journey of a whole year.

Xuanzang studied in Tianzhu (today's India) and stayed there for as long as 15 years, rendering homage to six Buddhist Holy Lands successively. His sincere commitment to Buddhism and unswerving determination moved many Tianzhu people. Some kings even sent several people to copy Buddhist sutra for him. In return, Xuanzang introduced them some Buddhist scripture that had been lost. Xuanzang also learned the language of Tianzhu, attended huge gatherings concerning Buddhist learning and delivered speeches on many occasions. Xuanzang's erudition won the respect of the Tianzhu people.

At the age of 42, Xuanzang returned to Chang'an, bringing back 657 Buddhist scriptures. He then commenced the work of translating the Buddhist scriptures. He translated 74 Buddhist scriptures altogether, amounting to about 1 305 volumes.

Xuanzang was not only an eminent monk, but also a great translator and an envoy for friendship between China and India. He made great contributions to the development of Chinese culture, and for cultural exchanges between China and India and other countries.

1 | 2

1. 西安大雁塔（玄奘在此翻译从印度带回的佛经）
   The Greater Goose Pogoda of Xi'an stores the Buddhist scriptures that Xuanzang brought back from India.
2. 西安大唐芙蓉园，唐玄奘“西游记”雕塑
   Sculptures of Xuanzang's Journey to the West in Xi'an Datang Lotus Park

鉴真东渡

Jianzhen Crosses the Ocean to Japan

当玄奘西游取经返回长安差不多100年以后，唐代另一位佛教大师鉴真，决心东渡日本，传播佛法。

鉴真，扬州人，少年时出家当和尚。他学问渊博，有深厚的佛学基础，曾担任扬州大明寺住持。

742年，日本天皇派人来到大明寺，请鉴真去日本传播佛法。当时海上交通十分艰险，有人表示疑虑，鉴真果断地说："为了传播佛法，我怎么能怜惜自己的生命呢？"但是，鉴真去日本的计划一次又一次受阻。一次出海不久，船只触礁（chùjiāo），又有一次被官府扣留。当他第5次东渡时，遇上狂风大浪，航向发生偏差，船在海上漂流14天后才获救，这次东渡又没有成功。

不久，鉴真因病而双目失明，但他去日本传播佛法的决心没有丝毫动摇。753年，他已经66岁了，又开始了第6次航行。在海上与风浪搏斗了一个多月，鉴真终于登上日本岛，实现了自己的愿望。跟随鉴真渡海东去的还有23名弟子。他们随身带去许多书籍、佛像、经书和其他珍贵物品。

鉴真居留日本10年，不仅传播了佛法，而且对日本建筑、医学、艺术等方面都有突出贡献。鉴真在奈良（Nàiliáng）设计创建的唐招提寺，被日本人民看作艺术明珠。他的医术在日本也有很大影响，被日本人誉为"医术之祖"。后来他在日本去世。

Jianzhen Crosses the Ocean to Japan

Almost 100 years after Xuanzang returned to Chang'an, Jianzhen, another eminent Buddhist monk of the Tang Dynasty, crossed the ocean eastward to Japan, to spread Buddhism.

Jianzhen was born in Yangzhou. As the abbot of the Daming Temple in that city, he received envoys sent by the ruler of Japan in 742, who requested that teachers of Buddhism be sent to their homeland. Jianzhen decided to go by himself. However, the crossing was fraught with hazards, yet he said deceivably: "How can I give up my faith in order to protect my body?" It was only on his sixth attempt that Jianzhen arrived in Japan. At that time, he was already 66 years old, and blind. He, with his 23 disciples had brought a great amount of books, the image of Buddhism, Buddhistic scripture, and some other treasure.

Jianzhen lived in Japan for 10 years. He not only spread knowledge of Buddhism, he also made prominent contributions to Japanese architecture, medicine and art. He designed the Toshodai Temple in Nara, which was treasured as a "bright pearl". He had also exerted great influence on Japanese medicine; he was praised as the Founder of Medicine. Jianzhen died in Japan.

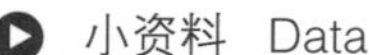

小资料 Data

遣唐使

唐朝时期，中国是东方最先进的国家，日本先后派了十几批遣唐使前往长安学习唐朝的政治制度、文化和佛法，人数多时达五六百人。这些遣唐使回国以后，积极传播中国的社会制度和文化，促进了中日友好关系和文化交流。

Envoys Sent to the Tang Empire

During the Tang Dynasty, China was the most advanced country in the East. On a dozen occasions, Japan sent groups of 500 to 600 students at a time to study in China. After these people returned to Japan, they spread knowledge of Chinese social institutions and culture, which did a great deal to promote the friendly relations and cultural exchanges between China and Japan.

1 | 2

1. 鉴真六次东渡日本传法的海船模型
   A vessel model taken by Jianzhen sailing to Japan six times to spread Buddhism
2. 江苏扬州鉴真纪念堂鉴真像
   A statue of Jianzhen in the Jianzhen Memorial Hall, Yangzhou, Jiangsu Province

三大石窟

The Three Famous Grottoes

佛教起源于古印度，在大约1世纪前后就传入中国。进入南北朝以后，统治者为宣扬佛教，在一些地方劈山削崖，开凿石窟。隋唐时期，石窟艺术又有很大的发展。著名的有山西大同的云冈石窟、河南洛阳的龙门石窟和甘肃敦煌的莫高窟，三大石窟中的最大的洞窟都是在这一时期开凿的。它们以藏有大量丰富多彩、千姿百态的佛教壁画与雕像塑像闻名于世，被称为艺术的宝库。

山西的云冈石窟在北魏佛教艺术中最有名。它依山开凿，东西长1 000米，雕刻着成千上万大大小小的佛像，最大的佛像高达17米。

龙门石窟里最大的洞窟是唐朝时开凿的，佛像的造型和服饰更加东方化，更加真实，体现

了唐代社会人们的审美观念。

莫高窟有1 000多个洞窟，又叫千佛洞，现有几百个洞窟，其中十分之六七的洞窟是隋唐时期开凿的。洞窟的四壁和顶上画满了彩色壁画，著名画家吴道子、阎立本等许多著名画派的作品，在莫高窟壁画中都有反映。现存壁画总面积有45 000多平方米，内容表现了佛教故事，不少画面反映出隋唐时期社会的繁荣。莫高窟的塑像共有2 400多尊，隋唐时期占了近一半。这些塑像都富于艺术魅力。

1 | 2

1. 敦煌莫高窟佛像
   The Buddhist Statues of Mogao Grottoes, Dunhuang, Gansu Province
2. 山西大同云冈石窟第20窟雕像
   The Buddhist statues (No.20 Yungang Grottoes at Datong, Shanxi Province)

The Three Famous Grottoes

Buddhism originated in India and spread into the hinterland of China around the first century. In the Southern and Northern dynasties, grottoes were carved in cliffs to house statues of Buddha and sacred murals. In the Sui and Tang dynasties, grotto art made great strides. The three most famous groups of grottoes are the Yungang Grottoes in

2

1 3

1. 洛阳龙门石窟奉先寺北壁塑像
The Buddhist statues in the Longmen Grottoes in Luoyang, Henan Province
2. 四川乐山大佛
The Great Statue of Buddha at Leshan, Sichuan Province
3. 敦煌莫高窟壁画
Murals of Mogao Grottoes, Dunhuang, Gansu Province

Datong, Shanxi Province, the Longmen Grottoes in Luoyang, Henan Province, and the Mogao Grottoes in Dunhuang, Gansu Province. They are world-famous for their great number of rich and colorful Buddhist frescos, sculptures and statues.

The Yungang Grottoes are the most eminent among the Buddhist artistic works of the Northern Wei Dynasty. They are cut into the foot of a mountain, and stretch 1 000 m from east to west. They contain thousands of Buddhist sculptures of various sizes, among which the biggest one is 17 m high.

The largest cave in the Longmen Grottoes was hollowed out during the Tang Dynasty. The Buddhist statues in these grottoes show the influence of the esthetic concepts of the people of India and Central Asia.

The Mogao Grottoes at Dunhuang used to have over 1 000 caves, but nowadays there remain only a few hundred, of which 60 to 70% were made in the Sui and Tang dynasties. The walls and ceilings of the grottoes are covered with colored frescos, including works of many famous painters such as Wu Daozi, Yan Liben, etc. totaling more than 45 000 m^2. The frescos depict Buddhist stories. Many of them reflect the prosperity of the Tang Dynasty. The Mogao Grottoes boast over 2 400 statues, almost half of which date from the Sui and Tang dynasties.

小资料 Data

乐山大佛

四川乐山的乐山大佛是世界上现存最大的一尊石刻坐佛像，于唐玄宗开元元年（713年）动工兴建，于唐德宗贞元十九年（803年）完工。乐山大佛是弥勒（Mílè）坐像，全身通高70.8米，肩宽24米。完工时的弥勒坐像全身彩绘，上面盖有宽60米的7层楼阁，这楼阁后来毁于战火。乐山大佛拥有“山是一尊佛，佛是一座山”的美誉。

The Great Statue of Buddha at Leshan, Sichuan Province

The Leshan Buddha is the biggest stone seated statue of Buddha in existence. Construction of the statue started in the first year (713) of the Kaiyuan reign period of Emperor Xuanzong of the Tang Dynasty, and it was completed in the 19th year (803) of the Zhenyuan reign period of Emperor Dezong. It is a seated statue of Maitreya (the Buddha of the Future). It is 70.8 m high, and the shoulder width is 24 m. When the statue was completed, it was painted in colors all over, and a seven-story tower 60 m wide was erected above it. This tower was destroyed in a war. There is a saying about the Leshan Buddha: the mountain is a Buddha, and the Buddha is a mountain.

科举制

The Imperial Civil Examination System

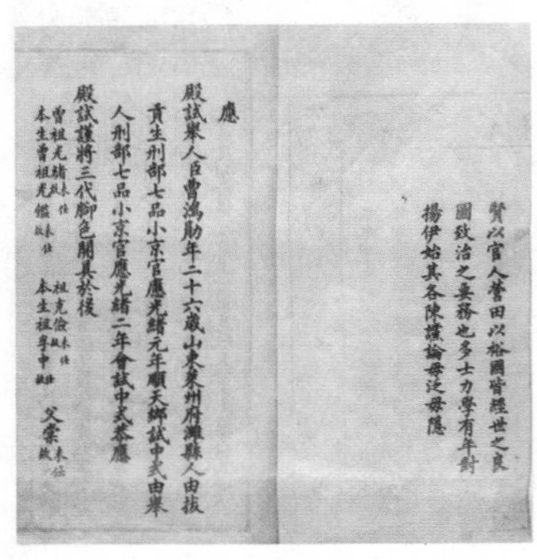

科举制也称“开科取士”，就是朝廷开设科目公开考试，然后根据考试成绩来选取人才，分别授予官职的一种制度。科举制产生于隋朝，唐朝继承了这一制度，并进一步完善，成为国家选拔官员的主要方式。

唐朝科举考试分为常科和制科两种。常科每年举行，考试科目有秀才、明经、进士等。在众多科目中考进士科难度最大，往往百人中才取一两名，因此特别受到读书人的重视。进士科考试合格称为“及第”。及第的人要在曲江池参加庆祝宴会，并在长安慈恩寺大雁塔下题名，十分荣耀。制科是皇帝临时诏令设置的科目，名目也很多，通常由皇帝亲自主持，但在士人眼里往往被视为非正途出身，不受重视。

唐代考生有两个来源：一是由学馆选送的学生，称为生徒；二是经州县初考合格后，再进京参加考试，称为乡贡。唐代科举考试一般由礼部主持，考生录取以后，再经吏部复试，根据成绩授予各种官职。

隋唐时期形成的科举制，使普通的读书人获得参加考试然后被选拔做官的机会。这就使封建王朝能在更大的范围内选拔官员。科举制历经隋、唐、宋、元、明、清，一直为历代王朝所采用。许多历史学家都认为，科举制是一项很好的文官选拔制度，也是中国从隋唐到明清一千多年顺利发展的一个保证。不过到了明清时，科举制演变成一种刻板、僵化的制度，也束缚了中国读书人的思想，对历史发展产生了消极的影响。

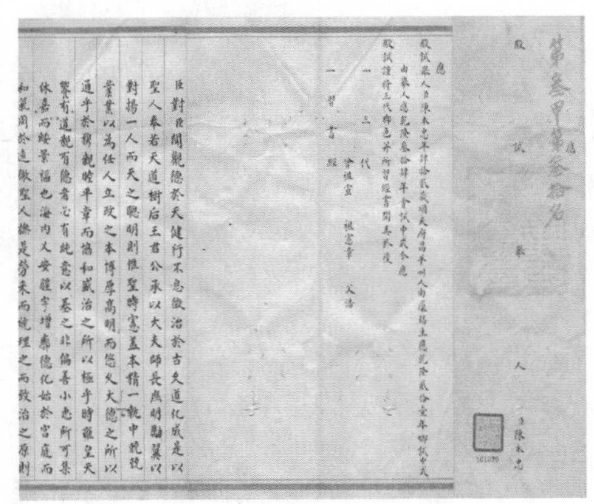

The Imperial Civil Examination System

Starting in the Sui Dynasty, the imperial government selected its officials from the ranks of the successful candidates in the imperial civil examinations.

The imperial civil examination in the Tang Dynasty was classified into two types: the regular one and the irregular one. The regular examination was held every year. It had many levels, such as *Xiucai*, *Mingjing* and *Jinshi*. The *Jinshi* degree was the most difficult to attain. Every year hundreds of men took the *Jinshi* examination, but only one or two passed. Those who passed the *Jinshi* examination would attend a lavish banquet held by the Qujiang Pond, and their names would be announced under the Greater Goose Pagoda in the Ci'en Temple. The irregular examination was set spontaneously by the emperor himself, who acted as the chief examiner. However, it was of less importance than the regular one.

There were two kinds of people who took the imperial civil examination. One consisted of students chosen by academies, who were called *shengtu*; the other kind, called *xianggong*, consisted of those who had passed the examinations held by prefectures and counties. The imperial civil examination in the Tang Dynasty was usually presided over by the Board of Rites. Those who passed the examination would be re-examined by the Board of Rites, and then receive various kinds of official positions according to their examination results.

The imperial civil examination system was the method used until the late years of Chinese last feudal dynasty, the Qing, which fell in 1911, to choose talented men for official positions. Many historians thought that the imperial civil examination system was an excellent system for selecting civilians and it has been the guarantee of the sound development from the Sui and Tang dynasties to the Ming and Qing dynasties for more than 1 000 years. However, during the Ming and Qing dynasties, the imperial civil examination system, which stressed knowledge of the Confucian classics exclusively, became a rigid and stultifying institution which kept China from adopting modern scientific methods.

1. 状元殿试策
   An examination paper of a Number One Scholar
2. 清代殿试试卷局部
   Part of an examination paper of the palace examination of the Qing Dynasty
3. 宋人科举考试图
   A portrait of the Imperial Civil Examination System

封建社会的继续发展和民族政权并立时期——五代、辽、宋、夏、金、元

The Continued Development of Feudal Society and the Coexistence of Ethnic Regimes — The Five Dynasties, and the Liao, Song, Xia, Jin and Yuan Dynasties

概述

Introduction

五代、辽、宋、夏、金、元时期，从907年后梁建立开始，到1368年元朝灭亡为止，长达460多年。从朱温废掉唐朝皇帝，建立梁朝（史称后梁）以后的50多年里，中国北部先后出现后梁、后唐、后晋、后汉、后周五个朝代，史称五代。南方各地和北方的山西，还先后出现了前蜀、吴、闽（Mǐn）、吴越、楚、南汉、南平、后蜀、南唐、北汉等十个割据政权，总称十国。

960年，后周大将赵匡胤（Zhào kuāngyìn）发动陈桥兵变，建立宋朝，都城在今天的开封，历史上称北宋。当时，中国还有辽、西夏等几个少数民族政权。1127年，女真贵族建立的金朝派军队攻入开封，北宋灭亡，继位的皇帝赵构逃往南方，后来在今天的杭州定都，史称南宋，出现了宋、金对峙的局面。1206年，铁木真统一蒙古，称成吉思汗。蒙古先后灭西夏、金，并一直打到多瑙河流域。1260年，忽必烈继承汗位，后来定都于今天的北京。1271年，忽必烈正式定国号为元。元军于1276年攻占杭州，1279年消灭了南宋残余势力，统一了中国。1368年，朱元璋的军队攻占北京，元朝灭亡。

这一时期，欧洲经济、文化的发展很不平衡。中国的经济、文化在世界上继续处于领先地位。北宋商品经济发达，科技水平高超。出现了世界上最早的纸币，火药兵器广泛应用，罗盘针（指南针）用于航海，发明了活字印刷。这些都极大地推动了世界历史的进步。元朝的疆域比过去的任何朝代都要辽阔，北京是当时闻名世界的大商业都市，意大利人马可·波罗在元世祖当朝时来到中国，居住了十几年，在《马可·波罗行纪》一书里描述了大都（今北京）的繁华景象。

The Continued Development of Feudal Society and the Coexistence of Ethnic Regimes — The Five Dynasties, and the Liao, Song, Xia, Jin and Yuan Dynasties

The period of the Five Dynasties (the Later Liang, Later Tang, Later Jin, Later Han and Later Zhou) and Ten Kingdoms (Former shu, Wu, Min, Wu-Yue, Chu, Southern Han, Southern Ping, Later Shu, Southern Tang Northern Han started in 907, when the Later Liang Dynasty was established. It ended in 960, when the Later Zhou fell and the Northern Song Dynasty was established.

Northern Song was under threat for most of its existence from states set up by minority ethnic groups, such as Liao and Jin in the northeast and Western Xia in the northwest. In 1127, the Jin army captured Kaifeng, the Northern Song capital. Zhao Gou, the emperor, escaped to the south, and set up what is historically known as the Southern Song Dynasty, with Hangzhou as its capital. In 1206, Temujin united the Mongolian tribes and was addressed Genghis Khan. The Mongols went on to build a huge empire. In 1260, Genghis Khan's grandson Kublai founded the Yuan Dynasty, with its capital in Beijing. The Yuan army seized Hangzhou in 1276, and in 1279 it crushed the remaining forces of the Southern Song Dynasty and united the whole of China. The Yuan Dynasty continued to exist until 1368, when a rebel army led by Zhu Yuanzhang seized Beijing and established the Ming Dynasty.

Trade flourished in the Northern Song period, as did science and technology. In China, there appeared the earliest paper currency in the world. Firearms were widely used, and the compass assisted navigation. Moveable type was used to print large numbers of books. The territory of the Yuan Dynasty was broader than that of any of the preceding dynasties, and Beijing became a world-renowned commercial metropolis. An Italian merchant named Marco Polo came to China during the reign of Emperor Shizu (1271—1294). He stayed for over 10 years. He described the prosperity of Dadu (today's Beijing) and other parts of China in his book *The Travels of Marco Polo*.

杯酒释兵权

Relieving the Generals of Their Commands at a Feast

唐朝灭亡以后，中国的历史进入五代十国的混乱时期。到了后周（951—960年）的时候，周世宗让赵匡胤掌握了军事大权。周世宗死后由他年幼的儿子继位，赵匡胤趁机夺取了皇权，建立了宋朝。他就是宋太祖。

宋太祖赵匡胤当上皇帝以后没多久，就有两个地方节度使反叛宋朝。宋太祖花了很大劲儿，才平定了叛乱。因为这件事，宋太祖心里总不踏实。有一次，他找跟随他多年的赵普说话，问他说："自从唐朝以后，换了许多朝代，不停地打仗，不知道死了多少百姓。这到底是为什么呢？"赵普说："这道理很简单。国家混乱，毛病就出在军事权力不集中，如果把兵权集中到中央，天下就太平了。"宋太祖听了连连点头。他自己就是利用手中的兵权夺取皇位的。为了防止这样的事情再次发生，宋太祖决定收回兵权。

961年秋天的一个晚上，宋太祖在宫中举行宴会，请石守信等几位老将喝酒。他举起一杯酒，先请大家干了杯，说："我要不是有你们的帮助，也不会有今天。但是你们哪里知道，做皇帝日子也不好过呀，还不如做个节度使快乐！"石守信等人听了十分惊奇，连忙问这是什么缘故。宋太祖接着说："这还不明白？皇帝这个位子，哪个不想坐呀？"石守信等人听出话中有话。大家着了慌，跪在地上说："我们决不会对您三心二意。"宋太祖摇摇头说："对你们几位难道我还信不过？只怕你们的部下将士当中，有人贪图富贵，把黄袍披在你们身上。你们想不干，能行吗？"石守信等人吓得满头大汗，连连磕头，第二天就说自己年老多病请求辞职。宋太祖马上同意了，给他们一大笔财物，收回了他们的兵权。历史上把这件事称为"杯酒释（shì，解除的意思）兵权"。

1. 宋太祖像
A portrait of Emperor Taizu
2. 宋太祖请大臣喝酒，言谈间解除他们的兵权，史称"杯酒释兵权"
To prevent revolt against the central authority, emperor Taizu took back the military power from his ministers at a banquet. This incident is referred to as "Relieving the Generals of Their Commands at a Feast"

Relieving the Generals of Their Commands at a Feast

After the downfall of the Tang Dynasty, China entered a chaotic period of the Five Dynasties and Ten Kingdoms. In the Later Zhou Dynasty (951—960), Emperor Shizong let Zhao Kuangyin control the military leadership. After Emperor Shizong died, his young son succeeded to the throne. Taking this chance, Zhao Kuangyin seized the imperial power and established the Song Dynasty as Emperor Taizu.

Not long after Zhao Kuangyin came to the throne, two local military governors revolted against the central authority. It took Zhao Kuangyin a lot of energy to suppress the revolt, which upset him very much. Once he talked with Zhao Pu who had been with him for many years. He said that since the downfall of the Tang Dynasty there had appeared many dynasties with endless wars. Numerous People had died. What was the reason for all of these? Zhao Pu said the reason was very simple. The chaotic situation in a country lay in the scattering of the military power. The country would be restored to peace as soon as the military power was returned to the overall control of the central authority. Emperor Taizu agreed with this opinion, and it was by controlling the military leadership that he had seized the imperial power. In order to prevent the same thing from happening again, Emperor Taizu decided to take back military power from local authorities. In an autumn evening in 961, Emperor Taizu held a banquet in the imperial palace and invited Shi Shouxin and other senior generals. The emperor held up the cup and said, "But for your help, I wouldn't be what I am like nowadays. But you don't know that it is very difficult being an emperor. In fact, it's happier being a local military governor than being an emperor." Shi Shouxin and the other generals were very surprised when they heard this and asked why. Emperor Taizu said, "It is quite obvious. Who does not want to be the emperor?" The generals got the underlying meaning of his words and became flustered. They knelt on the ground hurriedly and said, "we won't betray you at any time." Emperor Taizu shook his head and said, "I have confidence in all of you. But I'm afraid your subordinates may be ambitious and hanker after riches and honors. When they wrap the yellow gown (a symbol for emperor) around you and support you to be the emperor, can you refuse them?" The generals were so frightened that their faces were covered with beads of perspiration. The next day they asked to resign and the emperor agreed immediately. He gave them a large amount of money and took back their military power. This was called "relieving the generals of their commands at a feast" in history.

赤胆忠心的杨家将

The Loyal Generals of the Yang Family

历史上杨家将的主要人物是杨业。北宋初年，北方的辽国不断进扰宋朝边境。杨业带领部队守卫边境重镇雁门关。980年，辽国派10万大军攻打雁门关。那时候，杨业只有几千人马。他就让大部分人马守卫雁门关，自己带领几百名骑兵，悄悄绕到辽军背后，给辽军一个突然袭击。辽军毫无防备，心惊胆战，大败而归。

雁门关一仗取得胜利后，杨业又带领宋兵打了几个大胜仗。从此以后，辽军一看到“杨”字旗号，就吓得不敢再战。人们给杨业起了个外号，叫“杨无敌”。

过了两年，宋太宗决定大举攻辽，令宋军分三路进军。杨业担任西路军副帅。开始，三路军进展顺利。后来，东路军轻率冒进，导致溃败，宋军只得撤退。撤退时，由于西路主帅指挥错误，杨业的部队遭到辽国大军伏击。士兵们都战死了，杨业孤军奋战，身受几十处创伤仍坚持战斗，最后被俘。杨业在辽营里宁死不肯投降，绝食了三天三夜，就牺牲了。

杨业死后，杨家子孙继承了他的事业。儿子杨延昭、孙子杨文广都在保卫宋朝边境的战争中立了功。民间传说的杨家将的故事就是根据他们的事迹加工而成的。

1

1. 雁门关
Yanmen Pass

The Loyal Generals of the Yang Family

There are many stories about the exploits of the generals from the Yang Family and their faithful service to the Northern Song Dynasty. In the early days of Northern Song, people in the frontier had always been annoyed by the Liao. Yang Ye led his army to guard Yanmen Pass, a town of military importance. In 980, Liao commanded 100 000 troops to attack on Yanmen Pass. At that time, he had only several thousands of troops. However, leaving the major troops in camp to hold their ground, he, with his only hundreds of cavalries, rounded the back of Liao troops, and launched a surprise assault. The Liao army were unprepared and suffered a crushing defeat.

In addition, Yang Ye achieved other great victories. From then on, the Liao troops had hardly seen his battle flags when they began to shiver. And people nicknamed him "Mr Invincibility".

Two years later, Song Taizong was determined to launch a large scale offensive attack to Liao. Yang Ye was appointed as the assistant of the Chief Commander in the western route. Everything went well at the very beginning. However, since the eastern route had made a rash advance to the enemy, Song lost its battle and had to retreat. Due to a mortal failure in a strategic decision, Yang Ye suffered an ambuscade. After all of his soldiers died, he still insisted on fighting, but was wounded and captured at last. In the camp of the Liao troops, Yang Ye rejected hauling down his colors. He died in a hunger strike.

After he died, his offspring inherited his unfulfilled wish, safeguarding the border of the Song Dynasty. His son Yang Yanzhao and his grandson Yang Wenguang fought many glorious battles to repel the incursions by the Liao. The deeds of the Yang Family generals became the stuff of folk legend.

小资料 Data

澶渊之盟

契丹（Qìdān）族是生活在辽河流域的一支游牧民族。916年耶律阿保机建契丹国，后改国号为“辽”，定都上京（今内蒙古境内）。五代与契丹对峙时期，辽得到石敬瑭割让的幽云十六州后势力壮大起来，对北宋构成严重的威胁。1004年，辽的太后和辽圣宗耶律隆绪亲自发兵南下，连破宋军，11月已抵达黄河边的重镇澶州（Chánzhōu），威胁北宋的都城东京，北宋朝野人心惶惶。宋真宗在寇准的坚持下亲自出征，鼓舞士气。宋、辽两军出现对峙局面。不久，双方达成和议，北宋朝廷每年输送给辽国岁币银10万两，绢20万匹。历史上把这次议和称为“澶渊（chányuān）之盟”。此后，宋辽百余年间不再有大规模的战事，这对中原与北部边疆经济文化的交流和民族的融合有积极的意义。

The Pact of Chanyuan

Khitan was an ancient nomadic tribe in the Liaohe River valley. In 916, Yelu Abaoji founded the State of Khitan, then renamed as the "Liao", choosing Shang Du (in today's Inner Mongolia) as its capital. In the time of the military confrontation between Khitan and the Five Dynasties, the Liao expanded its forces after it had got the 16 prefectures of You and Yun ceded by Shi Jingtang. This posed a threat to the security of the Northern Song. In 1004, the empress dowager and the emperor Shengzong of Liao (Yelu Longxu) declared a war on the Northern Song. The Northern Song army suffered several defeats and the Liao army marched south. In the 11th month, the Liao army reached Chanzhou, a place of strategic importance by the Yellow River, posing a threat to Dongjing, the capital of the Northern Song. Both the government and populace were on tenterhooks. At this very moment, Song Zhenzong, under the insistence of his minister Kou Zhun, decided to go out to battle. His action did encourage the morale of his soldiers when the two armies were locked in a face-off. Shortly after, they signed a pact. According to it, the government of the Northern Song would send 100 000 taels of silver coin, 200 000 bolts of thin silk. Historically, this is what we call "the Pact of Chanyuan". From then on, there was no large scale war being waged. Economic and cultural communication had been further developed.

秉公执法的“包青天”

Bao the Upright Judge

中国民间流传着许多有关包公的传说，称他为“包青天”、“青天大老爷”，称赞他执法严明，铁面无私，为老百姓做主。确实，历史上有这样一个清官，他就是宋朝的包拯（Bāo Zhěng）。

包拯（999—1062年）是安徽合肥人，在地方和朝廷都做过官。他在做县官时，有一次，他的堂舅犯了法。包拯不讲私情，照样依法办事，派人把他抓到官府，判了死刑。许多亲戚赶来求情，包拯说：“不是我没有情义，谁叫他犯法呢？”

1 | 2

1. 安徽合肥包公墓
   The Tomb of Lord Bao, Hefei, Anhui Province
2. 安徽合肥包公祠内的包公铜像
   A bronze statue of Lord Bao in his memorial temple of Hefei, Anhui Province

后来，包拯又到朝廷做官，他依然秉公执法。有一年开封发大水，威胁到老百姓的安全。包拯发现涨水的原因是河道被阻塞了。原来一些大官在河道上修筑了花园亭台。为了保证开封的安全，包拯立刻下令，要这些人把河道上的建筑全部拆掉。即使是皇亲国戚，违反了法令，包拯也毫不留情，他向皇帝提出自己的意见，直到让这些人受到应有的惩罚，才肯罢休。

对受冤枉的老百姓，包拯却充满了同情。每次遇到这样的案情，他总是深入调查，详细分析，替百姓伸冤。人们感激他公正执法，都称他为“包青天”。

包拯做了大官，家里的生活也没什么变化，穿衣吃饭，跟普通老百姓一样。包拯死了以后，留下一份遗嘱（yízhǔ）说：“后代子孙做了官，如果犯了贪污罪，不许回老家；死了以后，也不许葬在包家坟地上。”

包拯一生做官清清白白，受到老百姓的敬仰，民间流传着许多他的故事，大家习惯上都叫他“包公”，包拯的本名倒很少有人提起了。

Bao the Upright Judge

Many stories have been handed down among the Chinese people about a judge known for his fearless espousal of justice. He was known as "Clear Sky Bao" or "Clear Sky Bao Milord", meaning that no wrongdoing could be hidden from his impartial eye and that he gave justice to the common people. Indeed, there was a virtuous official in history during the Song Dynasty named Bao Zheng.

Bao Zheng (999—1062) was from Hefei, in today's Anhui Province. He served in the local government as well as in the court. When he was a county magistrate, his uncle once violated the law. Bao Zheng showed no partiality for friends or relatives, and he treated him according to the law. He sent runners to take his uncle to the local official, and even sentenced his uncle to death. Many relatives pleaded for his uncle, but Bao Zheng said, "It is not because I am ruthless, it is he who violated the law."

When Lord Bao became a court official, he upheld the law firmly. One year, there occurred a flood in the capital, Kaifeng, which threatened to engulf the poorer quarters of the city. Bao Zheng found that the flood had been caused by the intrusion of waterside gardens and pavilions built for the pleasure of senior officials. For the safety of Kaifeng, without any hesitation, he ordered that these constructions be removed. Whoever violated the law, even if they were relatives of the emperor, Bao Zheng did not show any mercy. He kept proposing his opinion to the emperor till those people were punished.

Bao Zheng had great sympathy for those who were unjustly convicted. He would determinedly carry out detailed investigations and bring justice to the victims. People admired his character so much that they praised him as the "Clear Sky Bao".

Although Bao was a highranking official, there was little change in his house and he lived a simple and frugal life just like commoners. His will declared that if his descendants were to be corrupted officials, they would be forbidden to return home and they would be denied the right to be buried in the family graveyard.

Bao was well respected by people because of his righteousness, and his legend was spread among the regions. Since people were used to calling him Lord Bao, his real name was rarely mentioned.

1 | 2

1. 河南开封包公祠内的狗头铡等
   The guillotines found in Lord Bao's Memorial Temple, Kaifeng, Henan Province
2. 广东肇庆端砚
   A Duan inkstone made in Zhaoqing, Guangdong Province

小资料 Data

包拯小故事

包拯一生清廉，从不贪污受贿。他在端州（今广东肇庆，Zhàoqìng）当了将近3年官。端州有一种著名的特产——端砚（duānyàn）。笔、墨、纸、砚合称为文房四宝，而湖笔、徽墨、宣纸、端砚被称为四宝之最。端砚石质坚实温润，纹理细密，发墨快而不易干，书写流利生辉，从唐代起就很有名，是上贡皇帝的贡品。包拯以前的县官常征收老百姓的端砚，用来贿赂（huìlù）朝中权贵。包拯当县官时不加征端砚，也不贿赂权贵。虽然他十分喜爱书法，但他离开端州时竟然连一块端砚也没带走。

Lord Bao and the Inkstones

Bao Zheng was incorruptible and never received a bribe in all his life. He had been the magistrate of Duanzhou (today's Zhaoqing in Guangdong Province) for almost three years. Duanzhou was famous for its Duan inkstones. Writing brush, ink, paper and inkstones are altogether called "the four treasures of study", and Hu writing brush, Hui ink, Xuan paper and Duan inkstones are the best of all. The stone of Duan inkstone is hard as well as smooth, and its texture is fine. As Duan inkstone is easy to grind the ink with and hard to dry, writing used with the ink ground by it is rather smooth and convenient. These inkstones were so fine that they were even presented as tribute to emperors since the Tang dynasty. Bao Zheng's predecessors had often extorted inkstones from the people and used them to bribe court officials. But when Bao Zheng governed there he did not extort any Duan inkstones and refused to stoop to flattery. In fact, although he was a keen calligrapher himself, he did not take a single inkstone with him when he left Duanzhou.

忠心报国的岳飞

General Yue Fei, a Paragon of Loyalty

岳飞是南宋时期抗击金朝进犯的名将。他从小刻苦读书，特别爱读兵法，20岁时参加了军队，以勇敢出名。

岳飞一心想收复被金朝占领的中原大地，对自己要求十分严格，又关心爱护士兵。他领导的岳家军作战十分勇猛，从没打过败仗。

1140年，金大将兀术（Wūzhú）带领金朝的军队向南宋进攻。岳飞带领岳家军与金兀术作战。兀术有一支经过专门训练的骑兵，人马都披上厚厚的铁甲，叫做“拐子马”，向岳家军进攻。岳飞看准了拐子马的弱点，等敌人冲过来，命令士兵弯着身子，专砍马腿。马砍倒了，金兵跌下马来，这样就把拐子马打败了。兀术听到这个消息，伤心地哭了。他说，自从带兵打仗以来，全靠拐子马打胜仗，这下全完了。岳家军乘胜收复了许多中原失地。那时候金兵中流传着一句话：“撼（hàn）山易，撼岳家军难！”意思是，推倒一座山很容易，可是想打败岳飞率领的军队太难了！

但后来，昏庸的宋高宗却与金朝讲和，命令岳飞从前线撤兵，又解除了他的兵权。1142年，奸臣秦桧（Qín Huì）又以“莫须有”（即当地语言“可能有”的意思）的罪名把岳飞害死了。岳飞死时只有39岁。

1. 浙江杭州岳王庙内的岳飞塑像
A statue of Yue Fei in Yuewang Temple, Hangzhou, Zhejiang Province
2. 奸臣秦桧等铸铁像长跪在岳飞坟前
Statues of the kneeled treacherous ministers including Qin Hui, are placed in front of Yue Fei Mausoleum.

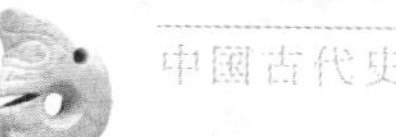

General Yue Fei,

a Paragon of Loyalty

Yue Fei was a general of the Southern Song Dynasty, who fought victoriously against the invading forces of the Jin Dynasty. He studied hard since he was a child, and was particularly interested in strategics. He joined the army when he was 20 and became famous for his bravery. Yue Fei wanted to reoccupy the territory of middle China which had been occupied by the Jin Dynasty with all his heart. While he was rather strict with himself, he cared for and cherished the soldiers. The Yue army led by him was very intrepid and never lost in the battlefield.

In 1140, the Jin army under General Wu Zhu attacked the Southern Song Dynasty. Yue Fei commanded the Yue Army to fight against them. Wu Zhu had cavalries with special training. The soldiers and warhorses were all clad in thick armor called "*guaizi* horse" and had them to attack the Yue army. Yue Fei found out the weakness of "*guaizi* horse" and instructed his men to bend and to hack at the horses' unprotected legs. In this way, the Jin troops fell down from the horses and were crushingly defeated. When Wuzhu heard about this sad news, he burst into a cry bitterly. He said that since he commanded the army to fight, his victories all depended on the "*guaizi* horse", that all was over. The Yue army reoccupied a lot of lost territory of the Central Plains. There was a saying in the Jin army that, "It is easier to shake a mountain than to shake the Yue army", which means it is easy to push down a mountain, but it is too hard to beat the army led by Yue Fei!

Later, however, the fatuous Emperor Gaozong of the Southern Song Dynasty made peace with the Jin and asked Yue Fei to retreat from the battlefront. Yue Fei was dismissed, and in 1142 executed on a trumped-up charge of "*moxuyou*" (a local dialect meaning "perhaps having guilt"). Yue Fei was only 39 years old when he died.

小资料 Data

靖康之变

金灭辽以后，看到北宋统治腐朽，防备空虚，决定一鼓作气，灭掉宋朝，统一中国。1125年10月，金兵从北方长驱直入，直逼东京。宋徽宗惊惶失措，不敢承担抗敌的重任，于1126年1月让太子赵桓（Zhāo Huán，即宋钦宗）继位，改年号为靖康（Jìngkāng）。第二年，金军攻陷了北宋的都城东京，掳走宋徽宗、宋钦宗以及后妃、宗室、大臣等三千多人，北宋灭亡，历史上称这一变故为"靖康之变"。这一年，宋钦宗的弟弟赵构在应天府（今河南商丘）即位，后来定都临安（今浙江杭州），这就是历史上的"南宋"。

Jingkang Incident

After the Jin conquered the Liao, seeing that the Northern Song was corrupt as well as weakly defended, the Jin decided to take the chance to overthrow the Song Dynasty and unify China. In October 1125, the Jin troops came directly from the north, and marched towards Dong Jing, the capital of the Song Dynasty. Emperor Huizong of the Song Dynasty was in a panic and did not dare to burden the duty of fighting back. In January 1126, he issued an imperial edict of abdication and let the prince Zhao Huan (Emperor Qinzong of the Song Dynasty) succeed the throne, and changed the reign title into Jingkang. The next year, the Jin army breached Dongjing, and captured over 30 000 people, including Emperor Huizong, Emperor Qinzong, imperial concubines, imperial relatives, and ministers. The Northern Song Dynasty was over and this was called the "Jingkang Incident" in history. In the same year, Zhaogou (the brother of Emperor Qinzong) succeeded in Yingtianfu (today's Shangqiu, Henan Province), and later moved the capital to Lin'an (today's Hangzhou, Zhejiang province). This is the "Southern Song Dynasty" in history.

历史名臣文天祥

Wen Tianxiang, a Renowned Minister

文天祥是中国历史上的名臣，江西人。他从小爱读历史上忠臣烈士的传记，立志要向他们学习，年轻时就考中了状元。

忽必烈建立元朝以后，开始进攻南宋，一路南下逼近临安（南宋首都，今杭州）。这时南宋朝廷连忙号召各地派兵救援。文天祥在江西响应，组织了几万义兵，准备赶到临安去。有个朋友劝他说："你用这些临时招来的人马去抵抗元军，好比赶着羊群去跟猛虎搏斗，还是不要去吧！"文天祥说："国家危急，却没有人为国出力，难道不叫人痛心吗？我明知道自己力量有限，宁愿为国献身。"

南宋朝廷在危急中任命文天祥为右丞相，去和元军谈判。文天祥被元军扣留，在押往大都的途中，他趁机逃走。

文天祥逃到福州、广东，重新组织力量抗击元军，最终因力量悬殊，被元军抓住，随后被押往大都。

文天祥在大都被关了3年多，宁愿死也不肯投降。最后元世祖忽必烈亲自劝他说："你的忠心，我也完全了解。现在你如果能改变主意，做元朝的臣子，我仍旧让你当丞相。"文天祥回答说："宋朝已经灭亡，我只求一死，别的没有什么可说了。"1283年，

年仅47岁的文天祥去世。

文天祥在监狱中写下的《正气歌》，成为千古传诵的不朽诗篇。

《正气歌》

天地有正气，杂然赋流形。下则为河岳，上则为日星。于人曰浩然，沛乎塞苍冥。
皇路当清夷，含和吐明庭。时穷节乃见，一一垂丹青。在齐太史简，在晋董狐笔。
在秦张良椎，在汉苏武节。为严将军头，为嵇侍中血。为张睢阳齿，为颜常山舌。
或为辽东帽，清操厉冰雪。或为出师表，鬼神泣壮烈。或为渡江楫，慷慨吞胡羯。
或为击贼笏，逆竖头破裂。是气所磅礴，凛烈万古存。当其贯日月，生死安足论。
地维赖以立，天柱赖以尊。三纲实系命，道义为之根。嗟余遘阳九，隶也实不力。
楚囚缨其冠，传车送穷北。鼎镬甘如饴，求之不可得。阴房阒鬼火，春院閟天黑。
牛骥同一皂，鸡栖凤凰食。一朝蒙雾露，分作沟中瘠。如此再寒暑，百沴自辟易。
哀哉沮洳场，为我安乐国。岂有他谬巧，阴阳不能贼。顾此耿耿在，仰视浮云白。
悠悠我心忧，苍天曷有极。哲人日已远，典刑在夙昔。风檐展书读，古道照颜色。

1

1. 江西吉安文天祥纪念馆
Wen Tianxiang Memorial Hall, Ji'an, Jiangxi Province

Wen Tianxiang,

a Renowned Minister

Wen Tianxiang, who was born in Jiangxi Province, was a renowned minister in history. In his youth, he was fond of reading biographies of loyal ministers, and made up his mind to model himself on them. Later, he achieved the first place in the imperial civil examination.

When Kublai Khan founded the Yuan Dynasty and commanded armies to approach Lin'an (the capital of the Southern Song Dynasty, today's Hangzhou). The Northern Song Dynasty called on troops from all over the country to rescue the emperor, Wen Tianxiang raised a volunteer force of more than ten thousand in Jiangxi Province and prepared to go to Lin'an. A friend of his dissuaded him that, fighting against the Yuan army with the temporarily organized army was like fighting against a furious tiger with a group of sheep. However, Wen Tianxiang said, "How harrowing it will be when the country is in danger but nobody is willing to do anything about it! I know that my ability was limited, but I would rather die for my country."

Appointed the Prime Minister by the Southern Song in the emergency situation, Wen Tianxiang went to negotiate with the Yuan army. However, Wen was detained by the Yuan side, but managed to escape on the way of being escorted to Dadu. Wen Tianxiang escaped to Fuzhou and Guangdong, where he reorganized forces to fight against the Yuan army. He was captured once more because of the great disparity between the two sides, and was sent to Dadu. Wen Tianxiang spent three years as a prisoner in Dadu. He would rather die than surrender. Emperor Shizu, Kublai Khan told Wen by himself that, "I fully understand your loyalty. If you can change your mind now and are willing to hold an official position in the Yuan Dynasty, I will keep you as the Prime Minister." Wen Tianxiang replied that, "Now that the Song Dynasty is over, all I want is death, and I have nothing more to say." Wen Tianxiang died in 1283 at the age of 47. The *Song of Integrity*, which he wrote behind prison bars, is regarded as a classic of its kind.

1

1. 文天祥像
A statue of Wen Tianxiang

Song of Integrity

There is integrity that is embodied in various forms.
On the earth it is mountains and rivers, in the sky it is the sun and stars.
In man it is the noble spirit that fills up the whole world.
The imperial road should be cleared of barbarians and be flooded with light.
In times of great danger man's high moral principle shows itself and leaves its record in history.
This is revealed in the records of Qi, the writings of Dong Hu of Jin.
Zhang Liang's service to Qin and Su Wu's moral courage in the Han Dynasty.
It was General Yan's head, Ji Kang's blood, Zhang Suiyang's teeth and Yan Changshan's tongue.
It was the Liaodong hat that could withstand ice and snow.
It was Zhuge Liang's memorial which was so heroic that it moved the immortals.
It was the river-crossing oar that wiped out the nomad invaders.
It was the Mongolian scepter that crushed treacherous vassals' heads.
Integrity is so majestic that it will never die out.
It shoots up to the sun and the moon, and life and death are of no importance before it.
It supports both the earth and the sky.
Our lives hinge on our cardinal guides and our foundation rests on our morality.
But now everything is upside down.
Divested of his headgear this prisoner is kept behind prison bars in the north.
He would be only glad to be burned in the barbarians' crucible.
Ghost flame rages in the room and the courtyard is wrapped in darkness.
Oxen and steeds live in the same fold and chickens and phoenixes share the same food.
The earth is shrouded in mist and fog.
If things go on like this, miseries and disasters will spread.
I am sad that this swamp used to be my paradise-like homeland.
Fallacies cannot become truth nor can Yin and Yang be confused.
So I am worried and look up at the white clouds floating in the sky.
My heart is full of sorrow and I wonder where the sky will end.
The ancient sages are far away, my execution is nearing.
I open a book to read, and there is sunshine on the ancient words.

成吉思汗与忽必烈

Genghis Khan and Kublai Khan

蒙古族是中国北方一个古老的民族。12世纪末，铁木真经过10多年战争统一了蒙古各部，1206年被推举为蒙古的大汗（dàhān），被尊称为“成吉思汗”，意思是“坚强的君主”。成吉思汗建立横跨亚欧大陆的大蒙古国以后，国力强盛，军事行动波及欧洲的多瑙河流域，对世界历史发展进程产生了重大影响。成吉思汗死后，蒙古军队相继灭西夏和金，统一了中国整个北方地区。

1260年，忽必烈（成吉思汗的孙子）继承了汗位，1264年，建都大都（今北京）。到1271年，忽必烈正式称皇帝，建立了元朝（1271—1368年），他就是元世祖。元世祖逐步巩固对北方的统治之后，就集中力量攻打南宋，终于灭了南宋。1279年，实现了中国南北大统一。

元世祖忽必烈做了皇帝以后，就对中央和地方的行政机构进行改革。他先在中央设立中书省，为最高的行政机构。在全国各地设立了行中书省，简称“行省”，在全国各地共设立10个行中书省，正式作为地方最高的行政机构。另外，吐蕃（今西藏）地区在元朝时也正式成为中国的一个行政区，由中央的宣政院管辖。元朝政府还设置了澎湖巡检司，管辖台湾与澎湖，这是台湾归属中国中央政府管辖的开始。

元朝行省制度的建立，加强了中央与行省、行省与行省之间的联系，使元朝中央对边疆少数民族地区的管理比以前任何朝代都有效，有利于多民族统一国家的稳定和发展。这是元世祖忽必烈的一项创举。

元朝创设的行省制度一直沿用到今天。

1. 内蒙古伊金霍洛旗成吉思汗陵
Genghis Khan Mausoleum, Ejin Horo Banner, Inner Mongolia Autonomous Region
2. 成吉思汗像
A portrait of Genghis Khan
3. 元世祖忽必烈像
A portrait of Kublai Khan, Emperor Shizu of the Yuan Dynasty

Genghis Khan and Kublai Khan

The Mongol was an ancient nationality in the north of China. At the end of the 12th century, Temujin united all the Mongolian tribes after 10 years of warfare. In 1206, he was chosen their khan, with the title of Genghis Khan which means "tough monarch". Under Genghis Khan, the Mongol Empire which crossed the Eurasian land mass was very strong with its military action affecting the Danube River in Europe and having great influence in the developing of the world history. After Genghis Khan's death, the Mongols continued to wipe out the Western Xia kingdom and the Jin Dynasty, and incorporated northern China into their empire.

In 1260, Kublai (the grandson of Genghis Khan), succeeded to the position of khan, and in 1264, he decided on Dadu (today's Beijing) as his capital. In 1271, Kublai Khan formally proclaimed himself emperor, historically known as Emperor Shizu, of the newly established Yuan Dynasty (1271—1368). After consolidating his rule over the north, he moved south to attack the Southern Song Dynasty, which fell in 1279, and China was unified into one nation once again.

Kublai Khan reformed the system of administration at both the local and central levels after he became the emperor. First, he established the *Zhongshusheng* (Metropolitan Secretariat) in the central government as the highest administrative institution, and *Xingzhongshusheng* in local governments officially as the highest local administrative institutions, called *Xingsheng* for short. There were 10 *Xingsheng* altogether in the whole country. In addition, Tubo (today's Tibet) officially became one of China's administrative regions in the Yuan Dynasty, under the direct administration of *Xuanzhengyuan* (Commission for Buddhist and Tibetan Affairs) in the central government. In the Yuan Dynasty, too, the government set up Penghu *Xunjiansi*, which ruled the Island of Taiwan and Penghu. This was the beginning of the Chinese central government administration over Taiwan.

The setting up of the *Xingsheng* system strengthened the relations between the central and local governments, as well as those between different local govern-

ments. It made the central govern-ment administration over border areas more effective than that of any previous dynasty, solidifying the unity of China as a multi-ethnic country. This was a pioneering work of Kublai, Emperor Shizu. Moreover, it was the basis of the administrative systems of later dynasties, and even of today's China.

1

1. 成吉思汗陵内以成吉思汗为主题的大型壁画
Full-length murals with Genghis Khan as the theme in the Mausoleum of Genghis Khan

小资料 Data

元大都

大都是元代的首都，蒙古人称为“汗八里”，就是“大汗之城”的意思。元灭金后，忽必烈在1246年，以中都（金的首都）东北风景秀丽的离宫为中心，着手规划建设新都城。1276年元大都建成完工。大都城采用外城、皇城和宫城三城相套形制，规模宏伟整齐，功能分区明确。大都是元代最大的商业中心，也是当时世界上最宏伟和繁华的城市之一。城中各种市集多达三十余处，有综合性的商业中心，也有各行业的街市。明清北京城就是在元大都的基础上改建和扩建而成的，有许多建筑仍保留到现在。

Dadu in the Yuan Dynasty

Dadu was the capital of the Yuan Dynasty. The Mongol called it "*Hanbali*", which means "the city of Khan". After conquering the Jin Dynasty, in 1246, Kublai Khan embarked on laying out and building a new capital city centered on the Provisional Imperial Palace with a great view in northeast, on the site of the Jin capital, Zhongdu. The construction of Dadu was completed in 1276. The new capital consisted of the Outer City, the Imperial City and the Palace City. With grand buildings and a strictly ordered pattern of streets and quarters, Dadu was the largest commercial center in the Yuan Dynasty and one of the most grandiose and most prosperous cities of that time in the world. There were over 30 markets of various types, comprehensive commercial centers and downtown streets devoted to different trades. The city of Beijing during the Ming and Qing dynasties was rebuilt and extended on the basis of Dadu, and many of the Yuan Dynasty buildings are still preserved.

马可·波罗来华

Marco Polo's Travels in China

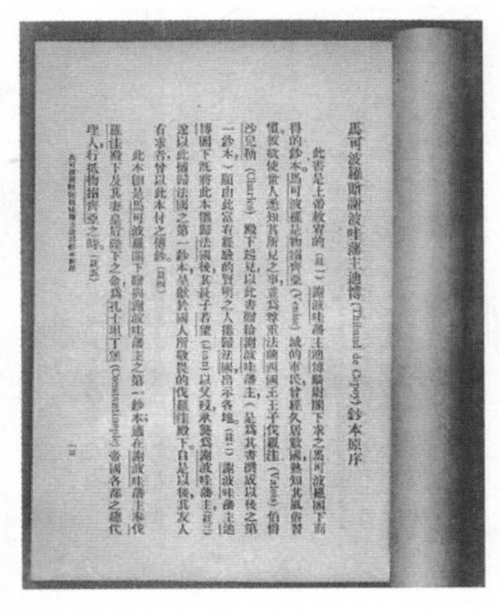
馬可波羅贈謝波吐藩主迪博(Thibaud de Cepoy)鈔本原序

此書是上帝教寵的（註一）謝波吐藩主迪博騎尉閣下求之馬可波羅閣下而得的鈔本。馬可波羅是物搦齊亞(Venise)城的市民，曾經久居數國，熟知其風俗習慣，數欲使衆人悉知其所見之事，並爲尊重法蘭西國王王子伐羅注(Valois)伯爵沙兒勒(Charles)殿下起見，以此書贈給謝波吐藩主。（是爲其書撰成以後之第一鈔本。）願由此富有經驗的賢明之人攜歸法國，指示各地。（註二）謝波吐藩主迪博閣下既將此本攜歸法國後，其長子若望(Jean)以父歿承襲爲謝波吐藩主，（註三）遂以此攜歸法國之第一鈔本呈獻於國人所敬畏的伐羅注殿下。自是以後，其友人有求者，曾以此本付之傳鈔。（註四）

此本卽是馬可波羅閣下贈與謝波吐藩主之第一鈔本，適在謝波吐藩主奉伐羅注殿下及其妻皇后陛下之命爲孔士坦丁堡(Constantinople)帝國各部之總代理人，行抵物搦齊亞之時。（註五）

元朝同亚、非、欧各国的交往很多，在当时来中国的外国人之中，最著名的是意大利威尼斯人马可·波罗（Marco Polo，1254—1324年）。

1271年夏天，马可·波罗的父亲和叔父带着他离开故乡，经过4年的艰辛旅程，来到了中国。

马可·波罗聪明好学，来到中国以后，很快学会了蒙古语、骑马和射箭。忽必烈很喜欢他，经常派他出去视察。马可·波罗后来在书中描述了中国西北、华北、西南、中南和华东的许多地方，其中多数是他游历过的，但也有一些可能来自传闻。据说，他在扬州呆过，还当了3年总管呢。

在中国时间久了，3个欧洲人非常怀念故乡，一再要求回国。获得批准后，他们再次踏上了充满艰险的归途。经过4年多的时间，终于在1295年回到了威尼斯。

这时他们已经远离故土24年，当地人以为他们已经死在国外了。现在他们却穿着东方的服装回来了。人们认为他们带回了无数黄金珠宝，给马可起了个外号，叫“百万”。

没有多久，威尼斯和另外一个城邦热那亚发生了战争。马可·波罗自己花钱买了一条船，亲自驾船参加威尼斯的舰队。结果威尼斯打了败仗，他做了俘虏，被热那亚人关进了监狱。热那亚人听说他到过东方，常常到监狱里听他讲东方和中国的见闻。牢里关着一个作家，把马可讲的事都记了下来，编成了一本书，叫《马可·波罗行纪》。

在这本游记里，马可·波罗描绘了一个新奇的东方世界，详细介绍了中国忽必烈时期的一些重大政治事件、风俗习惯、宗教信仰、著名城市、物产和商业活动等。这本书一出版，就受到了欧洲人的欢迎，激起了他们对东方文明的向往。

15世纪以后，欧洲的航海家、探险家，普遍受到了马可·波罗的影响，去东方寻找一个遍地黄金的国家。

Marco Polo's
Travels in China

The Yuan Dynasty had worldwide contacts with different countries in Asia, Africa and Europe. Among the many foreigners who came to China at that time, Marco Polo (1254—1324), an Italian from Venice, Italy, was the most famous.

In the summer of 1271, Marco Polo arrived in China with his father and uncle after a journey which had taken them four years.

Marco Polo was very smart and hard-working. Soon he acquired Mongolian, equitation and toxophily, and became a favorite of Kublai Khan, who often sent him on inspection tours. Later, he wrote a book which described many places in the northwest, southwest, the middle south of China as well as northern China and eastern China. It is said that he served as the magistrate of Yangzhou for three years.

After their long settlement in China, the three Europeans missed their homeland very much, and pleaded to return back several times. They got permission and began an adventurous journey home. The three Europeans finally returned to their homeland in 1295.

They had left their homeland for 24 years. The local people believed they had died abroad. However, they came back in

eastern clothes. People thought they had brought back countless treasure and gave Marco the nickname, "a millionaire".

Soon, Venice had a war with another city Genoa. Marco Polo bought a ship with his own money and sailed it himself to join the armada of Venice. Unfortunately, Venice lost the battle and he was captured and thrown into prison. The Genoa people heard about his travels to the East and often went to jail to listen to his stories of the East and China. There was a writer in jail who wrote down the stories told by Marco Polo and edited it into a book called *The Travels of Marco Polo*.

Marco Polo described a fabulous eastern world in his travel, and introduced the great political events, customs, beliefs, famous cities, productions and commercial activities in detail. Since the book was published, it had been popular with Europeans and roused their interest in eastern civilization.

Since 15th century, European navigators and explorers, generally influenced by Marco Polo, went to the East to search for a country full of gold.

1 | 2

1. 《马可·波罗行纪》汉译本
   Chinese version of *The Travels of Marco Polo*
2. 马可·波罗像
   A portrait of Marco Polo

四大发明

The Four Great Inventions

造纸术

西汉时期已经出现植物纤维纸，但比较粗糙，书写不方便。东汉时的宦官（huànguān）蔡伦，改进了造纸方法，用树皮、麻头、破布和旧鱼网作原料，制造出既美观又便宜，并且书写方便的纸张，并使这种以麻为主要原料的纸得到推广，对书写起到了重要的推动作用。造纸术逐步推广开来，到了三四世纪，纸取代竹简和丝帛成为中国的主要书写材料。

指南针

战国时，人们用天然磁石磨成“司南”，这是世界上最早的指南针，到今天已经有两千多年了。司南磁性较弱，指南效果比较差。

到了宋朝，发明了人造磁铁，磁性比天然磁铁稳定。指南针的装置也有很大改进，人们发明了指南鱼、指南龟、水浮指南针等指南工具。

在宋代，海外贸易非常发达。为了克服在海洋中航行的困难，到北宋末年，在航海上已经应用了指南针。南宋时还出现了将指南针安装在刻着度数和方位的圆盘上的罗盘针，使海上航行的人，在没有太阳的白天，没有月亮的夜晚，也能辨别方向。

印刷术

在人类文明发展史上，印刷术的地位非常重要。大约在隋朝的时候，雕版印刷术被发明了出来。但雕版印刷费时长，花钱多。

毕昇是北宋时一个聪明能干的印刷工人，发明了泥活字。先在粘土制成的一个个小方块上刻出反字。制成一批后，就放在火中烧硬成为陶字。排版时，在一块铁板上铺上一层用松香、蜡和纸灰混合的粉末，把一个个陶字排在

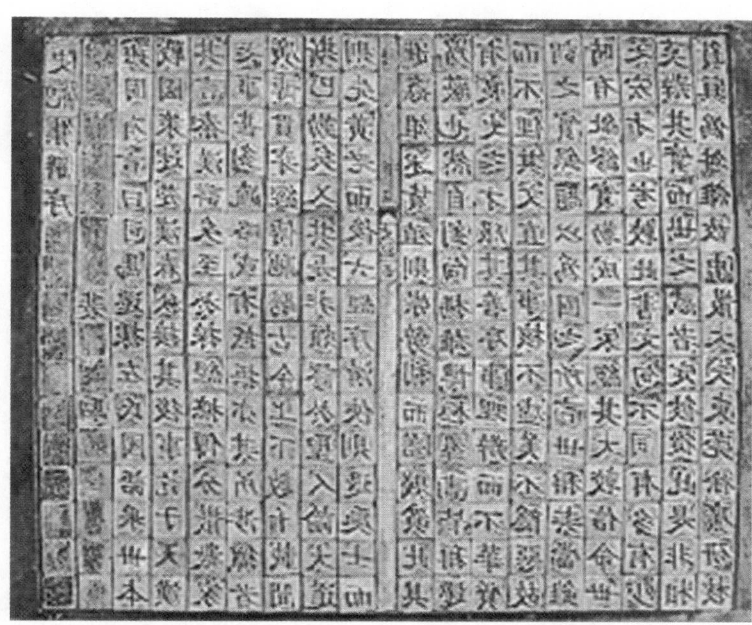

有框的铁板上，然后把铁板放到火上加温，等粉末熔化后，用一块平板把字压平。铁板温度降低后，活字固定，就可以印刷了。印版中如果有错别字，可以随时更换，印完一版，活字拆了，铁板可以再用。

毕昇为印刷术的改进打下了基础，西夏有了木活字，明代改成铜活字，直到后来使用的铅活字。

火药与火器

中国古代有专门炼丹的人，他们中有人把硫磺（liúhuáng）、硝石、木炭放在一起烧炼，引起了燃烧和爆炸，人们把这三种物质的混合叫做“火药”。唐朝中期的书籍里记载了制成火药的方法。唐朝末年，火药开始用于军事。

在宋代，火药得到了广泛使用。火药不仅被用在生活中，狩猎、开石、采石，制造爆竹和焰火，也被用在军事上。火器的制造技术也提高到了一个新的阶段。北宋制造的火药武器主要是燃烧性的、爆炸性的，如火箭、霹雳（pīlì）火球、蒺藜（jílí）火球等。到了南宋，发明了管状火器，把火药装在竹筒里点火喷射。有一次，宋朝军队和蒙古军队打仗，宋军发明了管状“突火枪”，即把火药装在竹筒里，然后装上“子窠（zǐkē）”。“子窠”和子弹的性质差不多，是用石子和铁块做的。这是世界上最早使用的原始步枪。它的出现是火器制造历史上划时代的进步。

1. 蔡伦像
A portrait of Cai Lun
2. 罗盘针
A compass needle
3. 泥版活字
Clay moveable types

The Four Great Inventions

The Technique of Making Paper

A crude type of paper was used for writing on as early as in the Western Han Dynasty. It was made from plant fiber, and was rather rough, which was inconvenient to write on. Cai Lun, a eunuch of the Eastern Han Dynasty, improved the technique of making paper using tree bark, rags and old fishing nets as raw materials, and produced a cheaper, more beautiful and more convenient type of paper. This kind of paper which used hemp as main material greatly generalized and promoted writing. By the third or fourth century, paper had replaced bamboo slips and silk as the main material for writing on.

The Invention of the Compass

Natural magnets were ground into crude compasses which called "*Sinan*" (a device pointing the south) as early as in the Warring States Period, and that was the oldest compass in the world, 2 000 years ago from now. The magnetic effect of *Sinan* was weak, as was its ability to guide south.

By the Song Dynasty, artificial magnets had been invented, whose magnetism was more stable than that of natural magnets. The equipment of the compass had been improved a lot and people invented several guiding tools such as the compass fish, the compass turtle, and the floating compass.

In the Song Dynasty, the maritime trade was prosperous. In order to overcome the difficulties of traveling in ocean, at the end of the Song Dynasty, compasses were used for navigation. There was even compass needles which was made by putting a compass on a dial with degree markings. This helped the sailors to find out the direction even during those days without sunlight and nights without moonlight.

The Technique of Printing

Printing has played a very important role in the history of civilization. Woodblock printing was in use at the time of the Sui Dynasty. But it involved a laborious and expensive process.

Bi Sheng of the Northern Song Dynasty was a smart printing

worker, and he invented moveable type of printing. He carved characters in reverse on blocks of clay. When a group was finished, the blocks were baked in a kiln. The slugs of type were pressed onto a coating of rosin, wax and paper ash spread on an iron tray, which was then heated and cooled to fix the slugs. If there was a wrong character, it could easily be replaced, and the tray, slugs and coating could be used over and over again.

Bi Sheng laid the foundation for improving the technique of printing. There was wooden type in West Xia, and in the Ming Dynasty, bronze type was invented, and later lead type was used.

Gunpowder and Firearms

Alchemists were the first people in ancient China to dabble in chemistry. In the search for "pills of immortality", it was found that a mixture of sulfur, saltpeter and charcoal could cause an explosion. People called the mixture of these three materials "gunpowder". A book in the middle of the Tang Dynasty recorded the method to make gunpowder. At the end of the Tang Dynasty, gunpowder was applied for military use.

In the Song Dynasty, gunpowder was widely used. Not only was it used in daily life, such as for hunting, stone-mining and fireworks, but also for military actions. The technique of making firearms had entered a new stage. The gunpowder weapons made in the Northern Song Dynasty were mainly for burning and explosions, such as fire arrows, *pili* burning balls and *jili* burning balls. In the Southern Song Dynasty, the fistulous firearms were invented. The Song army had invented a fistular kind of "fire guns" and used them to fight against the Mongolian army. The fire gun was made by putting the gunpowder into bamboo canisters, and then adding "*zike*" into them. *Zike* resembled bullets in character, but was made of stone and iron block. This was the oldest crude muskets in the world, which showed great progress in the history of firearm making.

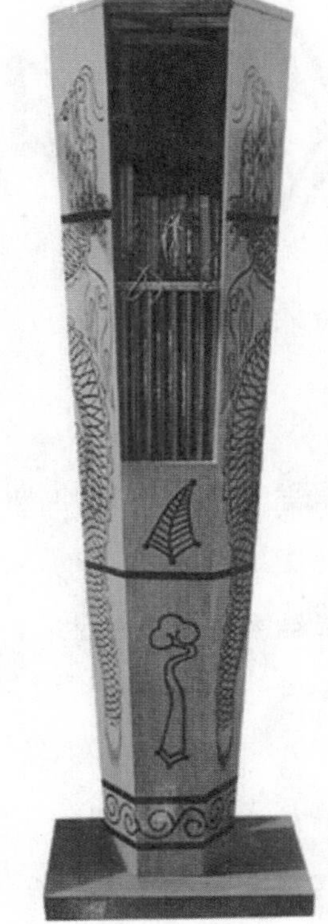

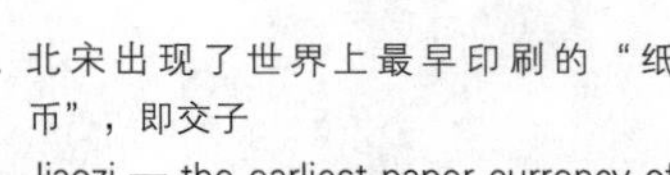

1 | 2 / 3

1. 北宋出现了世界上最早印刷的"纸币"，即交子
   Jiaozi — the earliest paper currency of the world — was printed in Northern Song Dynasty.
2. 突火枪
   A sudden fire gun
3. 火箭
   A fire arrow

《清明上河图》

Riverside Scene on the Pure Brightness Festival

宋朝绘画，除了人物画、山水画、花鸟画之外，还出现了描写城乡生活的社会风俗画。生活在北宋末年南宋初年的张择端所画的《清明上河图》是其中最优秀、最有名的。《清明上河图》描绘了北宋首都东京（今河南开封）汴河（Biànhé）两岸清明节前后的风貌。

《清明上河图》现收藏在北京故宫博物院。长卷共分3部分：第一部分画着晨光下，郊外河岸上慢慢行进着的一支驮着重物的驴队；第二部分描写汴河交通繁忙的景象，尤其引人注目的是像彩虹般横跨汴河两岸的“虹桥”，桥上熙（xī）熙攘（rǎng）攘，车水马龙，非常热闹；第三部分描绘了市区街景，各行各业，应有尽有，街上行人，来来往往。整幅画宽25.5厘米，长525厘米，共画了各类人物800多个，牲畜94头，树木170多棵。它把汴京郊外的菜园风光、汴河上的交通运输、街头的买卖状况、沿街房屋的建筑特征、船夫们的紧张劳动、士大夫们的悠闲自得、雄伟的虹桥、巍峨的城楼以及车子、轿子、骆驼，一一描绘得十分逼真。这幅画感染力强，欣赏价值高，受到人们的普遍喜爱，并被很多画家摹仿。

《清明上河图》直观地反映了北宋时代东京的城市面貌。它不仅欣赏价值高，而且是研究北宋时期东京的重要材料。

2

1

1. 《清明上河图》局部
The Rainbow Bridge, from *Riverside Scene on the Pure Brightness Festival*
2. 《清明上河图》局部
Street scene, from *Riverside Scene on the Pure Brightness Festival*

Riverside Scene on the Pure Brightness Festival

Apart from the masterpieces of figure painting, landscape, flower-and-bird painting, the Song Dynasty also produced social genre paintings describing both urban and rural life. The most famous of the latter works is one known as the *Riverside Scene on the Pure Brightness Festival*. It was painted by Zhang Zeduan, who lived in the late Northern Song Dynasty and early Southern Song Dynasty. It depicts scenes along the Bianhe River at Dongjing (today's Kaifeng in Henan Province), the capital of the Northern Song Dynasty, at the time of the Pure Brightness Festival.

Now it belongs to the collection of the Palace Museum in Beijing. The painting is divided into three parts: the first part shows a team of pack mules plodding along the river bank in the suburbs in the morning light; the second part shows the bustling scene of the transportation on Bianhe, especially the Rainbow Bridge spanning the river like a rainbow. There are many people and traffic on the bridge, so it is very busy there; the third part depicts the downtown streets, thronged with people plying all sorts of trades, and their customers. The whole scroll is 25.5 cm wide and 525 cm long, and has over 800 human and 94 animal figures, and 170 trees. This fascinating painting shows vegetable garden scenes, transportation over the Bianhe, business in the streets, architecture along the river and the tense labor of boatmen, the leisure of officials, the grand Rainbow Bridge, lofty buildings as well as vehicles, sedan-chairs and camels, all of which are portrayed vividly. This painting is affective with a high value of appreciation. It is popular with common people and copied by many painters.

The *Riverside Scene on the Pure Brightness Festival* directly reflected the city visage of Dongjing during the North Song Dynasty. It is not only valuable for appreciation, but also provides valuable material for the study of Dongjing during the North Song Dynasty.

司马光与《资治通鉴》

Sima Guang and the Comprehensive Mirror for Aid in Government

司马光（1019—1086年），北宋政治家、史学家，陕州夏县人（今属山西省）。他出生在一个官僚的家庭，曾经做过宰相。

司马光平生最大的成就之一就是主持编写了《资治通鉴》。司马光认为治理国家的人一定要了解历史，他用了两年的时间，写成了一部从战国到秦末的史书，名叫《通志》。后来他把《通志》拿给宋英宗看，宋英宗很满意，让他把这本书编下去。宋英宗允许司马光自己挑选编写人员，阅读官府藏书。司马光非常高兴，马上成立书局，邀请当时许多著名史学家做助手，共同编写通史。他们收集了大量材料，其中有很多在以前的历史书中都没有见到过的历史资料，非常珍贵。

为了编写这本书，司马光花费了大量心血。为了防止自己睡觉过多，耽误编书，他还特意请人用圆木做了一个枕头。睡觉时，只要一翻身，枕头就会滚掉，人也就醒了。这个枕头被称为“警枕”。

司马光用了19年完成了这部历史巨著。继位的宋神宗觉得很好，定名为《资治通鉴》。《资治通鉴》是一部编年体通史，记载了从公元前403到公元959年间1 362年的历史，共294卷，300多万字，材料详细真实，文字优美通畅，是后人编写编年体史书的典范，也是中国古代宝贵的文化遗产。

小资料 Data

司马光砸缸

传说司马光7岁那年，跟小伙伴在院子里玩。院子里有一口大水缸，有个小孩爬到缸沿上，不小心掉进了水缸。缸很大，水很深，眼看孩子快被淹死了，别的孩子都哭喊着往外跑。司马光没有慌，想出了一个主意，拿起一块大石头，用尽力气砸向水缸，缸破了，水流了出来，小孩得救了。

Smashing the Vat by Sima Guang

It is said that one day at the age of seven Sima Guang was playing with other children in the courtyard of his house. There was a big vat of water in the courtyard. One child climbed to the edge of the vat and fell into it. The vat was big and the water was deep, the child was drowning. While the other children were running around howling in a panic, Sima Guang coolly picked up a large stone, and smashed the side of the vat with it. The vat was broken, water flowed out through the hole, and the drowning child was saved.

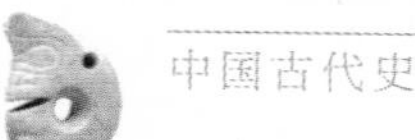

Sima Guang and the *Comprehensive Mirror for Aid in Government*

Sima Guang (1019—1086) was a statesman and historian of the Northern Song Dynasty. He was born in Xiaxian county, Shan Prefecture (belonging to Shanxi Province today) and he was born in an official family. He served as a prime minister at one time.

The most extraordinary achievement of Sima Guang was compiling the *Comprehensive Mirror for Aid in Government*. Sima Guang was convinced that those governing the country should be well versed in history. He spent two years in writing a history book including the history from the Warring States Period to the end of the Qin Dynasty, which was called *General History*. Later, when he submitted the book to Emperor Yingzong of the Song Dynasty, the Emperor was satisfied and encouraged him to continue to compile the book. Emperor Yingzong allowed Sima Guang to choose the compiling crew by himself and read the collected books of the library. Sima Guang was so delighted that he set up a press immediately and invited many famous historians of that time to be his assistants, and began to compile the general history together. They collected a lot of materials, many of which had never been recorded in other history books, making them very precious.

It took Sima Guang's painstaking effort to compile this book. He was afraid too much sleep would delay the work, so he ordered a pillow made of a round log. If he turned over during sleep, the pillow would slip from his head and he would wake up. This pillow was called the "alarm pillow".

Sima Guang spent a total of 19 years on this book. The succeeded Emperor Shenzong of the Song Dynasty thought highly of the book and named it *Comprehensive Mirror for Aid in Government*. The book is a comprehensive history of China in chronological style covering 1 362 years from 403 BC to 959 AD. This magnum opus comprises 294 volumes containing more than 3 000 000 words. The material was very detailed, and the words were exquisite and fluent. This book became the model for later chronicle history books, and is a precious cultural inheritance of ancient China.

1 | 2

1. 司马光因编《资治通鉴》被后人公认为司马迁之后又一史学大家
   A portrait of Sima Guang (His book, *Comprehensive Mirror for Aid in Government,* is an outstanding masterpiece that made him the greatest historian after Sima Qian.)
2. 元刊本《资治通鉴》
   The Yuan Dynasty block-printed edition of *Comprehensive Mirror for Aid in Government*

统一的多民族国家进一步发展和封建社会由盛而衰时期——明、清（鸦片战争以前）

The Period of Further Development of the Unitary Multi-ethnic Country and the Decline of Feudal Society — The Ming and Qing Dynasties (Before the Opium War of 1840)

概述

Introduction

14至19世纪，是中国封建社会衰落的明清时期。明朝从朱元璋在南京建立政权（1368年），到1644年崇祯皇帝在北京煤山上吊自杀，历时280多年。从1644年清朝顺治皇帝入主北京，到1840年鸦片战争爆发，清朝前期的统治长达190多年。明朝时，统一的多民族国家进一步发展。明朝前期经济发展，社会繁荣，郑和多次出使西洋各国，促进了中外友好交往。清朝的康熙（Kāngxī）、雍正（Yōngzhèng）和乾隆（Qiánlóng）时期，出现了繁荣的“盛世”。明清时期，中国人民创造了丰富的物质财富和精神财富，涌现出许多政治家、思想家、军事家、探险家和科学家，他们在中华民族的史册上谱写了光辉的篇章。

这一时期，世界历史进展迅猛，东西方经济文化接触日益频繁，新航路的开辟使世界密切联系起来。14至15世纪，欧洲地中海沿岸一些城市出现了资本主义萌芽。17至18世纪，英、美、法三国先后发生资产阶级革命，世界历史进入新的时期。西方先进国家已经进入工业革命的成熟阶段，资本主义发展迅速。相比之下，中国却未能同步发展。虽然中国从明朝中后期产生资本主义萌芽，但由于封建制度的束缚，生产力发展受到严重阻碍，商品经济发展艰难，封建社会由盛而衰。随着中国社会发展的逐步落伍和西方殖民主义侵略势力的到来，中国封建统治者对外部世界的态度，逐渐由交往转向闭关锁国，同西方国家的差距迅速拉大。

The Period of Further Development of the Unitary Multi-ethnic Country and the Decline of Feudal Society — The Ming and Qing Dynasties (Before the Opium War of 1840)

The decline of the Chinese feudal society occurred during the period of the Ming and Qing dynasties, from the 14th to the 19th centuries. The Ming Dynasty lasted over 280 years from its establishment by Zhu Yuanzhang in Nanjing in 1368 to when Emperor Chongzhen hanged himself on the Coal Hill of Beijing in 1644. The early reign of the Qing Dynasty lasted over 190 years from Emperor Shunzhi's entry into Beijing in 1644 to the outbreak of the Opium War in 1840. In the Ming Dynasty, there was a closer integration of the many ethnic groups that composed China. In the first half of the dynasty, the economy developed rapidly, and society was prosperous. Admiral Zheng He made seven long-distance voyages to the countries in the Western Seas to promote China's friendly relations with foreign countries. The reigns of emperors Kangxi, Yongzheng and Qianlong of the Qing Dynasty are regarded as a golden age, in which the Chinese people created enormous material and spiritual wealth, and there emerged great numbers of statesmen, thinkers, strategists, explorers and scientists. They wrote a glorious page on Chinese history.

During this period, the whole world developed rapidly, as economic and cultural contacts between the East and the West became more and more frequent with the opening of new navigation routes making the world much closer. The growth of capitalism appeared in some cities along the Miditerranean coast of Europe during 14th and 15th centuries. The Bourgeois Revolution broke out successively in Britain, the USA and France during 17th and 18th centuries. World history had entered a new period. The developing countries in the west had entered the mature stage of the Industrial Revolution, and capitalism developed rapidly. However, China was left behind during this phase of history. Although the beginnings of capitalism had appeared at the end of the Ming Dynasty, restrictions imposed by the feudal political system hampered the development of productivity and commerce, causing the feudal society to decline. With the draggling of the development of Chinese society and the coming aggression by Western colonialists, the Chinese feudal rulers were forced to change their attitude to the outside world. They changed from opening intercourse to a closed-door policy, making the gap between China and the western countries bigger and bigger.

明朝开国皇帝 朱元璋

Zhu Yuanzhang, the First Emperor of the Ming Dynasty

元朝末年，统治者昏庸无能，社会经济发展迟缓，甚至倒退，黄河又多次决口。连年的天灾人祸，农民几乎没有办法生活下去，于是在14世纪中叶爆发了大规模的农民起义。

朱元璋（1328—1398年），是元末农民起义领袖之一，他出生于濠州（Háozhōu，今安徽凤阳）一个贫苦的农民家庭。1352年，郭子兴率领农民在濠州起义，朱元璋参加到这支队伍中来，作战勇敢又足智多谋，很快就得到郭子兴的重用。郭子兴死后，朱元璋成了这支队伍的首领。1356年3月，朱元璋亲自带领大军，攻占了集庆（今江苏南京），并改名为“应天府”。他接受谋士的建议，在应天召集了许多有才能的人。同时朱元璋以应天为中心，采取先易后难的战斗策略，一个一个地消灭附近的元军。这时候，其他起义队伍也都各霸一方，割地称王。1364年，朱元璋消灭了他最强大的敌人——陈友谅的起义队伍，此后，其他农民起义队伍都被他一个个打败。

1368年，朱元璋在应天称帝，定国号为“明”，史称明朝，朱元璋就是明太祖。同年秋天，明军攻克元大都，结束了元朝在全国的统治。此后，他又用近20年的时间，完成了统一大业。

朱元璋说，国家刚刚稳定，就像小鸟刚出窝不可以拔毛一样，需要好好管理。他重视农业生产，命令在战争中流亡的农民回家种田，鼓励他们开垦新的农田；提倡种植棉、桑、麻等经济作物，免除他们3年的赋税。到1393年，全国可耕种的土地是元末的4倍。他恢复了手工匠人的自由身份，推动手工业的发展。他还重视水利，建国后，修建了许多水利工程。这些措施为全国社会经济文化的进一步发展提供了有利的条件。

明太祖废除丞相，在中央设立六部，六部直接对皇帝负责，加强了中央集权；他设立新的特务机构锦衣卫等，强化

皇权；他以猛治国，制定严酷的法律，严惩贪官污吏和骄横的武将，为巩固明朝的统治打下了良好的基础。

1 | 2

1. 朱元璋像
   A portrait of Zhu Yuanzhang
2. 江苏南京明孝陵
   Xiaoling Mausoleum of the Ming Dynasty, Nanjing, Jiangsu Province

小资料 Data

明孝陵

朱元璋和皇后马氏的合葬陵墓，位于南京城外的紫金山南。1382年马皇后死后，葬在这里。因她死后被封为“孝慈”，所以称为“明孝陵”。1389年朱元璋死后，与马皇后合葬。明孝陵于1381年开始动工，历时32年才修建完成，至今已有600多年的历史。它由下马坊、大金门、碑亭、方城、宝城等组成，是中国现存的最大的皇帝陵墓之一。明孝陵壮观宏伟，代表了明初建筑和石刻艺术的最高成就，直接影响了明清两代500多年帝王陵寝的形制。2003年明孝陵作为明清皇家陵寝的一部分被联合国教科文组织列入世界文化遗产名录中。

Xiaoling Mausoleum of the Ming Dynasty

Located in the south of Purple Gold Mountain in the suburb of Nanjing, Xiaoling Mausoleum of the Ming Dynasty is the tomb of Zhu Yuanzhang and Empress Ma. Empress Ma died in 1382 and was buried there. After she died, she was given the title "*Xiaoci*" (filial and kind), hence the name Xiaoling Mausoleum. After Zhu Yuanzhang died, he was buried together with Empress Ma in the tomb. The construction of the Xiaoling Mausoleum began in 1381, and took 32 years to finish. It has had a history of more than 600 years so far. It is composed of the Xiama (Dismount) Archway, Dajin (Great Gold) Gate, Tablet Pavilion, Square City and Bao (Treasure) City. It is one of the largest imperial tombs existing in China. Xiaoling Mausoleum is so spectacular and grandiose that it represents the highest level of the architecture and stone inscriptions of the early period of the Ming Dynasty. It directly influenced the tomb of more than 500 emperors in the Ming and Qing Dynasties. As a part of the imperial tombs of the Ming and Qing Dynasties, it was included in the World Cultural Heritage List by the UNESCO in 2003.

Zhu Yuanzhang, the First Emperor of the Ming Dynasty

A combination of incompetent rulers and natural disasters led to peasant uprisings which overthrew the Yuan Dynasty. Zhu Yuanzhang (1328—1398) was a leader of one of these peasant uprisings. He was born into a poor peasant's family in Haozhou (today's Fengyang, Anhui Province). In 1352, Guo Zixing led a peasant uprising in Haozhou, and Zhu Yuanzhang joined the troops. Later, he was put in a very important position because of his bravery and wisdom. He became the leader of the troops after Guo Zixing's death. In March 1356, Zhu Yuanzhang captured Jiqing (today's Nanjing) and changed its name to Yingtian. He took his advisors' suggestions and summoned many talented people in Yingtian. Meanwhile, with Yingtian as his base, he followed the strategy of wiping out the less powerful enemy first and the powerful ones later. He defeated the Yuan armies around him one by one. At the same time, the other uprising armies all took certain territory and proclaimed themselves as emperor. In 1364, Zhu Yuanzhang defeated the most powerful enemy, i.e. the uprising troops of Chen Youliang. Later, other peasant uprising troops were defeated one by one.

In 1368, Zhu Yuanzhang proclaimed himself emperor. He was historically known as Emperor Taizu of the Ming Dynasty, in Nanjing. In the autumn of the same year, the Ming army took Dadu, the capital of the Yuan Empire, putting an end to the rule of the Mongols. However, it took Zhu Yuanzhang nearly 20 more years to consolidate his hold over the whole country.

Zhu Yuanzhang said that since the country had just been stabilized, it was the same as a little bird that just left its nest and needed great care. His first concern was to restore agricultural production, which had been severely disrupted during the wars. He encouraged peasants who had fled from their homes during the fighting to return to their fields and to open up new land. He advocated that the planting of cash crops such as cotton, mulberries and hemp. He offered tax exemptions as an incentive. By 1393, the area of agricultural land had grown to four times as big as that at the end of the Yuan Dynasty. Also irrigation works had been expanded greatly. Emperor

Taizu also extended preferential treatment to craftsmen. All these measures provided advantageous conditions for the further overall development of society, economy and culture nationwide.

Emperor Taizu abolished the position of the Prime Minister, and set up six offices known as the "six boards" in the central government, which were directly responsible to the emperor. This method strengthened the centralization of authority. He set up a new institution of spies called "Guards in Embroidered Coats", which strengthened the imperial power. At the same time, the emperor made a thorough overhaul of the existing laws, increasing the penalties for offenders and thus laid a good foundation for the rule of the Ming Dynasty.

小资料 Data

明成祖迁都

明成祖朱棣（Zhū Dì）是明朝的第三个皇帝。明太祖朱元璋60多岁的时候，太子朱标死了，于是立朱标的长子朱允炆（Zhū Yǔnwén）为皇太孙。朱元璋死后，朱允炆即位（即建文帝）。朱元璋的四子燕王朱棣正拥兵驻守北方，抵御蒙古入侵。朱棣看到皇位落到了侄子的手里，心中不服。1399年7月，朱棣以帮助皇帝除掉奸臣为理由，从北平起兵南下，发动"靖难之役"。1402年攻入了都城南京，建文帝在兵乱中下落不明。朱棣夺取了帝位，为了防范元朝残余势力，把政治、军事中心移向北方，他把都城从南京迁到北平，改北平为北京。

Emperor Chengzu Moves the Capital

Zhu Di, Emperor Chengzu, was the third emperor of the Ming Dynasty. Zhu Biao, Emperor Taizu's crown prince, died when his father was at the age of over 60, and his place was taken by Zhu Biao's eldest son, Zhu Yunwen. After the new emperor came to the throne, Zhu Yunwen's uncle, Zhu Di, the fourth son of Zhu Yuanzhang, dispatched an army from his power base of Yan (the present-day Beijing area) in July 1399, on the pretext of helping to restore order. In 1402, this army captured Nanjing. Zhu Yunwen disappeared in the turmoil, and Zhu Di declared himself Emperor Chengzu. Feeling insecure in Nanjing, Emperor Chengzu moved the capital to Beiping, and changed its name to Beijing.

1. 江苏南京天妃宫（由明成祖朱棣赐建）
Palace of Heaven's Goddess built by Zhudi, Emperor Chengzu of the Ming Dynasty

郑和下西洋

Zheng He's Voyages

明朝前期，中国是世界上最先进、最发达的国家之一。为了显示中国富强，扩大明朝在海外各国的政治影响，加强与世界各国的联系，明成祖朱棣派郑和多次出使西洋（指文莱以西的东南亚和印度洋一带）。

郑和（1371—1435年），云南回族人，小名三保，又称三宝太监。他聪明好学，立过战功，明成祖非常信任他，派他出使西洋。1405年6月，郑和奉命第一次出使西洋。他率领两万多人，包括水手和士兵，还有技术人员、翻译等，携带大量的金、帛等货物乘坐200多艘海船，从江苏太仓刘家港出发，先到占城（今越南中南部），一路经过爪哇、孟加拉等地，到达红海沿岸，后从锡兰、古里（今印度卡里卡特）回国，历经两年，于1407年秋，返回南京。

郑和的船队满载着金银珠宝、丝绸、瓷器等中国特产，每到一个国家或地区，郑和都把这些东西当作明朝的礼物送给他们，表达了和他们友好交往的愿望。西洋各国非常友好地接待了郑和和他的船队，有些国家还派使者跟随他前来朝见中国皇帝。同时，郑和也从各国换回了珠宝、香料等特产。明成祖对郑和的成绩非常满意。郑和前后7次出使西洋，最远到达了非洲东海岸和红海沿岸。

这一时期南洋、西洋许多国家的国王、使臣和商队纷纷来到中国。郑和的出航也为人类航海史作出了巨大的贡献，他的第一次远航，比哥伦布发现美洲大陆早87年，比达·伽马开辟东方新航路早93年，比麦哲伦航行菲律宾早116年。因此郑和下西洋是世界航海史上的创举，现在东南亚一带还有许多纪念郑和的建筑物，表达了人们对他的崇敬。

郑和航海图

Sketch Map of Zheng He's Voyages

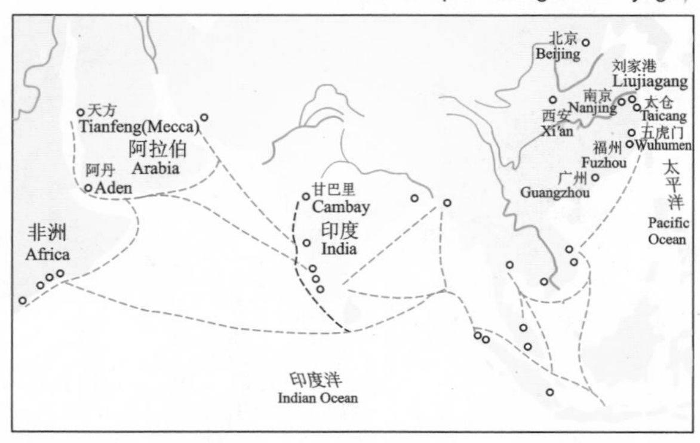

Zheng He's Voyages

In the early Ming Dynasty, China was one of the most advanced and developed countries in the world. In order to display the national power and strengthen contacts with other countries, Emperor Chengzu sent Zheng He, a senior general and eunuch, on six voyages to the Western Seas (Southeast Asia, west of Brunei and the Indian Ocean) on diplomatic missions.

Zheng He (1371—1435), an ethnic Hui (Moslem) petnamed Sanbao or Eunuch Sanbao, was born in Yunnan Province. Due to his brightness and diligence, as well as his achievement in the battle, he won the trust of Emperor Chengzu and was sent to the Western Seas on diplomatic missions. In June 1405, Zheng He embarked on his first voyage. His fleet of more than 200 ships carried well over 20 000 men, including sailors, soldiers, technical personnel, interpreters, etc., and large amounts of gold and silk. The fleet set out from Liujiagang in Jiangsu Province, and sailed westward as far to the Red Sea, areas along the way including Zhancheng (a Vietnamese city), Java, and Bengal. Then the fleet went back by way of Ceylon and Guli (today's Calicut in Indian). The round trip took two years. In the autumn of 1407, the fleet retuned to Nanjing.

Zheng He's fleets were loaded with large amounts of gold, precious stones, porcelain and silk which were used as gifts to express goodwill. Some of the countries Zheng He visited also dispatched envoys bearing tribute to the Ming court on his ships. Meanwhile Zheng He exchanged with these countries special local products such as jewellery, spice and so on. Emperor Chengzu was satisfied with Zhen He's achievements. During the Seven voyages to the Western Seas, Zheng He sailed as far as the eastern coast of Africa and the Red Sea coast.

During this period, many kings, ambassadors and businessmen came to China. Zheng He's voyages also made great contributions to the world's navigational history. His first voyage was 87 years earlier than Columbus' discovery of America, 93 years earlier than Da Gama's route to the East, 116 years earlier than Magellan's voyage to the Philippines. Zheng He's voyages were a great feat in the history of world. There are still many buildings in present Southeast Asia dedicated to his memory and respect.

小资料 Data

郑和七次下西洋

第一次　1405—1407年到锡兰山、古里等地。
第二次　1407—1409年到古里、小葛兰等地。
第三次　1409—1411年到忽鲁莫斯（波斯湾）、阿拉伯等地。
第四次　1413—1415年到非洲东海岸。
第五次　1417—1419年到东非。
第六次　1421—1422年到忽鲁莫斯（波斯湾）、阿拉伯等地。
第七次　1431—1433年到红海、麦加等地。

Zheng He' s Seven Voyages to the Western Seas

First: 1405-1407 reached Sri Lanka
Second: 1407-1409 called at Calcutta and Sri Lanka
Third: 1409-1411 reached Hormuz on the Persian Gulf and Arabia
Fourth: 1413-1415 reached the east coast of Africa
Fifth: 1417-1419 revisited East Africa
Sixth: 1421-1422 revisited Hormuz (Persian Gulf) and Arabia
Seventh: 1431-1433 reached the Red Sea and Mecca

戚继光抗倭

Qi Jiguang Repels Japanese Pirates

1. 戚继光塑像
A statue of Qi Jiguang
2. 为抗倭寇而建的福建惠安崇武古城（戚继光曾在此操练兵马）
Chongwu Stone Fortress (Hui'an, Fujian Province) was built to defend itself against the Japanese Pirates. Qi Jiguang was here to raise and train his own army.

元末明初，一些日本海盗时常骚扰中国沿海地区，威胁沿海人民的生命安全。当时的人们把这些人叫做“倭寇”（Wōkòu）。明朝建立后，实行了严厉的“海禁”政策，除了政府与海外国家保持朝贡关系外，其他海上贸易一概禁止。到了明朝中期，倭寇与中国海盗勾结在一起从事海上武装走私贸易，大肆抢掠，杀人放火，无恶不作，对沿海人民的危害越来越大。朝廷下决心整治海防，命令戚继光平定倭寇。

戚继光（1528—1587年），山东蓬莱人，是中国历史上著名的民族英雄。1556年，年轻的将领戚继光被派到浙江东部沿海地区抗击倭寇。他到了浙江以后，发现明朝军队纪律不严，战斗力不强，于是决定重新招募军队，训练精兵，他很快就召集了一支4 000人左右的队伍。戚继光根据沿海地区的特点，精心训练士兵。经过两个月的严格训练，队伍纪律严明，战斗力很强，与敌人作战屡战屡胜，当地的人们亲切地称他们为“戚家军”。

1561年倭寇假装侵犯奉化、宁海，实际想进攻台州。戚继光识破了倭寇的诡计，在台州打败了倭寇。戚继光在台州先后九战九捷，消灭了浙东的倭寇。以后，倭寇到哪里，戚继光就打到哪里，打得倭寇落花流水。经过近10年的艰苦作战，到1565年，倭寇基本上被赶出了东南沿海。

Qi Jiguang Repels Japanese Pirates

At the end of the Yuan Dynasty and in the early years of the Ming Dynasty, Japanese pirates often harassed China's coastal areas, threatening people's lives. Local people called these pirates "Wokou". Since the establishment of the Ming Dynasty, strict restrictions on maritime trade and intercourse with foreign countries were carried out. Except for government links with foreign countries, all business over the sea was forbidden. During the middle Ming Dynasty, Wokou sometimes even colluded with Chinese pirates, smuggling arms over the sea, plundering and slaughtering. Finally, the Ming court resolved to bolster the coastal defenses, and ordered Qi Jiguang to put an end to the pirate menace.

Qi Jiguang (1528—1587) was born in Penglai, Shandong Province. In 1556, he was assigned to deal with the problem of Japanese pirates in the coastal areas of Zhejiang Province. Dismayed at the low morale and the lack of training of the soldiers, Qi decided to raise and train his own army. Soon, he had a force of about 4 000 crack troops. They were known locally as "Qi's army" and soon distinguished themselves.

In 1561, the Japanese pirates pretended to invade Fenghua and Ninghai with the real aim of attacking Taizhou. Qi Jiguang saw through the enemy's trick and defeated the invaders at Taizhou. He fought nine battles and won nine times. After ridding Zhejiang of the pirate scourge, Qi Jiguang fought Japanese pirates wherever they appeared along the Chinese coastal areas. After nearly 10 years of hard fighting, he succeeded in driving the Japanese pirates out from the coastal areas of southeast China by 1565.

清官海瑞

Hai Rui, an Upright and Incorruptible Official

海瑞（1514—1587年），海南琼州人。1558年，他被任命为浙江淳安县知县。在他来之前，县里的官吏贪赃枉法，处理案件都是胡乱结案。海瑞到任后，认真处理案件，纠正了许多冤案错案，老百姓非常敬重他。

1564年，海瑞被调到京城做官。当时的皇帝明世宗相信长生不老，整天跟道士在皇宫里修炼，有20多年没上朝处理国家大事了，但大臣们都不敢劝皇帝。海瑞官虽不大，胆子却不小，他在1565年写了一道奏章批评明世宗。海瑞估计明世宗看了这一道奏章以后，可能杀自己的头，于是自己买了一口棺材，告别妻子，并且把他死后的事都交代好了。明世宗看到他的奏章后，果然大怒，把海瑞逮捕入狱。明世宗死后，海瑞获释。

1569年，海瑞又被任命为江南巡抚，巡视应天十府（包括苏州、应天、松江、常州、镇江、徽州等地）。应天府是明朝经济、文化最发达的地区，但也是大官僚、大地主最集中，国家最难管理的地方。大官僚、大地主霸占了大量的良田。海瑞坚决要求他们把霸占的土地无偿退还给农民，大官僚、大地主因此非常仇恨海瑞，于是和朝廷内的一些官员相勾结，在皇帝面前说海瑞的坏话，皇帝被这些人欺骗了，罢免了海瑞的官职，海瑞从此闲居10多年。

明神宗时，年迈的海瑞又被起用。1587年，海瑞死于南京任上。海瑞做官几十年，一生清廉，为人民做了许多好事，人们都叫他“海青天”。

1 | 2

1. 海瑞塑像
   A statue of Hai Rui
2. 海瑞墓（一代清官长眠于海南家乡）
   Hai Rui's Tomb (The incorruptible official is buried at his hometown of Hainan Province.)

Hai Rui, an Upright and Incorruptible Official

Hai Rui (1514—1587) was born in Qiongzhou, Hainan Province. In 1558, he was appointed county magistrate of Chun'an County in Zhejiang Province. Previously, many county officials took bribes and bent the law. They often wound up cases carelessly. Hai Rui cleaned up this notoriously corrupt county, setting an example of honest government.

In 1564, Hai Rui was transferred to an official post in the capital. Emperor Shizong was obsessed with Taoism and the research for immortality and completely neglected state affairs. Though only a very junior official, Hai Rui had the courage to send a memorial to the throne, censuring the emperor. Fully convinced that the emperor would have him executed, Hai Rui bought a coffin, bade farewell to his wife, and settled his affairs. He was not, in fact, executed, but thrown into prison and not released until after Emperor Shizong's death.

In 1569, Hai Rui was appointed imperial inspector of the 10 areas under the administration of Yingtian (including Suzhou, Yingtian, Songjiang, Changzhou, Zhenjiang, Huizhou, and others). Yingtian was the most advanced region in both economy and culture in the Ming Dynasty. Senior officials there had carved out large estates for themselves. This deprived the state of large amounts of fertile land. Hai Rui insisted unconditionally on breaking up these estates, and the returning the land to the peasants. His enemies thereupon banded together to slander him to the emperor, Muzong, and Hai Rui was stripped of his official rank.

After 10 years living in retirement, Hai Rui was employed again by the new emperor Shenzong. He held the post until his death in 1587. He was renowned far and wide as a model of an upright and incorruptible official.

闯王李自成

Daring King Li Zicheng

明朝后期，由于皇帝腐朽无能，宦官专权，政治黑暗腐败。官僚地主霸占了全国绝大部分的良田沃土，很多农民失去了土地，政府还不断地向农民征收赋税，困苦不堪的农民又遭到蝗灾、旱灾等自然灾害。在这种情况下，农民起义迅速地在全国酝酿（yùnniàng）。1627年，农民起义首先在灾情严重的陕北爆发。农民战争发展迅猛，短短几年内，就涌现出几十支起义军，其中以高迎祥领导的起义军规模最大。高迎祥死后，起义军主要有两支：一支由张献忠率领，另一支由李自成率领。

李自成（1606—1645年），陕西米脂人。1630年在家乡米脂起义，不久投奔高迎祥，成为高迎祥手下的一名闯将。高迎祥死后，李自成被拥为“闯王”，率领一支起义军转战于河南一带。当时，河南是灾情比较严重的地区，李自成在谋士的帮助下，提出“均田免粮”的口号，赢得了广大农民的支持，人们互相流传“杀牛羊，备酒浆，开了城门迎闯王”。起义军迅速壮大，发展到百万人。1641年，李自成起义军攻占了洛阳，活捉并杀死了福王朱常洵（Zhū Chángxún），没收王府中的财物，分给老百姓。1644年，李自成在西安建立了大顺政权，同年，乘胜进攻北京，明朝最后一个皇帝崇祯在煤山（今北京景山）上吊自杀，3月，李自成大军占领了北京。

农民军进了北京之后，严整军纪。大顺政权命令明朝的贵族、官僚、富户交出大量钱财，还镇压了一批罪大恶极的达官贵人，大顺政权控制了长城以南、淮河以北的广大地区。

李自成进北京的消息传到关外，满清摄政王多尔衮（Duōěrgǔn）急忙率兵南下，降服了驻守山海关的明将吴三桂。不久，李自成亲自率农民军同吴三桂的军队和清军在山海关展开大战，农民军战败。李自成被迫率军撤出北京，转战于河南、陕西等地。1645年，李自成战死于湖北九宫山。

1 | 2

1. 湖北通山县李自成墓墓碑
The gravestone of the Mausoleum of Li Zicheng, Tongshan County, Hubei Province
2. 陕西米脂县李自成行宫
Temporary Imperial Palace of Li Zicheng in Mizhi County, Shaanxi Province

Daring King Li Zicheng

The emperors in the late years of the Ming Dynasty were fatuous and incompetent, and power gradually slipped into the hands of eunuchs. Bureaucrats and landlords forcibly occupied large tracts of fertile land, leaving many peasants landless. Taxes and natural disasters, which officials did little to relieve, added to the burdens on the peasants, and eventually, in 1627, a large-scale uprising broke out in the area of what is now northern Shaanxi Province. The unrest spread throughout the country. The strongest of the rebel peasant armies was led by Gao Yingxiang. After Gao's death, his army was divided into two main parts: one was led by Zhang Xianzhong, and the other by Li Zicheng.

Li Zicheng (1606—1645) was born in Mizhi, Shaanxi Province. In 1630, he joined the uprising, rising rapidly to become a general under Gao Yingxiang. With the death of Gao, he took command of the rebel forces in present-day Henan Province. Li Zicheng won the support of the people in this disaster-stricken area by a policy of land reform and abolition of agricultural taxes. Li's army grew rapidly to become a million-strong force. Wherever Li Zicheng's army went, it distributed the property of the landlords among the people. In 1644, Li Zicheng established the Dashun Dynasty in Xi'an. In the same year, he marched on to Beijing. As

the rebels entered the capital, Emperor Chongzhen, the last Ming emperor, committed suicide by hanging himself on Coal Hill (today's Jingshan), just behind the Forbidden City.

Li Zicheng enforced strict military discipline, punished officials guilty of crimes and corruption. The regime controlled a vast area from the south of the Great Wall to the north of the Huaihe River.

Meanwhile, Dorgon, the prince regent of the Qing Dynasty, which had been set up in 1636 by the united Manchu tribes of northeast China, hurriedly led an army southward. Breaking through the strategic Shanhai Pass, Dorgon made the general Wu Sangui surrender. Li Zicheng was forced to withdraw from Beijing. In 1645, Li Zicheng was killed in the battle at Mount Jiugong, in today's Hubei Province.

小资料 Data

清军入关

1616年，女真首领努尔哈赤建立“金”，史称“后金”。1626年，皇太极继承皇位。1635年他改族名“女真”为“满洲”；次年，改国号为“清”，称皇帝。1644年，清军进攻山海关，山海关守将吴三桂投降。10月，清顺治皇帝从盛京（今沈阳）迁都北京，开始了对全中国的统治。

The Qing Army Pours Through Shanhai Pass

In 1616, Nurhachi, leader of the Jurchen (Nuzhen) tribes, established the Jin regime, called the Later Jin in history. In 1626, Huangtaiji succeeded to the throne. In 1635, he changed the name of Jurchen to Manchu; the next year, he changed the title of the regime to Qing, and proclaimed himself emperor. In 1644, the Qing army attacked Shanhai Pass. Wu Sangui, the general garrisoning the pass, submitted to the Qing army. In October, Emperor Shunzhi of the Qing Dynasty moved the capital from Shengjing (today's Shenyang) to Beijing, and commenced to reign over the whole of China.

郑成功收复台湾

Zheng Chenggong Recovers Taiwan

宝岛台湾自古以来就是中国不可分割的领土，它风景秀丽，物产丰富。

从1624年开始，荷兰殖民统治者采用欺骗的手段逐步侵占了台湾，欺压台湾人民。台湾人民忍受不了他们的压迫和掠夺，不断起而反抗，可是因为他们力量弱小，都没有成功，在东南沿海抗清的将领郑成功决心赶走荷兰殖民者。

1661年3月，郑成功亲自率领大军，从金门出发，在台湾当地人的带领下登上了台湾岛。台湾人民听说郑成功来了，成群结队，去迎接自己的亲人。等到荷兰人知道时，中国军队已经像神兵天将一样遍布岛上、海上。郑成功的军队与荷兰殖民者展开了激烈的战斗，把敌军包围在赤嵌（Chìkǎn）城（今台南市），断绝了他们的水源，守城的荷兰军队如果不投降就只能渴死、饿死。荷兰殖民头领提出给郑成功10万两白银，请求他退兵。郑成功断然拒绝，他说台湾历来是中国的领土，荷兰殖民者必须退出。荷兰人不甘心，又派了援兵，企图打败郑成功，可是早有防备的郑成功给敌人援军一个迎头痛击，彻底打碎了他们的梦想，殖民者最终向郑成功投降。1662年，中国收回了台湾。

收复台湾是中国军民抗击外来侵略的一次大胜利，郑成功也因此成为载入中国历史的民族英雄。

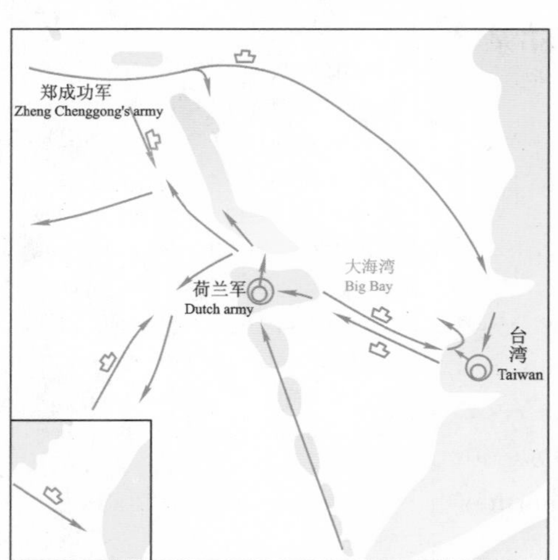

郑成功收复台湾略图
Sketch Map of Zheng Chenggong's Campaign to Recover Taiwan

1

1. 厦门鼓浪屿郑成功雕塑
A sculpture of Zheng Chenggong, Gulangyu, Xiamen

Zheng Chenggong Recovers Taiwan

Taiwan has been an inseparable part of China since ancient times. It has beautiful scenery and is rich in agricultural products.

In 1624, Dutch colonialists started to seize Taiwan gradually by cheating. The Taiwan people could not bear the pressure and plunder upon them. Though they never gave up resistance, they were too weak to beat the Dutch. Zheng Chenggong, a Ming general who was resisting the Qing Dynasty in the coastal area of southeast China. He resolved to drive the Dutch colonialists off Taiwan.

In 1661, Zheng Chenggong set out with an army from Jinmen and landed on the Taiwan Island by the guidance of the local people. Hearing of his arrival, the Taiwan people went in groups to welcome him as a family member. Zheng's forces had unimaginably spread all over the island and the sea before the Dutch began to respond. They besieged the Dutch in Chikan (today's Tainan City) and cut off their water supply. The Dutch commander offered Zheng 100 000 tael to retreat, but Zheng rebuffed and declared that Taiwan was always a part of China and the Dutch colonists had to withdraw at once. The Dutch increased the reinforcements, attempting to beat Zheng. However, the well-prepared Zheng made a head-on attack against the enemy and completely expelled them from Taiwan in 1662.

The recovery of Taiwan was a great victory for the Chinese people in their resistance to colonial invaders. For this, Zheng Chenggong became a national hero.

小资料 Data

中国对台湾的管辖简史

230年，吴主孙权派卫温到台湾。

607年，隋炀帝派朱宽到台湾安抚当地人。

1292年，元世祖忽必烈派大臣到台湾安抚当地人。

1335年，元朝设“澎湖巡检司”正式管辖台湾。

1684年，清朝设立台湾府。

A Brief History of China's Administration of Taiwan

In 230, Sun Quan, ruler of the State of Wu in the Three Kingdoms Period, sent his envoy Wei Wen to Taiwan.

In 607, Emperor Yangdi of the Sui Dynasty sent Zhu Kuan to Taiwan to reassure the local people.

In 1292, Kublai Khan, Emperor Shizu of the Yuan Dynasty, sent ministers to Taiwan to reassure the local people.

In 1335, the Yuan Dynasty set up the Penghu Inspectorate as the official administration of Taiwan.

In 1684, the Qing Dynasty set up the Taiwan Prefecture.

康乾盛世

The Golden Age of Three Emperors

清朝康熙（1661—1722年在位）、雍正（1722—1735年在位）和乾隆（1735—1796年在位）三位皇帝治理国家时，社会经济的发展水平达到了前所未有的高度，呈现出空前的繁荣和富强的局面，史称“康乾盛世”。

康熙是中国历史上在位时间最长的皇帝，同时也是清朝最贤明的君主，他的文治和武功几乎没有哪位皇帝可以和他相提

1. 故宫乾清宫外观
Outside of Qianqing Palace of the Palace Museum

并论。

1661年康熙即位时，还是一个小孩子，那时清朝的统治还不稳固，明朝的旧臣想推翻清朝，恢复明朝的统治，形势十分危急。为了缓和矛盾，稳定政治局面，康熙把儒家学说定为官方思想，任用汉人做官，提倡汉文化。在他的倡导下，编成了《康熙字典》；他还派遣耶稣（Yēsū）会士到各地测量，绘制了中国第一部实测地图《皇舆全览图》。

康熙还非常注重农业生产，并采取一系列措施减轻农民的负担，让被战争破坏的经济得到迅速恢复。他还经常巡视各地，了解民情，关心人民的疾苦。

康熙平定了三藩之乱（吴三桂、耿精忠、尚可喜的叛乱）、蒙古准噶尔部的分裂活动和西藏叛乱，从郑成功后代手中收回了台湾，两次与沙皇俄国在雅克萨作战，阻止了沙俄的扩张，维护了清朝领土的完整，康熙对国家统一作出了很大贡献。康熙在位期间，社会经济发展，人民生活安定。

雍正在位时间较短，他整顿吏治，重视用人，强调务实，使清朝的社会经济保持稳定和持续发展。

乾隆皇帝是雍正的儿子。1735年即位后，他鼓励农民开垦荒地，组织移民，并行农业生产，多次减免农民的赋税。他调整了雍正时中央与地方地主官僚的紧张关系。惩罚官吏结党营私，改善了官吏队伍。平定了回部贵族叛乱，并对西藏进行了政治和宗教改革，加强了对西藏的管理。消灭了西南少数民族地区的割据政权，这些措施奠定了近代中国的版图，把统一的多民族国家发展到一个新阶段。

乾隆在位期间，清朝经济发展，人口快速增长，进入了最强盛的时期。

小资料 Data

达赖与班禅

1653年，清政府册封达赖五世为“西天大善自在佛所领天下释教普通瓦赤喇怛喇达赖喇嘛（lǎma）”。正式确定达赖喇嘛为西藏佛教格鲁派（黄教）的宗教领袖。1713年又封班禅五世为“班禅额尔德尼”，颁发金印金册。从此以后，历世达赖、班禅必经中央政权册封，成为定制。

The Dalai and Panchen Lamas

In 1653, the Qing government officially recognized the fifth Dalai Lama as the head of the Gelugpa of Tibetan Buddhism, and in 1713, it recognized the fifth Panchen Lama as the head of the Tashilhunpo Monastery, the headquarters of a powerful sect of Tibetan Buddhism. From that time on, both the Dalai and Panchen lamas had to be confirmed by the central authority.

The Golden Age of Three Emperors

The reigns of the Qing emperors Kangxi (1661—1722), Yongzheng (1722—1735) and Qianlong (1735—1796) marked a period of unprecedented prosperity both politically and economically.

Kangxi enjoyed the longest reign in Chinese history. He was also the wisest emperor of the Qing Dynasty. When he ascended the throne in 1661 as a child, the rule of the Qing Dynasty was unstable. Many officials of the old regime wanted to overthrow the Qing Dynasty and resume the Ming's rule. Kangxi promoted a program of Sinicization of his government, including instituting Confucianism as the state ideology, appointing Han officials and promoting Han culture among the ruling Manchu class. It was also he who proposed to compile the *Kangxi Dictionary* and the first on-the-spot surveying map named the *Map of China in Kangxi's Reign*.

Kangxi also attached great importance to the restoration of agricultural production, which had been devastated by years of war. He adopted a series of measures to lighten the burden of the peasants. He often took imperial tours of inspection to know the conditions and sufferings of people.

Kangxi suppressed the Revolt of the Three Feudatories (Wu Sangui, Geng Jingzhong and Shang Kexi), separatist activities in Mongolia and Tibet, and wrested the control of Taiwan from the descendants of Zheng

Chenggong. In addition, encroachment from tsarist Russia was halted. Kangxi thus made great contributions to the territorial integrity of the country, as well as to its security and prosperity.

Emperor Yongzheng proved a worthy successor to Kangxi's policies. Emperor Qianlong, a son of Emperor Yongzheng, succeeded to the throne in 1735. He encouraged peasants to cultivate waste land, and lightened their tax burden. He mitigated the intense relations between the central and regional officials caused in Yongzheng's reign. He also strengthened the central government's control over the ethnic-minority areas, particularly in Tibet.

During Qianlong's reign, economy developed fast, the population also increased, and the Qing Dynasty entered its strongest phase.

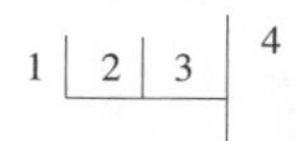

1. 康熙皇帝像
   A portrait of Emperor Kangxi
2. 雍正皇帝像
   A portrait of Emperor Yongzheng
3. 乾隆皇帝像
   A portrait of Emperor Qianlong
4. 乾清宫（清朝皇帝处理国家大事的地方）
   The throne room of the Qianqing Palace, where Qing emperors handled state affairs

清代强盛时期疆域略图

Sketch Map of the Qing Dynasty's Territory in its Heyday

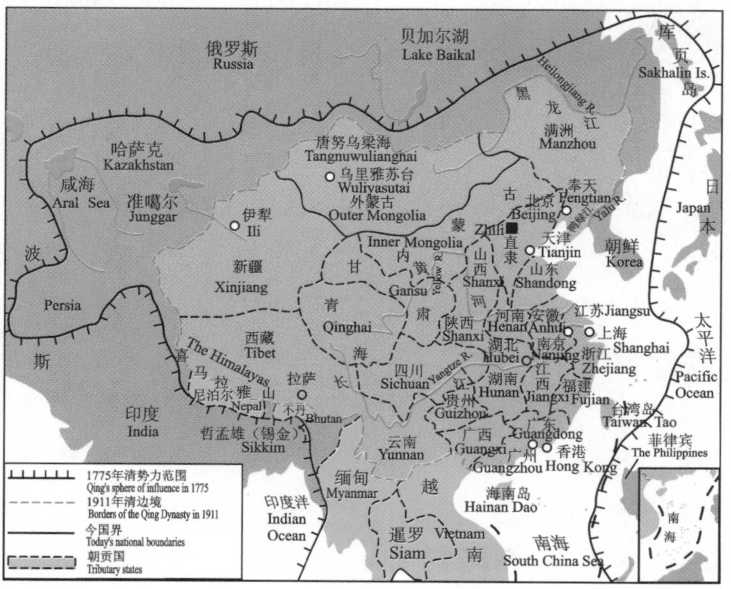

小资料 Data

闭关政策

清朝初年，为了防范东南沿海岛屿的反清势力，实行了比明朝更加严厉的海禁政策。后来虽有短暂的开放，允许商人进行有限制的贸易，但在1840年以前的大多时间里，清朝只有广州一地通商口岸，对丝绸、茶叶等传统商品的出口量严加限制，对国内商船到海外贸易规定了很多禁令，这就是“闭关政策”。由于清朝统治集团对当时世界大势缺乏足够的认识，以世界的中心自居，才在全球化贸易的背景下，采取了与西方资本主义自由贸易制度格格不入的消极防御政策，使中国丧失了与先进国家同步发展的机会。

Closed-door Policy

Early in the Qing Dynasty, the government adopted stricter policy against foreign communication in order to keep away the force against Qing government along the coastal areas. Though there were temporary openings allowing businessmen to trade in limited items, the Qing Dynasty had only one treaty port, Guangzhou, where traditional goods such as silk and tea were severely restricted. Bans on oversea commerce were also included in this policy which was called "Closed-door Policy". Due to the lack of knowledge about the current situation, the Qing Dynasty adopted negative policies different from free-trade systems of the West, causing China to lose opportunities to make the same progress with the developed countries.

科学巨匠与巨著

Great Scientists and Their Contributions

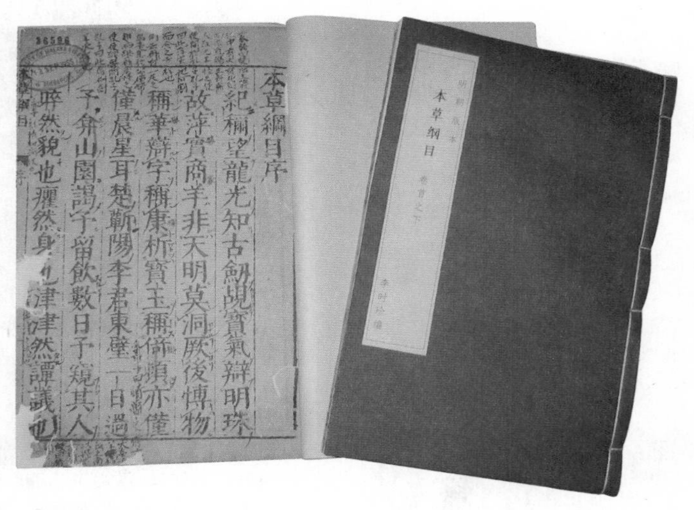

李时珍和《本草纲目》

李时珍（1518—1593年）是明代著名的医学家和药物学家，出生于湖广蕲州（Qízhōu，今湖北蕲春）一个世代行医的家庭。他受到家庭的影响，从小就对医学有着浓厚的兴趣，并决心做一个给人们解除病痛的好医生。李时珍24岁就开始正式给人治病，由于他刻苦钻研，医术高超，治好了许多疑难病症。

李时珍为了研究医术，读了很多古代的医书，他发现前人编著的医药书中有许多遗漏，甚至还有许多错误。他决心重编一本比较完备的药物著作。为了实现这一理想，李时珍阅读了大量的医学著作，还注重实地考察和采集草药。经过近30年的努力，他终于在60岁的时候写成了《本草纲目》一书。这本书内容十分丰富，收入药物1 800多种，新增药物3 700多种，医方1万多个，配有插图1 000多幅。书中关于植物的分类方法，也是当时世界最先进的。《本草纲目》是中国药物学研究的总结，已被译成多种文字，被誉为“东方医学巨典”。

徐光启和《农政全书》

徐光启（1562—1633年），上海人，明朝科学家，曾跟随意大利传教士利玛窦（Lìmǎdòu）学习西方的天文、数学、测量、火器等知识。他钻研科学文化知识，在介绍西方自然科学和发展中国

的农业、天文、数学等方面作出了重大贡献。

《农政全书》是一部关于农业科学的著作。在书中，徐光启用科学的方法总结了中国传统的技术，如农具、土壤、水利、施肥等等；他还介绍了欧洲的水利技术。书中有图，有批注，有说明，内容丰富，被称为中国古代的一部农业百科全书。

宋应星和《天工开物》

宋应星（1587—约1666年），江西人，明朝末年科学家。他一生写了许多著作，《天工开物》是其中影响最大的一部书。这本书是明朝农业和手工业生产技术的总结，内容十分广泛，几乎包括了当时社会生活的各个方面，反映了当时的社会发展水平，被誉为“中国17世纪的工艺百科全书”。

徐霞客和《徐霞客游记》

徐霞客（1586—1641年），江苏人，中国17世纪杰出的旅行家和地理学家。徐霞客读了很多书，对地理、历史、游记类的书特别感兴趣。他发现，有些地理书籍的记载是错误的，因而决心对祖国的地理情况进行实地考察。22岁那年，徐霞客开始了他的野外考察生活，直到他逝世的那一年。在30多年的考察生活中，徐霞客几乎跑遍了全中国。

《徐霞客游记》以日记的形式记录了作者旅行考察中的见闻和内心感受。徐霞客以实地考察的第一手资料，记录了中国的山川河流、地形地貌、矿产分布等。《徐霞客游记》是研究中国地貌、水文、动植物分布等的重要参考资料。

1. 明朝版本《本草纲目》
The Ming Dynasty edition of *Bencao Gangmu*
2. 《农政全书》书影
A copy of the *Encyclopedia of Agriculture*
3. 《天工开物》书影
A copy of the *Exploitation of the Works of Nature*

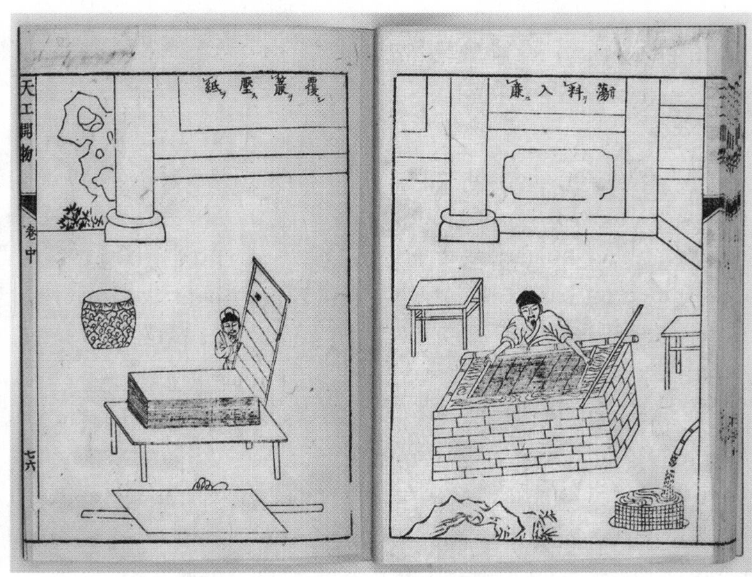

Great Scientists and Their Contributions

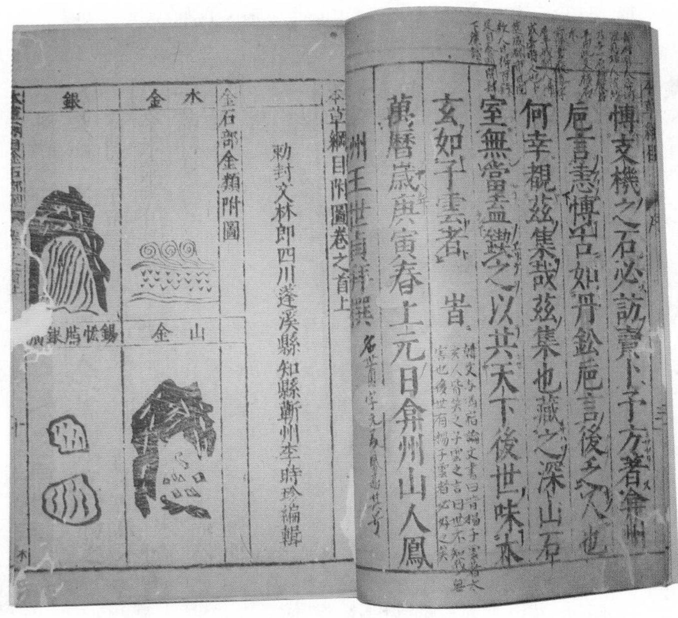

本草綱目附圖卷之首上

勅封文林郎四川蓬溪縣知縣蘄州李時珍編輯

金石部金類附圖

何幸覩茲集哉茲集也藏之深山石
室無當盍鍥之以共天下後世味太
玄如子雲者 旹
萬曆歲庚寅春上元日弇州山人鳳
洲王世貞拜撰

Li Shizhen and *Bencao Gangmu*

Li Shizhen (1518—1593) was born in Qizhou of Huguang (in today's Qichun, Hubei province). He was a well-known medical specialist and pharmacologist. Influenced by his family, he was deeply interested in medical treatment and decided to devote himself to the art of healing. At the age of 24, Li Shizhen formally began to make diagnoses and give medical treatment. Due to his diligence, his leechcraft was excellent and cured many complex diseases.

Noticing that the classical works on medicine contained many mistakes and obscurities, Li determined to write a definitive materia medica.

He read many medical books, and also paid close attention to site visits and collecting herbs. He spent 30 years on his work, which he completed at the age of 60. His book, titled *Bencao Gangmu (Compendium of Materia Medica)* contains details of over 1 800 kinds of herbs and other medicinal materials, 10 000 prescriptions and over 1 000 illustrations. It was the most scientific description of traditional Chinese medicine of its time, and is still used today. It has been translated into several major languages.

Xu Guangqi and *Encyclopedia of Agriculture*

Xu Guangqi (1562—1633), born in Shanghai, studied astronomy, mathematics and the art of making firearms under Matteo Ricci, an Italian missionary. He made great contributions to the introduction of Western natural science to China and to develop science in China, including scientific agriculture,

as embodied in his *Encyclopedia of Agriculture*.

In his book, with a scientific approach Xu summarized traditional Chinese technologies, such as agricultural tools, soil, irrigation and fertilization, etc. He also introduced the irrigation works in Europe. There are pictures, endorsements, and illustrations in his book. Rich in content, it was regarded as one of the best of the ancient Chinese Encyclopedias on agriculture.

Song Yingxing and *Exploitation of the Works of Nature*

Song Yingxing (1587—c.1666), born in Jiangxi, was one of the scientists of the late Ming Dynasty. Among the many books he wrote, his *Exploitation of the Works of Nature* was the most influential. Its contents cover almost every aspect of social and economic life of China in the 17th century, and it was praised as the technology encyclopedia of that time.

Xu Xiake and *Xu Xiake's Travels*

Xu Xiake (1586—1641), born in Jiangsu, was an eminent traveler and geographer of the 17th century. Puzzled by conflicting references in books of geography, history and travels, he decided to investigate for himself. From the age of 22, Xu Xiake spent 30 years traveling all over China. He recorded his observations in diary form in his *Xu Xiake's Travels*.

This book is still of great importance for the study of China's geomorphology, hydrology, distribution of animals, plants, mineral resources, etc.

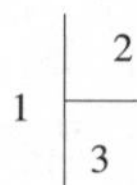

1. 明朝版本《本草纲目》
   The Ming Dynasty edition of *Bencao Gangmu*
2. 宋应星像
   A portrait of Song Yingxing
3. 徐霞客塑像
   A Statue of Xu Xiake

中国近代史
MODERN PERIOD

概述

Introduction

英国于19世纪30年代末在世界上率先完成了工业革命，成为当时最强大的资本主义国家。为了扩大工业品的销售市场，占领更广阔的工业原料产地，英国发动了侵略中国的鸦片战争。中国在鸦片战争中战败，被迫与英国签订了中英《南京条约》等不平等条约。从此，中国的主权与领土完整遭到破坏，开始沦为半殖民地半封建的国家。所以，史学界以1840年作为中国近代史的开端，此后110年的历史，是中国的近代史。鸦片战争后的100多年中，世界列强一次又一次发动对中国的侵略战争，使中国的主权与领土完整继续遭到破坏，使中国完全沦为半殖民地半封建国家；同时，中国也涌现出许许多多的抵抗侵略、挽救国家危亡的可歌可泣的事迹，如太平天国运动、戊戌变法、义和团运动等，特别是1911年孙中山领导的辛亥革命，推翻了中国两千多年的封建君主专制制度，建立了中华民国；1919年的“五四”运动，为中国共产党的诞生奠定了基础；1921年，中国共产党成立，中国革命出现了新局面。

1949年，在中国共产党的领导下，中国人民赶走了帝国主义侵略势力，推翻了国民党蒋介石为代表的帝国主义、封建主义、官僚资本主义的反动统治，结束了中国半殖民地半封建社会的历史，取得了民主革命的胜利。

In the late 1830s, being the first country in the world to accomplish the Industrial Revolution, Britain became the most powerful capitalist country of the time. In order to expand the markets for its industrial products and secure more resources of industrial raw materials, Britain launched a war against China — the Opium War, in which China was defeated and was forced to sign unequal treaties, including the *Treaty of Nanking*. From then on, China began to lose her sovereignty and territorial integrity and to decline to a semi-colonial, semi-feudal state. Therefore, historians regard 1840 as the beginning of the modern history of China, a history of 110 years. Ever since the Opium War, time and time again the imperialist powers waged aggressive wars against China, further violating her sovereignty and territorial integrity, and reduce China to a semi-colonial, semi-feudal country. At the same time, the Chinese people launched resistance movements one after another, such as the Taiping Heavenly Kingdom Movement, the Reform Movement of 1898, and the Yihetuan Movement, all intending to save the country. The greatest of all these was the Revolution of 1911 led by Dr. Sun Yat-sen, which brought to an end the 2 000-year-old autocratic, feudalist monarchy and established the Republic of China(1912—1949). The May 4th Movement of 1919 laid the groundwork for the establishment of the Communist Party of China (CPC), which was founded in 1921, thus epitomizing a new phase of revolutionary development in China.

In 1949, led by the Communist Party, the Chinese people managed to drive away the imperial powers and overthrew the government of the Nationalist Party (Kuomintang, KMT) led by Jiang Kai-shek, representative of imperialism, feudalism and bureaucrat capitalism. The history of the semi-colonial and semi-feudal society in China was replaced with the victory of a democratic revolution.

林则徐与虎门销烟

Lin Zexu and the Destruction of Opium at Humen

1839年6月3日，在广东虎门的海边，许多箱子堆得像小山一样高，周围有成千上万的群众，他们都在激动而兴奋地等待着……

原来，箱内装的都是大烟。大烟正式的名字叫鸦片，是一种毒品，人吸了就会上瘾（shàngyǐn）。常吸大烟的人身体虚弱，精神萎靡（wěimǐ）。从19世纪初开始，英国等西方国家大量向中国走私鸦片，在不到40年的时间里，就使中国吸鸦片

的人数达到200多万。鸦片给英国商人带来巨额的利润，却给中国社会带来了巨大的危害：它不但损害人民的健康，而且使中国的白银大量外流，社会经济受到很大影响。另外，由于军队中吸食鸦片的“大烟鬼”增多，军队的士气和战斗力也大大下降。

面对这种严重的形势，以湖广总督林则徐为代表的大臣们多次向道光皇帝上书，主张严禁鸦片。1839年，道光皇帝终于下决心派林则徐去广州禁烟。

林则徐（1785—1850年）在1838年任湖广总督时采取有效措施严厉禁止鸦片，成绩显著。林则徐到广州后，与外国烟贩展开了坚决的斗争。他先进行调查，摸清情况，然后命令烟贩们交出全部鸦片，并且保证永远不再走私。外国烟贩们不相信林则徐真能禁绝鸦片。他们不交鸦片，有的还准备逃跑。林则徐派兵抓回逃犯，包围了英国商馆，撤出了商馆里的中国雇工，断绝了商馆的饮食供应，并且说：“鸦片贸易一天没有断绝，我就一天也不离开这里！我发誓要把禁烟进行到底！”烟贩们这下害怕了，知道没有希望了，只好交出鸦片，一共有2万多箱，110多万公斤！

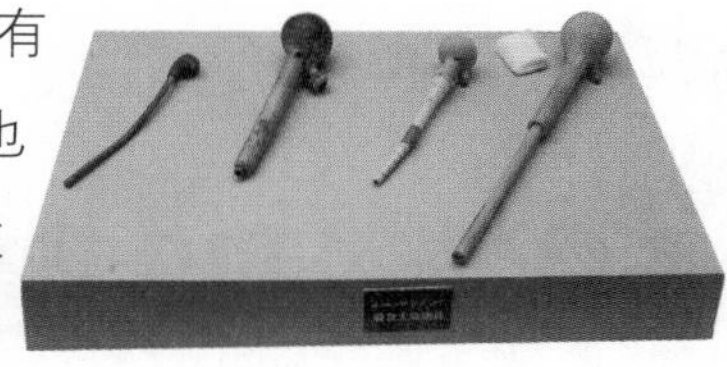

林则徐命令将这2万多箱鸦片全部销毁，于是就发生了开篇的那一幕。由于鸦片数量太多，销烟工作整整进行了23天。

虎门销烟是一件震撼世界的壮举，它向全世界表明了中国人民决心禁烟和反抗外来侵略的坚强意志，林则徐也因此成为中国近代史上的民族英雄。

1. 林则徐画像
A portrait of Lin Zexu
2. 澳门林则徐纪念馆内的虎门销烟塑像
Sculptures of Lin Zexu Destroying the Opium at Humen in Lin Zexu's Memorial Hall, Macau
3. 吸食鸦片的烟具
Smoking paraphernalia for taking opium
4. 烟膏
Opium paste
5. 罂粟壳和烟膏
Opium shell and opium paste

Lin Zexu and the Destruction of Opium at Humen

On June 3rd 1839, a lot of boxes were piled up high on the beach of Humen, Guangdong Province. Thousands of local people were waiting with great excitement ...

In fact, what was inside the boxes was *dayan*, the local term for opium, which is an addictive drug that causes great damage, physically and mentally. Britain and other Western countries began to smuggle opium into China in the early 19th century. In less than 40 years, the number of opium addicts in China amounted to over two million. Opium brought huge profits for British traders, but posed a great danger to Chinese society. It not only damaged people's health, but also drained off China's financial resources by the denomination of silver, thus undermining the socio-economic stability of the country. In addition, the morale and strength of the army were greatly reduced with the increase of opium addiction among the ranks.

Facing these threats, Emperor Daoguang was repeatedly urged by his ministers to ban the trade of opium. The prominent one among the ministers was Lin Zexu, Viceroy of Hubei and Hunan, who was dispatched by the Emperor in 1839 to Guangzhou to implement the banning of opium.

Lin Zexu (1785—1850) had been successful in banning opium in 1838 when he was Viceroy of Hubei and Hunan. After arriving in Guangzhou, he fought against the foreign opium traders by investigating and forcing them to turn in their stocks of opium together with a pledge of never smuggling again. At first,

the opium traders did not take Lin seriously by refusing to take his command. Some of them even tried to escape, but were caught by Lin's army. The army later besieged the British Chamber of Commerce and cut the food supply there after evacuating the Chinese employees inside. Lin made his voice clear, "I will stay so long as the opium trade is carried on! I swear to ban the opium thoroughly!" The opium traders felt scared and hopeless. They had no choice but to turn in the opium, which amounted to more than 1 100 000 kg in over 20 000 boxes.

Lin Zexu ordered to destruct the 20 000 boxes of confiscated opium, hence the scene on the beach of Humen. Starting from June 3rd, 1839, it took 23 days to complete the destruction of the drugs.

The destruction of opium at Humen stunned the world and highlighted the will of the Chinese people in banning the drug and in battling against foreign aggression. For his bold action, Lin Zexu became a national hero in modern Chinese history.

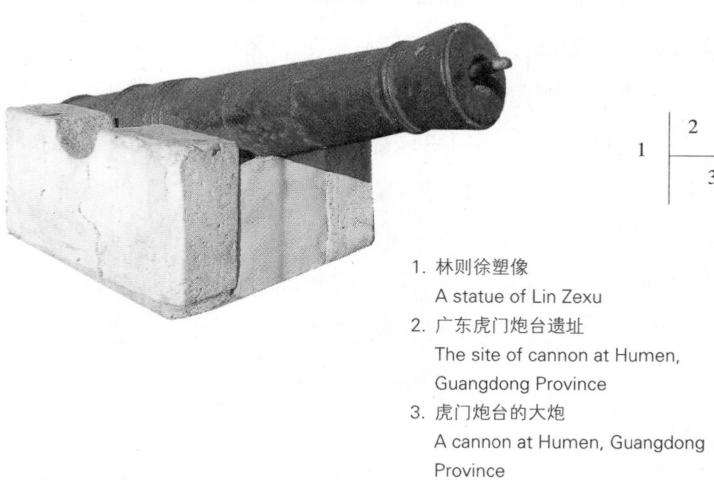

1 | 2 / 3

1. 林则徐塑像
   A statue of Lin Zexu
2. 广东虎门炮台遗址
   The site of cannon at Humen, Guangdong Province
3. 虎门炮台的大炮
   A cannon at Humen, Guangdong Province

第一次鸦片战争

The First Opium War

鸦片走私利润很高，不但英国商人能从中赚很多钱，而且英国政府也能从中得到很大好处。因此，林则徐在广州的禁烟措施，使他们遭受了巨大的损失。1840年6月，英国派出48艘共装备有540门大炮的舰队开到广东海面，发动了侵略中国的第一次鸦片战争。

由于林则徐率广州军民早已严加防备，英军只好沿海岸线北上，攻陷浙江的定海，8月到达天津。道光皇帝非常害怕，派主张

求和的大臣琦善前去谈判，保证只要英军退回广东，清政府就一定惩治林则徐。英军撤退后，朝廷就把林则徐撤职查办。

1841年1月，英军强行占领香港岛。清政府被迫宣战，并派大臣奕山到广州指挥。2月，英军猛攻虎门炮台，守将关天培在没有援军的情况下英勇奋战。炮台失守后，关天培和将士们用大刀和敌人拼杀，最后全部壮烈牺牲。5月，英军进攻广州城，胆小如鼠的奕山举白旗投降。攻下广州的英军作恶多端，激起了人民的反抗。广州郊区三元里人民自发地组织起来，与侵略者展开斗争，保卫家乡，给侵略者以沉重打击。

英军继续扩大侵华战争，进攻浙江的定海、镇海、宁波等地。以葛云飞为代表的沿海爱国军民拼死抵抗，但终因武器落后，加上朝廷腐败、指挥不利而连连失败。1842年6月，英军进攻上海吴淞口，年近70的老将陈化成率军迎战，虽身受重伤，血染战袍，仍紧握令旗指挥战斗，直到牺牲。吴淞失守后，英军沿长江入侵，8月打到南京。清政府慌忙投降，与英方签订了出卖中华民族权益的《南京条约》，内容有：清政府赔款2 100万银元；割让香港岛，开放广州、厦门、福州、宁波、上海5个城市为通商口岸等等。这是外国侵略者强迫清政府签订的第一个不平等条约。中国从此开始沦为半殖民地半封建国家。

The First Opium War

Not only did British traders profit greatly from the opium trade, the British government benefited from it as well. Therefore, the destruction of opium stocks in Guangzhou by Lin Zexu also meant huge losses to the British government. They dispatched 48 warships equipped with 540 cannons to the coast of Guangdong, launching the First Opium War against China in June 1840.

Under the command of Lin Zexu, the army and the people of Guangzhou were well prepared for the war. The British fleet then turned up north along the coast and captured Dinghai in Zhejiang Province. They reached Tianjin in August, when the panic-stricken Emperor Daoguang sent Minister Qi Shan to negotiate with the British. The emperor promised to dismiss Lin Zexu as long as the British troops went back to Guangdong. When they did so, Li Zexu was removed from his office.

In January 1841, the British occupied the Hong Kong Island. The Chinese government of the Qing Dynasty had to declare war against Britain and send Minister Yi Shan to Guangzhou to direct the battle. In February, the British troops bombarded the fort in Humen, where the Chinese defenders under General Guan Tianpei fought against the enemy without reinforcements. When the fort was lost, General Guan and his brave men continued to fight, using swords, but were overwhelmed and slaughtered. In May, the chicken-hearted Yi Shan surrendered Guangzhou to the British, who met the local people's strong resistance, notably from Sanyuanli in the suburb of Guangzhou, and incurred serious losses.

The war escalated with the British attack of several places in Zhejiang Province, including Dinghai, Zhenhai and Ningbo. Chinese forces, some led by the heroic General Ge Yunfei, could not stop the British troops because of outdated weapons, inexperienced army officers, and corrupted government officials. In June 1842, the British troops captured the Fort Wusong in Shanghai, where they met General Chen Huacheng, who was in his 70s, deeply wounded and bleeding all over, fighting to his last breath with the commanding flag still in his hand. From Fort Wusong the British went upstream along the Yangtze River and advanced on Nanjing (Nanking) in August. The Chinese government of the Qing Dynasty was forced to surrender by signing the *Treaty of Nanking*. Under the terms of the treaty, China was to pay 21 million silver dollars, to cede Hong Kong Island to Britain, and to open the cities of Guangzhou, Shanghai, Xiamen, Fuzhou and Ningbo as trading ports. The *Treaty of Nanking* was the first unequal treaty signed by the Qing Dynasty. It marked the start of China's decline into a semi-colonial and semi-feudal state.

1. 广东虎门鸦片战争博物馆，纪念作战牺牲的军民的雕像
Museum of Opium War, Humen, Guangdong Province, exhibits statues of soldiers killed in wars.
2. 在英国军舰上签订《南京条约》的场景
Signing the *Treaty of Nanking* on a British warship

太平天国农民运动

The Taiping Heavenly Kingdom Movement

鸦片战争以后，清政府的统治更加腐败，社会黑暗，广大劳动人民生活非常贫苦。1843年，一个名叫洪秀全的广东青年受基督（Jīdū）教思想的启发，创立了一个宗教组织——拜上帝会，宣传人人平等的思想，号召人民推翻清朝的统治。拜上帝会得到很快的发展，到1849年，会众已达到1万多人。1851年1月11日，这天正好是洪秀全38岁生日，他领导农民在广西桂平县金田村起义，建号“太平天国”。

太平军作战勇猛，连连打败清军，队伍也从2万人很快扩大到几十万人。1853年3月，太平军攻占南京。洪秀全把南京改名为天京，定为首都。太平天国颁布了《天朝田亩制度》，试图建立一个“有田同耕、有饭同食、有衣同穿、有钱同使，无处不均匀，无人不饱暖”的理想社会。

定都天京后，为了巩固和发展胜利成果，太平军又分别进行了北伐和西征，取得了累累战果。

1856年9月，就在各方面事业都轰轰烈烈地展开的时候，太平天国领导集团内部却为了争夺权力而爆发了自相残杀的“天京事变”。这场历时两个月的变乱大大削弱了

太平天国自身的力量，清军则趁机全面反攻，特别是曾国藩率领的湘军成为太平天国最强大的敌人。外国侵略分子也组成“洋枪队”等，帮助清政府镇压太平天国。虽然洪秀全为了扭转不利局面而选拔任用了陈玉成、李秀成等一批年轻的将领，并取得了一些成效，但最终没能挽救太平天国失败的命运。1863年底，湘军开始围困天京。1864年6月，洪秀全病逝。7月，湘军攻破天京。在中外反动势力联合绞杀下，历时近14年的太平天国农民运动失败了。

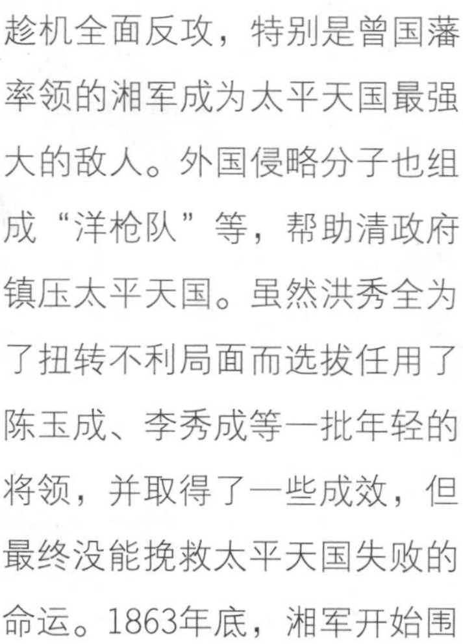

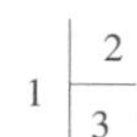

1. 洪秀全塑像
   A sculpture of Hong Xiuquan
2. 南京太平天国天王府石舫
   The stone boat in the royal palace of the Taiping Heavenly Kingdom in Nanjing
3. 太平天国农民运动图
   A paint of the Taiping Heavenly Kingdom Movement

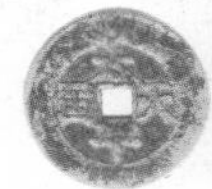

小资料 Data

打败洋枪队

1860年，李秀成率领的太平军占领了上海附近的青浦。美国人华尔组织“洋枪队”，帮助清军攻打太平军。李秀成率领太平军英勇作战，打死洋枪队六七百人，缴获洋枪两千多支，大炮十几门。洋枪队大败，华尔身受重伤逃跑。

Defeating the Foreign Musketeers Squad

In 1860, the Taiping army, led by Li Xiucheng, occupied Qingpu near Shanghai. An American named F. T. Ward organized Foreign Musketeers Squad to help the Qing army to attack the Taiping army. Under Li Xiucheng's leadership, the Taiping army routed the attackers, killed six to seven hundred musketeers while seizing over 2 000 rifles and a dozen cannons. The Foreign Musketeers Squad suffered a total loss while Ward himself, badly wounded, managed to flee for his life.

The Taiping Heavenly Kingdom Movement

太平天国运动形势图

Sketch Map of the Taiping Heavenly Kingdom Movement

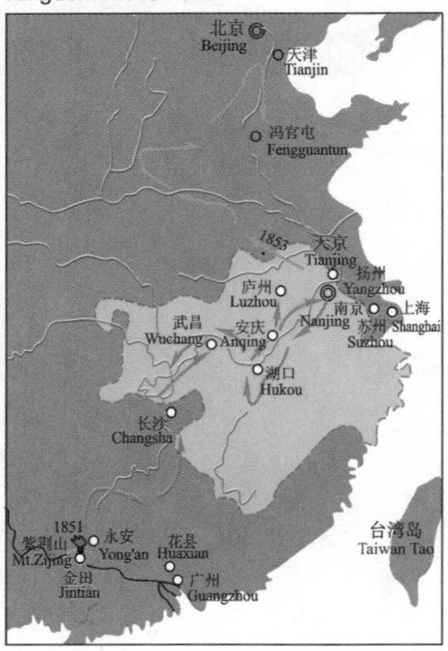

太平天国起义地点
Site of Hong Xiuquan's uprising

太平军从金田到南京进军路线
Taiping army's march on Nanjing from Jintian Village

北伐进军路线
The route of the northern expedition

西征路线
The route of the western expedition

拜上帝宗教活动地区
The areas of God Worship Society activities

太平军主要活动地区
The main areas of the Taiping army's operations

1. 曾国藩像
A statue of Zeng Guofan
2. 太平天国朝政宫殿
Palace of Taiping Heavenly Kingdom

Since China's disastrous defeats in the Opium War, the Qing Dynasty became more corrupt and weaker than ever, and there was widespread misery and poverty among the common people. In 1843, inspired by the ideas of Christianity, a young man named Hong Xiuquan from Guangdong Province set up a religious organization called the God Worship Society, which advocated human equality and called for the overthrow of the rulers of the Qing Dynasty. This organization quickly attracted many adherents, the number of which amounted to over 10 000 in 1849. On January 11th, 1851, Hong Xiuquan's 38th birthday, he initiated a peasant uprising in Jintian Village, Guiping County, in the present-day Guangxi Zhuang Autonomous Region, and declared the establishment of the Taiping Heavenly Kingdom. The Taiping army fought bravely and won a great number of battles against the army of the Qing Dynasty while growing from an army of 20 000 to that of several hundred thousand. In March 1853, the Taipings occupied Nanjing. Hong Xiuquan made the city their capital and changed its name to Tianjing (meaning "heavenly capital"). The Taiping Heavenly Kingdom promulgated the *System of Land Ownership of the Heavenly Kingdom*, aiming to achieve an ideal society here on earth, where all the people would share land, food, clothing and money, and where there would be no trace of iniquity, hunger and shabbiness.

The Taiping army, winning victories everywhere, marched northward and westward to secure and expand its domain around the capital of Tianjing.

In September 1856, when the Taiping Movement was developing vigorously, power struggles took place among the leaders. This was marked by the Tianjing Incident, which lasted two months and severely weakened the Taiping leadership. The Qing government took this opportunity to organize a full-fledged counterattack. The Taiping army's most powerful enemy was the Xiang (another name for Hunan Province) army organized and led by Zeng Guofan. Foreign aggressors even organized "Firearms Brigades" to help the Qing government suppress the Taiping Heavenly Kingdom. In order to turn the tide, Hong Xiuquan nominated a group of young generals, i.e. Chen Yucheng and Li Xiucheng, who did achieve something, but not enough to change the destiny of the Heavenly Kingdom. In late 1863, the Xiang army besieged Tianjing. On June 3rd, 1864, Hong Xiuquan died of illness, and in July Tianjing was captured by the Xiang army. Under the strangling of the united reactionary forces at home and abroad, after 14 years, the peasant uprising of the Taiping Heavenly Kingdom was finally quashed.

小资料 Data

曾国藩（1811—1872年）

中国近代史上最有影响的人物之一。湖南湘乡人，37岁时就担任礼部侍郎。太平天国运动爆发后，曾国藩在家乡训练乡兵，组建了一支规模庞大的湘军，成为镇压太平天国最主要的力量，他本人也成为清朝末年最重要的大臣之一。19世纪60年代，与李鸿章等人共同发起“洋务运动”。

Zeng Guofan (1811－1872)

Zeng Guofan was one of the most influential figures in modern Chinese history. He was born in Xiangxiang, Hunan Province and appointed chamberlain of the Board of Rites when he was only 37. When the Taiping Heavenly Kingdom Movement took place, Zeng went to his hometown to train a local militia, which was organized into the powerful Xiang army, the major force used to help crush the Taipings. He was also one of the important officials of the late Qing Dynasty. During 1860s, Zeng Guofan initiated the Westernization Movement together with Li Hongzhang.

第二次鸦片战争

The Second Opium War

1854年，英国要求全面修改1842年签订的中英《南京条约》，以进一步扩大其在中国已经取得的权益。英国的无理要求得到法国、美国的支持，但遭到清政府的拒绝。

1856年10月，英、法组成联军，发动了侵略中国的第二次鸦片战争。1857年12月，联军攻陷广州。随后北上，1858年5月攻占大沽炮台。咸丰皇帝惊慌失措，立即派大学士桂良等前往天津议和，6月，签订了中英、中法《天津条约》，主要内容包括：允许外国公使进驻北京，增开通商口岸，英法等外国人可以到中国内地通商、传教，向英法赔款等。

1859年，英、法两国又提出拆除白河防御等无理要求，再次遭到拒绝。6月，联军舰队突然袭击大沽炮台，中国守军奋起反击，击沉、击伤英法军舰十多艘，打死打伤侵略军600多人。联军狼狈逃窜。

1860年8月，兵力大增的英法联军卷土重来，相继攻占大沽炮台和天津，并进逼北京。咸丰皇帝仓皇逃往热河（今河北承德市）。10月6日，英法联军火烧圆明园。不久，清政府被迫与英、法、俄三国分别签订了《北京条约》，割让九龙，增开天津为商埠（shāngbù），增加赔款。历时4年的第二次鸦片战争仍以中国的失败、签订丧权辱国的不平等条约而告终。

The Second Opium War

1 | 2

1. 失陷的大沽炮台
A portrait of Dagu Fort affer it was captured
2. 圆明园遗址
Ruins of the Yuanmingyuan Garden

In 1854, Britain requested the ratification of the *Treaty of Nanking* signed in 1842 in order to advance its interests in China. The requests, though supported by France and the United States, were rejected by the government of the Qing Dynasty.

In October 1856, the allied troop of Britain and France waged the Second Opium War. Guangzhou was captured in December 1857, and so was Dagu Fort in May 1858. Emperor Xianfeng of the Qing Dynasty sent chief scholar Gui Liang to negotiate peace in Tianjin. In June, the *Treaty of Tianjin* was signed, granting the establishment of foreign legations in Beijing, the increasing number of trading ports, the rights of foreigners to trade and evangelize freely inside China, and the payment of reparations to Britain and France.

In 1859, Britain and France requested the removing of fortification around the Baihe River. They were rejected again by the Qing government. In June, the allied fleet launched a surprise attack on Dagu Fort, where they met considerable defense from the Chinese army. A dozen warships were lost with a total casualty of over 600. The allied troop retreated.

In August 1860, the British and French allied forces came back and managed to capture Dagu Fort and Tianjin. The capital of Beijing was threatened and Emperor Xianfeng fled to Rehe (today's Chengde, Hebei Province) in panic. On October 6th, the allied troops broke into the world-famous Yuanmingyuan Garden and burned it. Soon after, the Qing government was forced to sign the *Treaty of Peking* with Britain, France and Russia. By this treaty, Kowloon was ceded, Tianjin became a trading port, and reparations were increased. The Second Opium War lasted four years and ended again with China's defeat and the unequal treaties of humiliation and forfeiting sovereignty.

小资料 Data

火烧圆明园

圆明园是清朝皇帝的别宫，位于北京西北郊，是世界著名的皇家园林。第二次鸦片战争期间，1860年10月，英法联军攻陷北京后，闯入圆明园，将园内珍宝抢劫一空，并毁坏了无法运走的珍贵文物。为了掩盖罪行，他们最后放火烧毁了这座举世闻名的“万园之园”。大火延烧三天，烟云笼罩了整个北京城。

The Burning of the Yuanmingyuan Garden

Situated in the northwestern suburb of Beijing, the Yuanmingyuan Garden (the Old Summer Palace) was a resort for the Qing emperors during the height of summer. It was a world renowned imperial garden. In October 1860, during the Second Opium War, British and French allied forces captured Beijing. They plundered the Yuanmingyuan Garden and destroyed the treasures they could not take away. In order to cover their deeds, they burned the garden to the ground. Three days and nights, fire and smoke could be seen in northwest of Beijing.

洋务运动

The Westernization Movement

经过两次鸦片战争和太平天国运动的打击，清朝统治者感到了统治危机在一天天加深。19世纪60年代到90年代，以曾国藩、李鸿章、左宗棠、张之洞等为代表的清政府内掌握实权的官僚主张学习、采用一些西方先进的科学技术，发展生产，“求强”、“求富”，以图挽救清朝的封建统治，历史上称为“洋务运动”。

洋务运动大体分为三个阶段：

第一阶段是兴起阶段，从60年代初到70年代初，约10年时间，清政府以创办军事工业的“求强”活动为中心，安庆军械所、江南制造总局、金陵机器局、福州船政局、天津机器局、西安机器局等相继建立。

第二阶段是发展阶段，从70年代初到80年代中期，约15年时间，在继续创办军事工业的同时，大力兴办民用企业，如轮船招商局、机器织布局等，重心转为“求富”。

第三阶段是衰败阶段，从80年代中期到90年代中期，约10年时间，以“海防”为重点，建立北洋水师等。1895年中日甲午战争北洋水师全军覆没，宣告了历时30多年的洋务运动破产。

洋务运动涉及经济、军事、文化教育、政治、外交等许多领域，虽然没能使中国走上富强的道路，但它引进西方一些近代科学技术，在客观上刺激了中国资本主义的发展，加速了封建生产关系的瓦解，对外国经济势力的扩张也起到了一定的抵制作用。

1 | 2

1. 李鸿章像
   A portrait of Li Hongzhang
2. 江南制造总局大门
   Gate of the Jiangnan Machinery Factory

The Westernization Movement

Hit by two Opium Wars and the Taiping Heavenly Kingdom Movement, the rulers of the Qing Dynasty felt the deepening crisis. From the 1860s to the 1890s, high officials of the Qing government, represented by Zeng Guofan, Li Hongzhang, Zuo Zongtang and Zhang Zhidong, advocated learning and adopting advanced technology from the West in order to save the dynasty by promoting industrial production with "the pursuit of mightiness and prosperity". This is called the "Westernization Movement" by historians.

The Westernization Movement went through three stages:

The first stage was the formative stage, dating from early 1860s to early 1870s and marked by "the pursuit of mightiness", hence the setup of modern military industries, including the Anqing Weapon Factory, the Jiangnan Machinery Factory, the Jinling Machinery Factory, the Fuzhou Shipyard, the Tianjin Machinery Factory and the Xi'an Machinery Factory.

The second stage was the booming stage, dating from early 1870s to mid-1880s and marked by the shift of focus from military to civilian industries for "the pursuit of prosperity", hence the setup of the Shipping Merchandise Office and the Machinery Textile Office.

The third stage was the declining stage, dating from mid-1880s to mid-1890s and marked by the focus on coastal defense, hence the founding of the Northern Fleet. The overwhelming defeat of China's Northern Fleet in the Sino-Japanese War of 1894 sounded the death knell of the Westernization Movement, which lasted over 30 years.

The Westernization Movement took place in the fields of economy, military, culture, education, politics and foreign affairs. It did not bring China into prosperity. Yet, it did introduce modern science and technology from the West and contribute in a small way to the development of capitalism in China. It became the enzyme for the collapse of feudalism and also helped to contain the expansion of foreign economic power in China.

小资料 Data

李鸿章（1823—1901年）

中国近代史上最有影响的人物之一。他是曾国藩的得意门生和重要助手，淮军创始人和统帅，洋务运动的主要倡导者。多次领兵与太平军作战，和湘军一起镇压了太平天国。从19世纪60年代起，积极筹建新式军事工业，分别在上海、南京创立江南机器制造总局和金陵机器制造局等。1888年，建成北洋海军。在对外交涉中表现出严重的“惧外”倾向，始终坚持“委曲求全”的方针，曾多次代表清政府与外国列强签订不平等条约。

Li Hongzhang (1823—1901)

He was one of the most influential figures in modern Chinese history. Being the favorite disciple of and aide to Zeng Guofan, he was the founder and commander of the Huai army and the major advocate of the Westernization Movement. Together with the Xiang army, he helped to put down the Taiping Heavenly Kingdom Movement. Since the 1860s, he was in charge of setting up modern military industries, i.e. the Jiangnan Machinery Factory in Shanghai and the Jinling Machinery Factory in Nanjing. In 1888, he established the Northern Fleet. In terms of foreign affairs, he displayed "the fear of foreigners" and followed the policy of "stooping to compromise", representing the Qing government to sign the unequal treaties for several times.

中日甲午战争与《马关条约》

Sino-Japanese War of 1894 and the *Treaty of Shimonoseki*

日本是中国的近邻。明治维新以后，日本的资本主义经济得到迅速发展，国力大大增强，侵略扩张的野心也越来越大。1894年（农历甲午年）7月，日本出兵朝鲜，并袭击中国运兵船，中日甲午战争爆发。

战争初期，清朝军队在朝鲜的平壤（Píngrǎng）与日军展开激战，清军战败，日军占领了平壤，战火烧到了中国境内。

9月17日，中国北洋水师10艘军舰在丁汝昌、刘步蟾（Liú Bùchán）的指挥下，与由12艘日舰组成的日本海军在黄海展开激战。虽然敌舰数量多、航速快、速射炮多，但中国海军大部分将士都英勇奋战。“致远”号弹药用尽、船身中炮后，舰长邓世昌命令开足马力撞击敌舰，结果军舰不幸被鱼雷击中沉没，邓世昌和全舰200多名官兵壮烈牺牲。“经远”舰舰长林永升也率领将士战斗到生命的最后一刻。经过几个小时的激战，北洋水师损失严重，日方军舰也受到重创。

11月，日军攻占了大连、旅顺，并在旅顺进行了疯狂的屠杀。在4天时间里，用各种极为残忍的手段杀害了18 000多名中国同胞。

1895年2月，日军攻占威海卫，北洋海军全军覆没。

1895年4月，李鸿章代表清政府与日本签订了丧权辱国的《马关条约》，中国赔偿日本军费白银2亿两，还把辽东半岛、台湾等地割让给日本（由于沙俄等国出面干涉，日本把辽东半岛归还中国。中国则给日本3 000万两白银，作为“赎辽费”）。

甲午战败后，中国半殖民地化的程度进一步加深了。

Sino-Japanese War of 1894 and the *Treaty of Shimonoseki*

Japan is a close neighbor of China. After the Meiji Restoration, capitalism developed rapidly in Japan, making the country a major power bursting with ambitions to expand its orbit. In July 1894, Japan dispatched an army to the Korean Peninsula, which clashed with Chinese ships carrying troops to defend the Korean king. Thus, the Sino-Japanese War of 1894 broke out.

Defeated in the city of Pyongyang, the Qing army was forced to retreat, and the war was carried into China itself.

On the morning of September 17th, 1894, under the command of Ding Ruchang and Liu Buchan, 10 warships from China's Northern Fleet engaged 12 Japanese warships in the Yellow Sea. Outnumbered by the Japanese, most Chinese sailors fought bravely. When the warship *Zhiyuan* ran out of ammunition, its captain, Deng Shichang, tried to ram a Japanese ship. The *Zhiyuan* was torpedoed and sank, and all its 200 officers and men died heroically, including Deng Shichang himself. Lin Yongsheng, captain of the warship *Jingyuan*, also fought alongside his men to the last moment of his life. After a few hours of fighting, the Northern Fleet inflicted heavy loss while the Japanese side was also hit badly.

In November, the Japanese army occupied Dalian and Lushun. In a period of only four days, the Japanese massacred more than 18 000 inhabitants of Lushun.

In February 1895, the Japanese army took the port of Weihaiwei, hence the total destruction of the Northern Fleet.

In April 1895, Li Hongzhang represented China in signing the *Treaty of Shimonoseki*, a treaty of betrayal and humiliation, with Japan, according to which China had to pay Japan 200 million taels (unit of weight) of silver as war reparations and to cede the Liaodong Peninsula and Taiwan to Japan. (Due to pressure from Tsarist Russia and other countries, Japan returned the Liaodong Peninsula to China in return for 30 million taels of silver.)

This war accelerated the semi-colonization of China.

1. 甲午抗日名将丁汝昌塑像
   A statue of Ding Ruchang, the famous general of the Sino-Japanese War
2. 《马关条约》谈判现场
   The site of the negotiation of the *Treaty of Shimonoseki*
3. 山东威海甲午战争纪念馆甲午海战雕塑
   Sculptures of naval battle in the Sino-Japanese War of 1894 in the Sino-Japanese War of 1894 Museum
4. 日军在旅顺残杀中国平民
   Massacre of civilians by the Japanese army in Lushun

戊戌变法

The Reform Movement of 1898

公元1895年，《马关条约》签订的消息传到北京。当时正在北京参加科举考试的康有为，联合1 300多名考生一起给光绪皇帝上书，反对向日本求和，要求变法。上书虽然没有到达皇帝手中，但维新变法思想的影响迅速扩大。历史上称这一事件为“公车上书”。

康有为认为中国的危亡局势都是腐败的制度、落后的思想造成的。“公车上书”后，他和他的学生梁启超一起办报纸、组织强学会，宣传改革旧制、变法维新的新思想，在全国掀起了救亡图存运动。

1898年，中国农历叫戊戌（wùxū）年，光绪皇帝终于下决心重用维新派，在全国实

行变法。变法的主要内容有：政治上改革旧机构；经济上保护、奖励工商业；教育上创办新学校，改革科举考试，学习西方的文化和科学技术等等。

以慈禧（Cíxǐ）太后为代表的守旧派不能容忍维新运动的发展，他们要捕杀维新派，并准备废掉光绪皇帝。维新派向手握重兵的袁世凯求救，但是却被袁世凯出卖了。1898年9月21日，慈禧太后发动政变，派人把光绪皇帝关了起来，同时抓捕维新党人。康有为、梁启超逃到了国外。另一位重要的维新党人谭嗣同（Tán Sìtóng）本来也有机会逃走，但他说：“各国变法，没有不流血的，而中国还没有为变法而流血的人，所以国家不强盛，今天就从我开头吧。”不久，谭嗣同、康广仁等六人被杀害，历史上称他们为“戊戌六君子”。

戊戌变法从光绪皇帝颁布诏书宣布实行变法到政变发生、变法失败，一共只有103天，所以又叫“百日维新”。

1 | 2 | 3 / 4

1. 光绪皇帝像
   A portrait of Emperor Guangxu
2. 玉澜堂（慈禧太后软禁光绪的地方）
   Yulan Hall where Emperor Guangxu was put under house arrest by Empress Dowager Cixi
3. 梁启超像
   A portrait of Liang Qichao
4. 谭嗣同像
   A portrait of Tan Sitong

The Reform Movement of 1898

In 1895, when the news reached Beijing that the *Treaty of Shimonoseki* had been signed, Kang Youwei, who was then taking the imperial civil examinations in Beijing, rallied over 1 300 examinees to submit a petition to Emperor Guangxu to oppose the treaty to sue for peace with Japan and to demand political reform. Although their petition was not heard by the emperor, the reformist thoughts spread like wild fire. This event is named the "Joint Petition of Imperial Examination Candidates to the Emperor".

Kang Youwei thought that China's perilous situation had resulted from its corrupt bureaucracy and backward ideology. After he submitted the petition to the emperor, he and his student Liang Qichao started running newspapers and organized the Qiangxue (Learn-to-be-Strong) Society to press for political reform, thus initiating the national salvation and striving for survival movement all over the country.

In 1898, the year *wu-xu* by the Chinese lunar calendar, Emperor Guangxu decided to put reformers in important positions in the government, and to carry out reform measures all over the country. The main contents of the reform were: the overhaul of the traditional

government institutions; the protection, encouragement and rewards for industry and commerce; the introduction of modern educational methods; the abolition of the imperial civil examination system; and the study of Western science, technology and culture.

Represented by Empress Dowager Cixi, the conservatives could not tolerate this reform and decided to put the reformers under arrest and dethrone Emperor Guangxu. The reformers hoped to enlist the support of Yuan Shikai, a powerful general and minister, but were betrayed by Yuan. On September 21st, 1898, a palace coup masterminded by Cixi put Emperor Guangxu under house arrest, and most of the reformers were arrested. Kang Youwei and Liang Qichao fled abroad. Tan Sitong, another important reformer, who had the chance to escape, refused to do so. He said, "There can be no reform without blood. In China there is no one who has shed blood for the reform, and that is why our country is still poor and weak. Now I am willing to be the first to give my life for the reform." Before long, Tan Sitong, Kang Guangren and four other leading reformers were executed by the conservatives. They are known to history as the "Six Gentlemen of Wu-xu".

The Reform Movement lasted only 103 days from the promulgation of reform by Emperor Guangxu to the coup, the end of the Movement. Therefore, it is also called the "Hundred Days Reform".

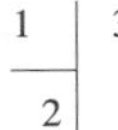

1. 山东青岛康有为故居
   Kang Youwei's residence in Qingdao, Shandong Province
2. 康有为像
   A portrait of Kang Youwei
3. 慈禧太后像
   A portrait of Empress Dowager Cixi

小资料 Data

慈禧太后（1835—1908年）
又称西太后。原为咸丰皇帝的妃子。1861年，咸丰去世，6岁的同治皇帝即位。慈禧作为同治皇帝的母亲垂帘听政，掌握了国家大权。1875年同治病死，5岁的光绪皇帝即位，仍由慈禧太后听政。慈禧太后是同治、光绪两朝实际的统治者。

Empress Dowager Cixi (1835—1908)
Empress Dowager Cixi, the West Queen Mother, was a concubine of Emperor Xianfeng. In 1861, Emperor Xianfeng died, and six-year-old Emperor Tongzhi succeeded to the throne. As the emperor's mother, shading with a screen, Empress Dowager Cixi sat behind the throne during the young emperor's office hour, thus wielding the actual power of the throne. In 1875, Tongzhi died of illness, and was succeeded by the five-year-old Emperor Guangxu. Cixi remained in her seat behind the screen. She managed to control the country for the period of the two emperors — Tongzhi and Guangxu.

义和团运动

The Yihetuan Movement

鸦片战争以后，外国传教士凭借不平等条约给他们的特权，强占中国的大量田地、房屋、庙宇，极力扩大教会势力。每当教民与平民发生矛盾时，教会总是无视中国法律，无条件地庇护教民。外国教会与中国平民之间的矛盾越来越尖锐。

1898年，在民间习武组织义和拳的基础上，山东兴起了反教会、反侵略的义和团运动。义和团遭到清军的严厉镇压。1900年，山东、河北两省义和团联合起来向北京进军。由于这场爱国运动得到了人民群众的广泛支持，义和团队伍迅速壮大。慈禧太后害怕继续镇压会危及自己的统治，于是想利用义和团来对付外国势力，暂时承认了义和团的合法地位。义和团先后进入北京、天津城内。

义和团运动的发展引起了外国势力的极大恐慌。他们先是逼迫清政府镇压，后来看到

清政府无法控制局面，就决定出兵。1900年6月，英、美、德、法、俄、日、意、奥八国组成联军向北京进犯。清政府向列强宣战。义和团与八国联军展开了激烈的战斗。但由于清政府缺乏坚定的抗敌决心，而义和团又组织松散，且作战的方式和武器都十分落后，最后只能归于失败。8月，北京陷落。慈禧太后带光绪皇帝逃到西安。八国联军在北京烧杀抢掠，犯下了滔天罪行。

为了向列强求和，清政府出卖了义和团，宣布义和团是“拳匪”，并与外国军队勾结一起绞杀义和团运动。1901年9月，列强强迫清政府签订了卖国的《辛丑条约》。从此以后，清政府完全成为帝国主义列强控制中国的工具。

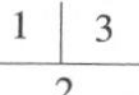

1. 武装起来的义和团员
   Yihetuan members
2. 八国联军入侵部队在大沽
   Invading troops of Eight Power Allied Forces in Dagu, Tianjin
3. 被捕后视死如归的义和团民
   Indomitable death-defying Yihetuan members after being captured

The Yihetuan Movement

Following the Opium Wars and enjoying the privileges given by the unequal treaties, foreign missionaries occupied a great deal of land, houses and temples all over China. Often in defiance of Chinese laws, they used their considerable influence to protect their converts. There were increasing conflicts between foreign missionaries and Chinese civilians.

In 1898, led by a martial arts group known as the Yihe Boxers, the Yihetuan (Society of Righteousness and Harmony) Movement took place in Shandong Province, which soon developed its anti-Christian and anti-aggression themes. The Qing government tried to suppress the Yihetuan at first. In 1900, the Yihetuan organizations in Shandong and Hebei joined forces to march to Beijing. Supported by the common people, their numbers grew rapidly all the time. Empress Dowager Cixi worried that the crackdown of the Yihetuan could be disadvantageous to her rule. Meanwhile, she wished to use them as a weapon against the foreign forces which may intend to disintegrate China. Hence, she gave her recognition to the Yihetuan as a patriotic movement, which spread to Beijing and Tianjin accordingly.

The Yihetuan brought about great anxiety to the foreign powers in China. When they realized that the Qing government neither could nor would contain the Yihetuan, they decided to dispatch troops to quash the movement on their own. In June 1900, eight countries, i.e. Britain, the United States, Germany, France, Tsarist Russia, Japan, Italy and Austria formed an allied army, which occupied the foreign legation quarters in Beijing. The Qing government declared war on these powers. With a half-hearted Qing army at its back, equipped with minimal leadership and primitive weapons, the inexperienced Yihetuan warriors fought hard against the allied forces, simply having no chance to win. In August, the whole of Beijing fell into the hands of the foreign allies. Empress Dowager Cixi and Emperor Guangxu fled to Xi'an.

The foreign troops committed burnings, killings, looting and other heinous crimes in Beijing.

The Qing government then betrayed the Yihetuan, calling them bandits and joined the foreign forces to suppress them. In September 1901, the foreign powers forced the Qing government to sign the *Protocol of 1901*. From then on, the Qing government was no more than an instrument with which the imperialists enforced their will on the Chinese people.

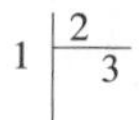

1. 签订《辛丑条约》的场景
   A picture of signing the *Protocol of 1901*
2. 八国联军在大沽口登陆
   Eight Power Allied Forces landed in Dagukou
3. 战斗中被击毁的清军炮阵地
   Destroyed artillery position of the Qing Government Army in a battle

小资料 Data

庚子赔款

根据《辛丑条约》的规定，清政府要向侵略者支付战争赔款4.5亿两白银，分39年还清，本息合计9.8亿两。由于八国联军入侵北京发生在1900年，农历为庚子（gēngzǐ）年，所以这笔巨额赔款又称“庚子赔款”。

The Geng-zi Reparations

According to the Protocol of 1901, the Qing government had to pay 450 million taels of silver to the invaders as war reparations over a 39-year period. The principal and interest amounted to 980 million taels altogether. The year when the eight imperial powers invaded Beijing was the year of *geng-zi* in Chinese lunar calendar, hence the huge amount of war reparations is called the Geng-zi Reparations.

孙中山与辛亥革命

Dr. Sun Yat-sen and the Revolution of 1911

1 | 2/3

1. 孙中山像
A portrait of Dr. Sun Yat-sen
2. 广州黄花岗七十二烈士陵园
The tomb of the 72 martyrs in Huanghuagang, Guangzhou, Guangdong Province
3. 江苏南京临时大总统孙中山办公室
The office of the interim President Sun Yat-sen, Nanjing, Jiangsu Province

孙中山，1866年出生，广东省香山县（今中山市）人。小时候喜欢听洪秀全的故事，非常崇拜这位敢于反抗清政府、创立新秩序的英雄。12岁时，孙中山到夏威夷，接触和学习到了西方的科学文化知识。通过读华盛顿（George Washington）和林肯（Abraham Lincoln）的传记，他进一步坚定了为国家和民族的大业而奋斗的志向。

1894年，孙中山在檀（tán）香山的爱国华侨中组织了一个反清革命团体——兴中会。1905年，孙中山又在日本联合一些革命团体的成员成立了全国规模的统一革命政党——中国同盟会，立志要推翻清政府，振兴中华，建立资产阶级民主共和国。孙中山还将他的革命理想概括为“民族、民权、民生”的“三民主义”。

孙中山和革命党人秘密组织了多次武装起义，但都失败了。大批革命党人献出了宝贵的生命，但他们的精神激励着国内外的爱国志士继续奋斗。

1911年10月10日，长期在军队中开展革命活动的湖北革命团体文学社和共进会联合发动了武昌起义，取得成功。武昌起义的胜利掀起了革命的高潮，各省纷纷响应。一个多月当中，共有十多个省宣布独立，清王朝的统治迅速崩溃。1911年是中国农历辛亥（xīnhài）年，历史上把这场推翻清朝统治的斗争叫辛亥革命。

1911年12月，孙中山回国。由于他对革命事业作出的巨大贡献和他在革命党人当中的崇高威望，孙中山被推选为临时大总统。1912年1月1日，孙中山在南京宣誓就职，中华民国临时政府成立。

中华民国成立不久，袁世凯在帝国主义的支持下窃取了临时大总统的职位，政权落入腐败的北洋军阀（jūnfá）的手中。为了对抗北洋军阀的统治，1912年8月，以中国同盟会为主的6个政治团体在北京合并，成立了中国国民党，孙中山被选为理事长。

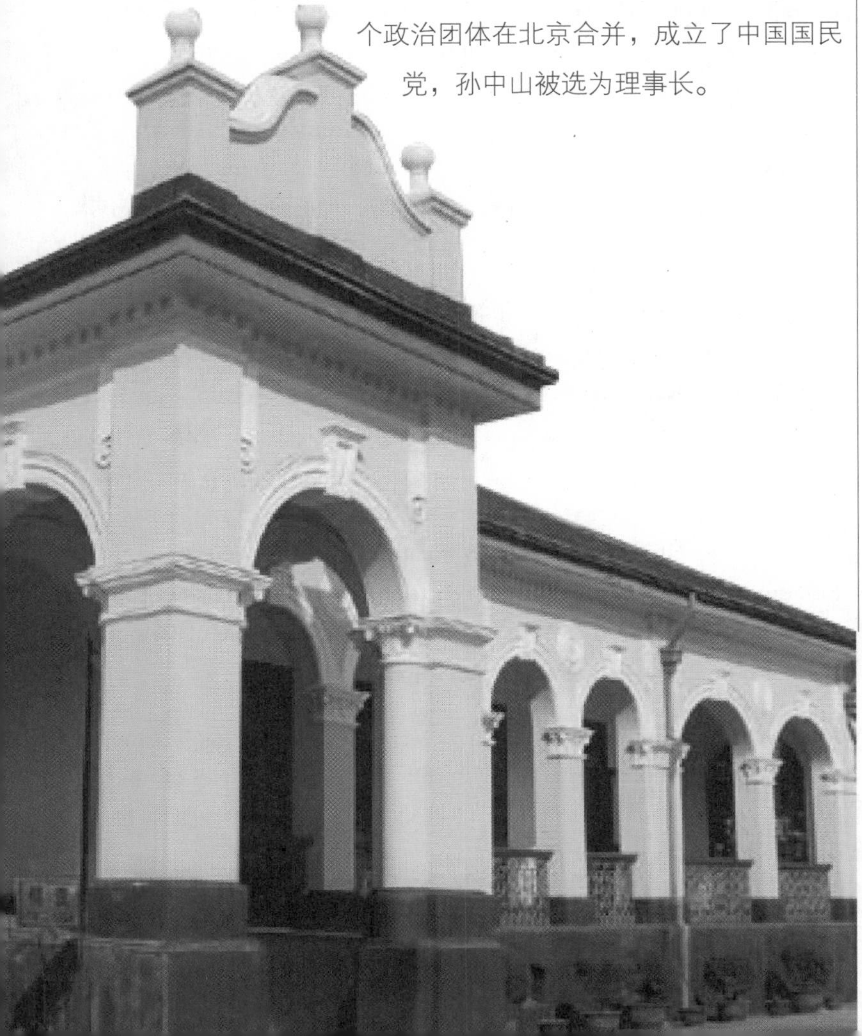

小资料 Data

黄花岗七十二烈士

1911年4月，革命党人在广州组织反对清政府的武装起义。起义之前，爱国华侨捐助了大量钱物，有的爱国华侨还回到广州，与国内的革命党人一起组成“敢死队”。起义遭到惨重失败，72人牺牲。烈士的遗体被合葬在广州黄花岗。这次起义也被称为“黄花岗起义”。七十二烈士的精神激励着爱国志士继续进行反清斗争。

72 Martyrs of Huanghuagang

In April 1911, a revolt against the Qing government broke out in Guangzhou. Patriotic overseas Chinese donated substantially to this event. Some overseas Chinese even went back to Guangzhou to form a suicide squad together with revolutionaries there. The revolt was crushed and 72 sacrificed their lives. The remains of these martyrs were buried together at Huanghuagang in Guangzhou, hence the name Huanghuagang Revolt. The spirit of the 72 martyrs impelled patriots at home and abroad to go on fighting against the Qing government.

Dr. Sun Yat-sen

and the Revolution of 1911

Sun Yat-sen was born in 1866 in Xiangshan County (today's Zhongshan City), Guangdong Province. In his childhood he heard stories about the Taiping Heavenly Kingdom, and developed an admiration for the Taiping leader Hong Xiuquan, who tried to overthrow the Qing government and set up a new system. At the age of 12, Sun went to Hawaii, where he studied Western sciences and culture. Among his favorite readings were biographies of George Washington and Abraham Lincoln, which planted in him a resolve to strive for his country and people.

In 1894, Sun Yat-sen organized an anti-Qing revolutionary organization, the "Society for the Revival of China" (*Xingzhonghui*), among the patriotic Chinese residing in Honolulu. In 1905, he set up a united revolutionary party, the "China Revolutionary League" (*Zhongguo Tongmenghui*) by allying some Chinese revolutionary group members all over Japan. He was determined to put an end to the Qing Dynasty, to rejuvenate China and establish a capitalist democratic republic. Sun summarized his revolutionary ideas into the "Three People's Principles" viz, the Principle of Nationalism, the Principle of Democracy and the Principle of the People's Livelihood.

Sun Yat-sen and other revolutionaries secretly organized many armed uprisings, but all of them failed with the sacrifice of the lives of many revolutionaries.

On October 10th, 1911, the revolutionary organizations in Hubei Province, known as the "Literary Association" (*Wenxueshe*) and the "Society for Mu-

tual Progress" (*Gongjinhui*), which had been developing revolutionary activities in the army, started the Wuchang Uprising. This triggered nationwide revolts against the Qing dynasty. Within one month, a dozen provinces had declared their independence from the Qing government, which resulted in the sudden collapse of the Qing Dynasty. The year 1911 was the year *xin-hai* by the Chinese lunar calendar, so this revolution which overthrew the Qing Dynasty is also called the Xin-hai Revolution.

In December 1911, Sun Yat-sen returned to China. Because of the enormous contributions he had made to the revolution and his prestige among the revolutionaries, he was elected Interim President of the Republic of China. His inauguration on January lst, 1912 in Nanjing marked the installment of the interim government of the Republic of China.

Not long after the founding of the Republic of China, with the support of the imperialist powers, Yuan Shikai managed to get himself elected President. Political power then fell into the hands of the Northern Warlords. As a counter to warlord rule, the Nationalist Party (Kuomintang, KMT) was founded in Beijing in August 1912 by the China Revolutionary League together with five other political parties. Sun Yat-sen was elected Chief Councilor of the new party.

1. 武昌起义军政府旧址
   The site of the Wuchang Uprising government
2. 秋瑾塑像
   A statue of Qiu Jin
3. 1912年1月1日，孙中山在南京宣誓就职时的誓词
   The oath Sun Yat-sen took when establishing the interim government of the Republic of China in Nanjing, Jan 1, 1912

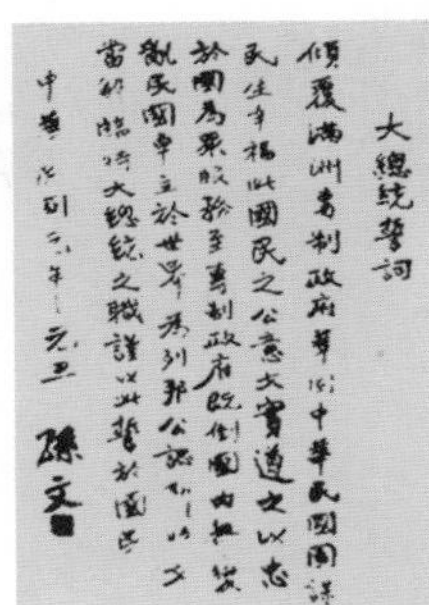

大總統誓詞

傾覆滿洲專制政府鞏固中華民國圖謀民生幸福此國民之公意文實遵之以忠於國為衆服務至專制政府既倒國內無變亂民國卓立於世界為列邦公認斯時文當解臨時大總統之職謹以此誓於國民

中華民國元年元旦 孫文

小资料 Data

秋瑾

浙江省绍兴人，是中国近代史上最著名的女英雄。她在日本留学时参加了革命党。秋瑾喜欢身着男装，骑马练剑，被人称为"鉴湖女侠"。1907年，秋瑾在浙江准备发动起义，不幸被捕，英勇牺牲。

Qiu Jin

Born in Shaoxing, Zhejiang Province, she is the most famous heroine in modern Chinese history. She joined the China Revolutionary League when she was studying in Japan. Qiu Jin liked to wear men's clothes and practiced horsemanship and fencing. People call her Jianhu Knight. In 1907, she was arrested and executed for preparing an uprising in Zhejiang.

"五四"运动

The May 4th Movement

1918年，德国战败，第一次世界大战结束。1919年，英、法、美等国在巴黎召开"巴黎和会"，中国作为战胜国之一也参加了。会上，中国代表团提出从德国手中收回山东的主权，但是这个合理的要求被拒绝了，列强决定把德国在山东的特权转交给日本，强迫中国代表签字。

消息传来，全国人民万分悲愤。1919年5月4日，北京大学等十几所北京的大专院校的学生在天安门集会，呼喊"还我青岛"、"打倒卖国贼"等口号抗议示威。愤怒的学生还冲进卖国贼曹汝霖（Cáo Rǔlín）的家，痛打了正在曹家的驻日公使章宗祥，并放火烧了曹宅。北洋政府派军警镇压，抓走了30多名学生。

第二天，北京大学生开始罢课，他们走上街头进行爱国讲演和宣传。山东、天津、上海等地的学生也纷纷起来声援。反动的北洋政府逮捕了近千名学生，激起了全国人民更大的愤怒。6月，上海工人首先罢工，支持学生的爱国行为。接着，学

1 | 2

1. 北大红楼（北京大学旧址，现为新文化运动纪念馆）
Honglou, the historical site of Beijing University, today's New Culture Movement Museum
2. 今北京大学校门
Western gate of Peking University

生罢课、工人罢工、商人罢市的运动在全国展开。同时，在巴黎参加和会的中国代表团收到几千份全国各界群众要求他们拒签和约的通电。6月28日，旅居法国的华侨和留学生还包围了中国代表团的住所，不让他们在卖国条约上签字。在巨大的压力面前，北洋政府只好释放了爱国学生，撤了卖国贼曹汝霖、章宗祥、陆宗舆（Lù Zōngyú）的官职，中国代表团也拒绝在条约上签字，“五四”运动取得了胜利。

“五四”运动的意义不仅仅在外交方面。在运动发生前的几年中，具有民主与科学精神的新思想、新文化在以北京大学为中心的知识界迅速传播。“五四”运动促进了马克思主义与中国工人运动的结合，加速了中国共产党建立的进程。

小资料 Data

北京大学

北京大学的前身是京师大学堂，1898年作为戊戌变法的“新政”措施之一正式建立，是中国近代最早由国家创办的大学。20世纪初年，北京大学是新文化运动的中心和“五四”运动的策源地，具有爱国、进步、民主、科学的传统精神和勤奋、严谨、求实、创新的学风。中华人民共和国成立后，北京大学成为一所以文理基础教学和研究为主的、著名的综合性大学，为国家培养了大批人才。

Peking University

Peking University, formerly the Metropolitan University, was founded in 1898 as an outcome of the Reform Movement of 1898 and the first national university in modern China. In the early 20th century, it became the cradle of the New Culture Movement and the May 4th Movement. With tradition of patriotism, progress, democracy and science, it has a style of study marked by diligence, preciseness, practicality and innovation. After the founding of the People's Republic of China, Peking University began to enjoy its fame as a comprehensive school based on the teaching and research of the natural and social sciences. It has trained many talents for the country.

The May 4th Movement

In 1918, the First World War ended with the defeat of Germany. In 1919, Britain, France, the United States and other victor countries held the Paris Peace Conference. As one of the victor countries, China also attended the conference. At the conference, China requested that she should take back Shandong Province, whose sovereignty was relinquished to Germany before the War. The imperialist powers turned down this request and handed over all claims of Shandong from Germany to Japan and compelled the Chinese representatives to sign.

This news caused explosions of outrage in China, and on May 4th, 1919, students of Peking University and other higher institutions gathered in Tiananmen Square to protest, shouting the slogans of "Restore our lost Qingdao Island" and "Down with the traitors". They stormed the house of Cao Rulin and beat someone they met there — the Chinese High Commissioner to Japan, Zhang Zongxiang — and then set fire to the house. The Northern government sent troops to suppress the students and put over thirty of them under arrest.

On the second day, students in Peking University went on strike by going into the streets to disseminate patriotic ideas. Students from Shandong, Tianjin and Shanghai came to Beijing to support them. The reactionary Northern Warlord government arrested nearly 1 000 students, which caused even greater turbulence all over the country. In June, workers in Shanghai went on strike to support the students' patriotic requests, to be followed in other cities by students suspending classes, workers downing tools and merchants closing shops. Meanwhile, the Chinese delegation to the Paris Peace Conference received thousands of telegrams sent by people from all walks of life in China asking them not to sign the treaty. On June 28th, overseas Chinese residents and students in France surrounded the residence of the Chinese delegation to urge them not to sign the treaty. Confronted with huge pressure, the Northern Warlord government had to release the arrested students and remove the pro-treaty ministers Cao Rulin, Zhang Zongxiang and Lu Zongyu from office. Finally, the Chinese delegation refused to sign the treaty, which marked the victory of the May 4th Movement.

However, the significance of the May 4th Movement lay not only in this diplomatic victory. Several years before the movement, new ways of thinking and new culture marked by democracy and science had been spreading rapidly among intellectuals, with Peking University notably as the center. The May 4th Movement promoted the combination of Marxism with the Chinese Workers' Movement and quickened the setting up of the Chinese Communist Party.

1 | 2/3

1. “五四”运动时学生使用的纪念章
A Badge bearing slogans worn by students during the May 4th Movement
2. 北京天安门广场人民英雄纪念碑“五四”运动浮雕
A relief sculpture featuring the May 4th movement on the Monument to the People's Heroes in Tiananmen Square, Beijing
3. “五四”运动中示威游行的青年学生
A portrait of students protesting in the May 4th Movement

中国共产党的成立

The Founding of the Communist Party of China

1 | 2 / 3

1. 上海中共“一大”会址
   The site of the First National Congress of the CPC in Shanghai
2. 中国共产党建党初期的毛泽东
   Mao Zedong as he looked when the CPC was founded in its early stage
3. 浙江嘉兴南湖游船内景(中国共产党第一次全国代表大会从上海移到此处举行)
   Inside the pleasure-boat on Nanhu Lake, Jiaxing, Zhejiang Province (the First National Congress of CPC adjourned from Shanghai to here)

1917年，俄国发生了十月革命，建立了世界上第一个社会主义国家。十月革命的胜利和社会主义思想引起了中国先进分子的高度关注。中国人民从十月革命的光辉实践中找到了马克思主义这一锐利的思想武器。

1919年，中国无产阶级积极参加“五四”爱国运动，并对斗争取得最后的胜利起到了重要作用，使全社会看到了无产阶级的力量。“五四”运动后，具有初步共产主义思想的知识分子主张以马克思主义为指导，依靠无产阶级，通过革命的方式来推翻旧制度，建立新社会。

1920年8月，陈独秀、李达、李汉俊等在上海发起成立中国第一个共产党组织。10月，李大钊（Lǐ Dàzhāo）、

张国焘（Zhāng Guótāo）、邓中夏等在北京成立了共产党组织。此后，湖北、山东、广东、湖南等省也相继成立了共产党组织，甚至在法国的中国留学生也成立了共产党组织。各地共产主义小组都积极进行建立统一的全国性共产党组织的准备工作。

1921年7月23日，毛泽东、何叔衡、董必武等来自全国各地的13位代表在上海秘密召开中国共产党的成立大会，也是中国共产党第一次全国代表大会。会议讨论通过了中国共产党的纲领，确定中国共产党的奋斗目标是：以无产阶级的革命军队推翻资产阶级，建立无产阶级专政，废除私有制，最终消灭阶级差别。大会选举陈独秀、张国焘、李达组成中央局，陈独秀为中央局书记。会议进行到7月30日时，会场受到了警察的搜查和密探的注意。为了安全，代表们离开上海，转移到浙江嘉兴南湖的一条游船上继续开会。

这次会议后，在中国的政治舞台上，正式出现了一支崭新的力量——中国共产党，它给灾难深重的中国人民带来了光明和希望。

The Founding of the Communist Party of China

In 1917, the October Revolution took place in Russia, and the first socialist state in the world was established. The victory of the October Revolution and the spread of socialist thought attracted the attention of progressive Chinese intellectuals. They found Marxism as an alternative to save China.

In 1919, the Chinese proletariat actively took part in the patriotic May 4th Movement, showing their decisive power in the final victory of the Movement. Since then, intellectuals with new communist ideas began to advocate breaking away from the old system and building a new society with the support of the proletariat and a revolution under the guidance of Marxism.

In August 1920, the first communist group was established in Shanghai by Chen Duxiu, Li Da and Li Hanjun. In October, another communist group was founded by Li Dazhao, Zhang Guotao and Deng Zhongxia in Beijing. Later on, communist organizations flourished

in the provinces of Hubei, Shandong, Guangdong, Hunan, and even among overseas students in France. All these groups were deliberating on forming a communist party on the national level.

On July 23rd, 1921, thirteen representatives from around the country including Mao Zedong, He Shuheng and Dong Biwu held a secret meeting in Shanghai as the first National Conference of the Communist Party of China (CPC). The first party constitution was reviewed and accepted, stipulating the goals of the party. The goals were to set up a proletariat revolutionary party to overthrow the ruling capitalist government and replace it with the dictatorship of the proletariat, marked by the abolishment of private ownership and social class distinction. Chen Duxiu, Zhang Guotao and Li Da were elected to form the Central Bureau of the party with Chen as the Secretary in Chief. On July 30th, to avoid attention from the secret police, the representatives left Shanghai, and the conference adjourned to a pleasure-boat on Nanhu Lake in nearby Jiaxing.

Following this conference, the CPC, a brand-new political force become active on China's political stage. The CPC brought hope to the suffering Chinese people.

1 | 2

1. 浙江嘉兴南湖
   Nanhu Lake, Jiaxing, Zhejiang Province
2. 李大钊像
   A portrait of Li Dazhao

小资料 Data

李大钊（1889—1927年）

李大钊，河北乐亭人，北京大学经济系教授和图书馆主任，《新青年》杂志编辑，中国最早的马克思主义者，中国共产党的创始人之一。1920年在北京组织共产党的早期组织。中国共产党成立后，他负责北方区党的工作。第一次国共合作期间，在帮助孙中山确定联俄、联共、扶助农工三大政策和改组国民党的工作中，起了重要作用。在中国共产党第二、三、四次代表大会上，均当选为中央委员。1927年4月被军阀张作霖逮捕，在北京英勇就义。

Li Dazhao（1889—1927）

Li Dazhao, born in Leting, Hebei Province, was a professor in the Department of Economics and the curator of the school library at Peking University. As an editor of the magazine New Youth, he was one of the first Marxists in China, and one of the founders of the CPC. In 1920, he organized communist activities in Beijing. After the founding of the CPC, he was responsible for activities in northern China. He played an important role in helping Dr. Sun Yat-sen to establish the three cardinal policies — allying with Russia, uniting with the CPC and assisting peasants and workers — and the reorganizing of the Nationalist Party (Kuomintang, KMT) during the first round of cooperation between the two parties. He was elected member of the Central Committee in the second, third and fourth national conferences of the CPC. In April 1927, he was arrested by the warlord, Zhang Zuolin, and was executed in Beijing.

第一次国共合作

The First Round of KMT-CPC Cooperation

20世纪20年代初，为了推翻帝国主义和北洋军阀在中国的统治，正在苦苦寻找正确革命道路的孙中山，得到了共产国际、苏俄和中国共产党的真诚帮助。他接受共产国际代表马林等人的建议，欢迎中国共产党同他合作，同意共产党员以个人身份加入国民党。中国共产党方面也于1923年6月召开第三次全国代表大会，集中讨论共产党员加入国民党问题，正式确定了国共合作的方针。

经过一系列的准备工作之后，1924年1月，中国国民党第一次全国代表大会在广州召开，李大钊、毛泽东等共产党员也参加了会议。大会确立了联俄、联共、扶助农工的三大政策，重新解释了三民主义，改组了国民党，第一次国共合作正式形成。

国共合作的建立，推动了反对军阀黑暗统治的国民革命高潮的到来。

小资料 Data

省港大罢工

1925年5月，英、日帝国主义在上海制造了枪杀中国群众的“五卅”（wǔsà）惨案，激起全国人民的极大愤慨，上海工人举行总罢工，表示抗议。为了支援上海人民的反帝斗争，在中国共产党的直接领导下，6月，广州、香港工人举行了反对英帝国主义的大罢工。这次罢工规模大，时间长，给英帝国主义以沉重打击。香港有25万工人参加了罢工。罢工坚持了16个月。

The Guangzhou-Hong Kong Strike

In May 1925, British and Japanese troops in Shanghai shot the local protesters in Shanghai, hence the May 30th Massacre, which aroused the anger of people from all over the country. Workers in Shanghai organized a united strike. In June 1925, to support the strike in Shanghai, the CPC directed workers in Guangzhou and Hong Kong to go on strike to protest British imperialism. The strike was massive in size and lasted a long time. 250 000 workers in Hong Kong participated in the strike, which lasted for 16 months and caused great loss to the British imperialists.

The First Round of KMT-CPC Cooperation

In the early 1920s, in search of a better way to end the ruling of the Northern Warlords and the imperial powers and to advance revolution in China, Sun Yat-sen accepted the help from the Communist International, Soviet Russia and the Communist Party of China (CPC). He also accepted the advice from Ma Lin, the representative from the Communist International to cooperate with the CPC by allowing CPC members to join the Nationalist Party (Kuomintang, KMT) as individual members. In June 1923, on the Third National Conference of CPC, the policy of cooperating with KMT by individual membership was discussed on and adopted.

After a series of preparation, in January 1924, the First National Congress of KMT was held in Guangzhou. Some CPC members, such as Li Dazhao and Mao Zedong, also attended the conference. The three cardinal policies i.e. allying with Russia, uniting with the CPC and assisting peasants and workers, were adopted. The Three People Principles were re-interpreted and the KMT was reorganized. The first KMT-CPC cooperation took place.

The KMT-CPC cooperation marked the climax of the national revolution against the rule of warlords.

1. 广州黄埔军校旧址
   The site of the Whampao Military Academy, Guangzhou
2. 1924年，任黄埔军校政治部主任的周恩来
   Zhou Enlai, director of the Political Department of the Whampoa Military Academy in 1924

小资料 Data

黄埔军校

国共合作实现后，为了培养军事人才，建立革命武装力量，孙中山在苏联和中国共产党的帮助下，1924年在广州创办了陆军军官学校——黄埔军校。校长由蒋介石担任，周恩来等许多共产党人在军校中担任了重要职务。学员入学后主要学习军事和政治两类课程。军校注重政治教育，培养学生的爱国思想和革命精神。在军事教育方面，主要采用当时苏联最新的军事理论和技术进行分学科的训练。从1924年到1927年，黄埔军校培养了6期共12 000多名毕业生，其中涌现了一批优秀的军事和政治人才，许多人成为国共两党的高级将领。黄埔军校为中国革命作出了巨大贡献。

The Whampoa Military Academy

Under the KMT-CPC cooperation and with the help of the Soviet Union and the CPC, Sun Yat-sen set up an academy for army officers — the Whampoa Military Academy in Guangzhou in 1924. The academy trained members of both the CPC and the KMT as the spearhead of the new revolutionary forces. Chiang Kai-shek was appointed president of the Academy, and many CPC members, including Zhou Enlai, held important posts in the Academy. Both military and political courses were taught. Whampoa stressed political education and cultivated the students' patriotism and revolutionary spirit. As for military education, it adopted the latest military theories and techniques from the Soviet Union to train students in various subject areas. From 1924 to 1927, the Whampoa Military Academy trained over 12 000 students in six terms, many of whom later became senior officers and political leaders of the two parties. In this way, the Whampoa contributed greatly to the Chinese revolution.

北伐战争

The Northern Expedition

1924年国共合作实现后，国共两党以广东为革命基地，准备进行北伐。北伐的目的是要推翻军阀的黑暗统治，打破帝国主义国家对中国的政治军事控制，使中国人民摆脱苦难。

1925年，国民党在广州成立广东国民政府。1926年国民政府正式决定北伐。为了全力支持北伐，中国共产党深入工人、农民当中，积极进行宣传和组织工作，为北伐战争打下了广泛而坚实的群众基础。

1926年7月，国民革命军在广州誓师，北伐战争正式开始。北伐军先攻占了湖南的省会长沙，接着直逼武汉。敌人在武汉外围选择地势极其险要的地方派重兵防守。北伐军浴血奋战，特别是叶挺领导的、以共产党员为主力的第四军独立团冲锋在前，英勇无比，为第四军赢得了“铁军”的称号。北伐军突破敌人的防线，渡过长江，占领武汉。1927年３月中旬，周恩来率领上海工人武装起义，使北伐军顺利进驻上海。3月下旬北伐军攻占南京。

北伐战争得到了全国人民的热烈拥护和支持。出师不到10个月，就消灭了军阀吴佩孚、孙传芳的主力部队，占领了长江以南的大部分地区，沉重地打击了反动军阀，使国民革命的火焰燃遍了半个中国。

The Northern Expedition

With a new alliance, the two parties (CPC and KMT) made Guangdong Province their revolutionary base, and prepared for the Northern Expedition, which would sweep away the rule of the warlords, break the military and political control of imperialist countries over China and end people's tribulation.

In 1925, the KMT formed the Guangdong National Government in Guangzhou. In 1926, the National Government decided to launch the Northern Expedition. In order to drum up support for the Northern Expedition, the CPC did active publicity and organizational work among the workers and peasants, establishing a broad and firm base among the masses for the Northern Expedition.

In July 1926, the National Revolution Army set off on its northward march, marking the beginning of the Northern Expedition. The Northern Expeditionary Army first captured Changsha, the capital of Hunan Province, and then pressed on toward Wuhan, which was heavily fortified. The prominent Independent Regiment, which was composed mainly of Communists and commanded by Ye Ting, fought courageously, and won for the Fourth Corps the title of "Iron Army". The Northern Expeditionary Army broke through the enemy's line of defense, crossed the Yangtze River and occupied Wuhan. In the middle of March 1927, Zhou Enlai led the workers of Shanghai in an armed uprising, ensuring the smooth entry of the Northern Expeditionary Army into Shanghai. At the end of March, the army also occupied Nanjing.

The Northern Expedition was warmly welcomed and supported by the people all over China. In less than ten months, it crushed the main forces of the major warlords Wu Peifu and Sun Chuanfang, and occupied most of the area south of the Yangtze River, all struck a heavy blow at the reactionary warlords and kindled the flame of revolution over half of China.

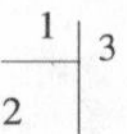

1. 江苏南京中山陵
   Sun Yat-sen's Mausoleum, Nanjing, Jiangsu Province
2. 第四军独立团团长叶挺
   Ye Ting, regimental commander of the Independent Regiment of New Fourth Corps
3. 广东肇庆阅江楼（叶挺独立团团部址）
   Yuejiang Tower in Zhaoqing, Guangdong Province, former headquarters of the Independent Regiment of New Fourth Corps

小资料 Data

孙中山逝世

1925年3月12日，孙中山先生在北京病逝。北伐胜利后，国民政府按照孙中山先生生前的愿望，将其遗体从北京运到南京。1929年安葬于中山陵。

The Passing away of Dr. Sun Yat-sen

On March 12th, 1925, Dr. Sun Yat-sen died of illness in Beijing. After the victory of the Northern Expedition, the National Government moved his remains from Beijing to Nanjing according to his will. In 1929, his remains were buried in the Sun Yat-sen Mausoleum.

南昌起义

The Nanchang Uprising

北伐战争的胜利打击了封建军阀和帝国主义在中国的统治。但是，随着形势的发展，国民党右派敌视共产党、破坏国共合作的面目日益暴露出来。1927年4月12日，蒋介石在上海发动反革命政变，杀害了300多名共产党员和革命群众，另外还有500多人被捕，数千人失踪。随后，广东、江苏、浙江、湖南等省都发生了屠杀共产党人的惨案。蒋介石叛变革命后，在南京建立了国民政府。7月15日，以汪精卫为首的武汉国民政府也背叛了革命，大规模逮捕杀害共产党人。至此，第一次国共合作彻底破裂，中国出现了白色恐怖的局面。

面对危急的形势，中国共产党人为了挽救革命进行了英勇顽强的斗争。1927年8月1日，周恩来、贺龙、叶挺、朱德、刘伯承等领导并发动了南昌起义。经过4个多小时的激战，起义军打败了国民政府的军队，占领了南昌城。

南昌起义引起了国民政府的恐慌，蒋介石调动军队进攻南昌。起义军撤离南昌，向广东进军，准备重建广东革命根据地。这一计划由于受到敌人的围攻而失败。

南昌起义打响了武装反抗国民党反动派的第一枪，中国共产党从此创建了自己的军队，开始走上独立领导革命、武装夺取政权的新道路。

1 | 2

1. 江西“八一”南昌起义纪念馆
   Memorial Hall of the Nanchang Uprising, Nanchang, Jiangxi Province
2. 周恩来等人领导的南昌起义
   The Nanchang Uprising led by Zhou Enlai

The Nanchang Uprising

The victory of the Northern Expedition greatly weakened the power of the warlords and imperialists in China. But as time went on, the right wing of the KMT began to show their hostility towards the CPC and sabotaged the KMT-CPC cooperation. On April 12th, 1927, Chiang Kai-shek staged a reactionary coup d'état in Shanghai, killing over 300 CPC members and other revolutionaries, and arresting over 500. In addition, thousands were missing. The purge spread to Guangdong, Jiangsu, Zhejiang, and Hunan provinces, where CPC members were slaughtered. After betraying the revolution, Chiang set up his National Government in Nanjing. On July 15th, the National Government in Wuhan, led by Wang Jingwei, also betrayed the revolution by arresting and killing CPC members en masse. At this time, the first KMT-CPC cooperation completely dissolved, and a period of white terror commenced in China.

At this critical moment, the Communists rose in a brave struggle to save the revolution. On August 1st, 1927, Zhou Enlai, He Long, Ye Ting, Zhu De, Liu Bocheng and others initiated and led the Nanchang Uprising. After four hours of fierce battle, the uprising army beat the National Army and seized the city of Nanchang.

The Nanchang Uprising caused panic in the National Government. Chiang dispatched an army which retook Nanchang. The insurgents then marched toward Guangdong, planning to rebuild the Guangdong revolutionary base. They failed to do so under siege of the enemy.

The Nanchang Uprising was the "first shot" of the CPC's armed struggle against the KMT reactionaries. From that time on, the CPC built its own army to lead the revolution independently and to seize the governing power through armed forces.

小资料 Data

“八七”会议

1927年8月7日，中国共产党中央委员会在武汉召开紧急会议，纠正了前一时期对国民党软弱退让的错误，确立了土地革命和武装反抗国民党反动派的方针。“八七”会议是一个转折点，它为中国革命指明了新的方向，在中国共产党的历史上有重要意义。

The August 7th Conference

On August 7th, 1927, the Central Committee of the CPC convened an emergency conference in Wuhan, correcting the mistake of being weak and concessionary to the KMT, and setting up the principles of an agrarian revolution and resisting the KMT reactionaries by armed forces. The August 7th Conference was a turning point by providing a new direction for the Chinese revolution, and was a meeting of great significance in the history of the CPC.

中国工农红军长征

The Long March of the Chinese Workers' and Peasants' Red Army

南昌起义后，毛泽东领导了湘赣边界秋收起义，并在江西的井冈山建立了第一块革命根据地。此后，共产党领导的革命根据地广泛建立，并得到广大农民的热烈支持和拥护，根据地不断扩大。

1930年到1932年，国民党南京政府调集重兵，对革命根据地发动了多次大规模的“围剿”（wéijiǎo），企图破坏根据地，消灭共产党。共产党领导的红军在根据地人民的支持下，一次又一次地粉碎了敌人的“围剿”。

1933年，蒋介石调集了100万军队，开始对红军进行第五次“围剿”。由于红军第五次反“围剿”失败，1934年10月，中央红军主力被迫撤离中央根据地，开始战略转移。

长征的道路十分艰难。红军爬雪山、过草地，没有粮食时就挖野菜，啃树皮，遇到了很多难以想象的困难。在国民党军队的围攻下，红军多次陷入被动挨打的局面。

1935年1月的遵义会议确立了毛泽东在红军和党中央的领导地位，红军变被动为主动，打了很多胜仗：四渡赤水、强渡大渡河、飞夺泸定桥……冲破了国民政府军队的围追堵截。1935年10月中央红军到达陕北吴起镇，与刘志丹领导的陕北红军胜利会师。1936年10月，红军三大主力在会宁等地会师，长征胜利结束。

1. 贵州遵义会议会址
The site of Zunyi Conference, Zunyi, Guizhou Province
2. 红军长征时通过的四川若尔盖水草地
The treacherous marshy grassland the Red Army had to cross during the Long March in Zoigê, Sichuan Province

长征路线图
Sketch Map of the Long March

小资料 Data

遵义会议

长征初期，由于当时中央领导人的错误领导和指挥，红军人员损失大半，中国革命陷入极大的危机之中。在危急的形势下，1935年1月中共中央在贵州遵义召开政治局扩大会议，及时纠正了第五次反"围剿"和长征以来中央在军事领导上的错误，确立了毛泽东在共产党和红军中的领导地位。遵义会议在危险的时刻挽救了党和红军，挽救了中国革命，成为中国共产党历史上一个生死攸关的转折点。

The Zunyi Conference

In the early period of the Long March, because of the poor leadership and command, the Red Army lost more than half of its members. Facing this critical situation, the Central Committee of the CPC convened the enlarged meeting of the Political Bureau in Zunyi, Guizhou Province, in January 1935. This conference corrected the mistakes in decision-making since the fifth campaign against the "encirclement and suppression", and established Mao Zedong's leadership of the Communist Party and the Red Army. At a particularly perilous moment, the Zunyi Conference served as a turning point to save the Red Army, the CPC and the Chinese revolution.

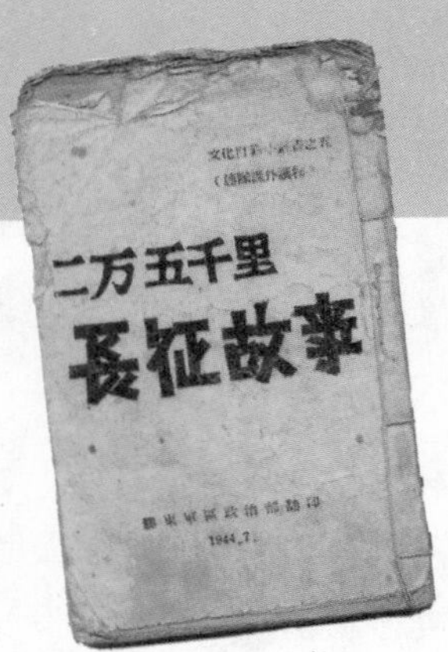

The Long March

of the Chinese Workers' and Peasants' Red Army

Soon after the Nanchang Uprising, Mao Zedong led the *Qiushou* (Autumn Harvest) Uprising in the border of Hunan and Jiangxi provinces and established the first revolutionary base area in the Jinggang Mountains in Jiangxi Province. This was followed by the setup of several other bases in other parts of China. With warm support from the peasants, these bases were enlarged.

From 1930 to 1932, the KMT Government in Nanjing launched many large-scale campaigns of "encirclement and suppression" of the revolutionary base, attempting to destroy these areas and eliminate the CPC. But with the support of the people in the base areas, the Red Army, directed by the CPC, repulsed the enemy time and again.

In 1933, Chiang Kai-shek assembled a force of one million men, and launched the "encirclement and suppression" campaign against the Red Army for the fifth time. Because the Red Army did not carry out the campaign against "encirclement and suppression", the main force of the Red Army was forced to retreat from its central base areas and began a strategic shift in October 1934.

The Long March was an arduous trek. The Red Army had to cross snow-covered mountains and uninhabited grassland. When

there was no food, the Red Army soldiers ate tree barks and wild herbs. Under siege, the Red Army often fell prey to the army of the KMT.

The Zunyi Conference in January 1935 established Mao Zedong in the leadership of the Red Army and the Party. The Red Army took the initiative in its hands resulting in the winning of many battles. Famous episodes at this time included crossing the Chishui River four times, forcing a way across the Dadu River and capturing the Luding Bridge. All of these highlighted the breakaway from the siege of the National Army. In October 1935, the central column of the Red Army reached Wuqi Town in northern Shaanxi Province and joined forces with the Red Army column of northern Shaanxi led by Liu Zhidan. In October 1936, the three major columns of the Red Army converged in the Huining area, which marked the victorious completion of the Long March.

1. 1937年，（右起）毛泽东、朱德、周恩来、博古在延安
   A group photo of (from right) Mao Zedong, Zhu De, Zhou Enlai, Bo Gu reaching Yan'an in 1937
2. 遵义会议的会议室
   The meeting room of the Zunyi Conference
3. 四川大渡河上的泸定桥
   Luding Bridge over Dadu River, Sichuan Province

小资料 Data

强渡大渡河

大渡河水深流急，地势极为险峻。1863年，太平天国翼王石达开的军队就是在这里遭到清军的前后夹攻，全军覆没。72年后，红军长征来到这里。国民党派重兵围追堵截，企图让毛泽东做“石达开第二”。毛泽东率领的红军英勇善战，打败了国民党军队，并成功地渡过了大渡河。

Forcing the Dadu River

The Dadu River is marked by its deep and fast current and precipitous banks. In 1863, a Taiping army led by Shi Dakai, the "King of Wings", was massacred by the Qing army as it tried to cross the river. The KMT forces tried to do the same to the Red Army 72 years later and to make Mao Zedong the second Shi Dakai. The Red Army led by Mao, however, outfought the KMT army bravely and crossed the river safely.

"九一八"事变

The September 18th Incident

1 | 2 / 3

1. 末代皇帝溥仪像
   A portrait of Puyi, the last emperor of China
2. 辽宁沈阳"九一八"纪念碑
   The Memorial Tablet of the September 18th Incident, Shenyang, Liaoning Province
3. 溥仪与日本天皇同乘一辆马车
   Puyi and Japanese Emperor riding in the same carriage

20世纪30年代，中国到处传唱着一首歌："九一八，九一八，从那个悲惨的时候，脱离了我的家乡……""九一八"到底是一个什么日子呢?

从19世纪后期开始，日本多次发动侵华战争，并且武装占领了台湾。但是，日本对这一切并不满足。20世纪日本准备大规模向国外军事扩张，中国是它的主要目标。为了首先侵占中国的东北三省，日本制造了"九一八"事变。

1931年9月18日晚上，沈阳附近的日军在一个叫柳条湖的地方炸毁了一段铁路，反而说是中国军队破坏铁路，想袭击日本军队，随即向中国的东北军大营和沈阳城发起了突然进攻。东北军伤亡很大。一夜之间，日军就占领了沈阳。

"九一八"事变发生时，国民党政府正忙于"剿共"（消灭共产党）。蒋介石一再命令东北军首领张学良：为避免事件扩大，绝对抱不抵抗主义。由于中国军队不抵抗，日军仅用了4个多月的时间就轻而易举地占领了中国的东北三省，3 000万同胞沦为亡国奴。

为了稳固统治，日本侵略者在东北三省成立了所谓"满洲国"，让早已退位的清朝末代皇帝溥仪（Pǔyí）来当傀儡（kuílěi）皇帝，实际上，权力完全控制在日本人手中。日本的侵略和统治激起了中国人民的激烈反抗，抗日义勇军在十分艰苦危险的环境中与日本侵略军展开了英勇的斗争。

The September 18th Incident

In the 1930s, a song became popular all over China. The lyrics go, "September 18th, September 18th. On that tragic day, I was forced to leave my hometown ..." What happened on September 18th?

Since the late 19th century, Japan had unleashed multiple wars of aggression against China, and seized Taiwan. China was the chief objective of its full-fledged military expansion in the 20th century. The three northeastern provinces of China became Japan's first target.

On the evening of September 18th, 1931, Japanese troops blew up part of a railway line at Liutiaohu, which is close to Shenyang. They then accused the Chinese army of trying to launch an attack against Japan. Soon after, the Japanese attacked the barracks of the Northeast Army and the city of Shenyang. With massive casualties, the city was lost overnight.

At this time, the National Government of the KMT was busy trying to eliminate the CPC. Chiang Kai-shek ordered Zhang Xueliang, leader of the Northeast Army, should adopt the policy of nonresistance to avoid broadening the scope of the event. Without any Chinese army standing against them, the Japanese army easily occupied the three provinces of northeast China, with a population of 30 million in only four months.

In order to consolidate their rule over northeast China, the Japanese invaders established a puppet state called Manchukuo, with Puyi, the abdicated last emperor of the Qing Dynasty as its puppet ruler within the complete control of Japan. This aroused great indignation among the local Chinese people, who formed army volunteers to fight against the invaders under extremely difficult circumstances.

小资料 Data

末代皇帝

溥仪（1906—1967年），满族，姓爱新觉罗。1908年光绪皇帝死后，不满3岁的溥仪登上皇位，年号宣统。1912年，中华民国成立，不久，溥仪退位，清朝灭亡。溥仪是中国2 000多年封建社会的最后一个皇帝。

The Last Emperor of China

Puyi (1906—1967) was of the Manchu nationality with family name of Aisin-Gioro. In 1908, after Emperor Guangxu had died, Puyi, who was only two years old then, came to the throne with the reign title Xuantong. In 1912, the Republic of China was founded. Soon after, Puyi gave up his throne, marking the end of the Qing Dynasty. Puyi was the last emperor of the feudal society in China, which lasted for more than 2 000 years.

华北事变与“一二·九”运动

The Huabei Incident and the December 9th Movement

1935年5月，日本寻找借口向国民党政府提出对华北统治权的无理要求，并调动日军入关，用武力相威胁。国民党政府妥协退让，使华北主权大部丧失，华北到了最危急的时刻，正如北平学生说的：“华北之大，已经安放不得一张平静的书桌了！”

8月1日，中国共产党发表“八一”宣言，11月发表《抗日救国宣言》，号召迅速建立抗日民族统一战线，推动了全国抗日民主运动的高涨。

12月9日，北平五六千名学生在中国共产党的领导下，举行了大规模的反日救国示威游行。示威学生遭到反动军警的镇压。学生一边同军警搏斗，一边向群众进行抗日救国宣传。第二天，北平全市学生举行总罢课，抗议反动政府的暴行。12月16日，北平1万多名学生和市民群众举行了更大规模的示威游行。

北平学生的爱国行动得到了全国各地学生、工人和知识分子的广泛响应和支持，全国抗日救亡运动空前高涨。

“一二·九”运动粉碎了日本占领华北进而全面侵略中国的计划，打击了国民党政府的妥协投降政策，进一步推动了全国抗日民主运动，标志着新的民族革命高潮的到来。

1. 北平前门西车站广场的市民大会场
   Grand scene of townpeople's protest rally assembly in West Station Square, Qianmen, Beiping
2. 学生的游行队伍
   Students' demonstration
3. 学生在进行抗日示威
   Students conducting anti-Japanese demonstration

The Huabei Incident and the December 9th Movement

In May 1935, in order to obtain dominance in *Huabei* (North China), Japan made political and military threats to the Nationalist Party's Government. The Nationalist Party's Government gave in and submitted governance of most of the Huabei area. The crisis of Huabei could not be more serious, as students in Beiping (today's Beijing) put it, "So spacious is Huabei, yet it cannot accommodate a peaceful school table!"

On August 1st, the CPC announced the "*August 1st Declaration*", which was followed by the "*Declaration of Fighting the Japanese and Saving the Nation*" in November, all calling upon the establishment of a united national front for anti-Japanese fighting. An upswing of anti-Japanese democratic movement was brought about through out the country.

On December 9th, led by the CPC, five to six thousand students held a massive demonstration in Beiping with the theme of fighting Japan and saving the nation. The police intervened brutally, causing a physical clash with the students who were carrying out their goal of fighting Japanese and saving the nation. On the second day, a general strike broke out among all schools in Beiping for the atrocity of the government. On December 16th, there came another demonstration of more than ten thousand people, both students and town folk.

The patriotic acts of students in Beiping gained nationwide response and support from students, workers and intellectuals all over the country, marking the unprecedented movement of fighting Japanese and saving the nation.

The December 9th Movement deterred the Japanese from its plan to occupy Huabei and all of China. It was a protest against the Nationalist Party Government's policy of compromise and surrender, a boost for the anti-Japanese democratic movement nationwide, and a signal of the forthcoming apex of the democratic revolution.

西安事变

The Xi'an Incident

日本占领中国东北三省后，又不断制造事端，准备侵略华北，形势十分危急。全国人民要求政府停止内战，共同抵抗日本侵略。但蒋介石却顽固地坚持先消灭共产党，再抵抗日本侵略者的政策。

1936年，蒋介石到西安逼迫张学良和杨虎城两位将军继续"剿共"。已经丢失了自己的故乡东北三省的张学良一再表示要去抗日，甚至哭着请求蒋介石不要再打内战了，救国要紧。可是他不但没能感动蒋介石，反而受到蒋的严厉训斥。张学良、杨虎城看到劝说无效，只好另想办法，逼蒋抗日。

12月9日，西安学生1万多人为纪念"一二·九"运动一周年，举行游行集会。他们步行前往蒋介石的住地，要求停止"剿共"，一致抗日。蒋介石大怒，命令张学良派兵把学生挡回去，如果学生不听，就开枪。张学良非常同情学生，他赶到学生们那儿，极力劝他们先回去，并且答应在一周之内用事实回答他们的要求。当天晚上，张学良向蒋介石反映学生们的要求，并再一次恳求抗日救国，但仍然遭到拒绝。

12月12日夜里，张学良、杨虎城发动兵变，在临潼华清池扣留了蒋介石。西安事变发生后，应张学良、杨虎城的邀请，共产党派周恩来到西安，商讨解决问题的办法。经过各方面的努力，终于迫使蒋介石答应停止内战，一致抗日，西安事变和平解决了，为国共两党第二次合作创造了条件。十年内战基本结束。

The Xi'an Incident

After occupying the three provinces in northeast China, the Japanese army indulged in a series of provocations to give itself an excuse to penetrate deeper into North China. Under such a dangerous situation, people throughout China demanded that the National Government stop the civil war and switch to resisting the Japanese army. But Chiang Kai-shek stubbornly persisted in his policy of eliminating the CPC first before standing against the Japanese.

In 1936, Chiang went to Xi'an to press the two generals, Zhang Xueliang and Yang Hucheng, to pursue the operations against the Communists more vigorously. Zhang Xueliang, who had lost his home base of the Northeast, insisted on fighting Japan and pleaded tearfully with Chiang to stop the Civil War for the sake of saving the nation. Not moved, Chiang blamed Zhang bitterly. When all attempts of persuasion turned out to be in vain, Zhang and Yang decided to force Chiang to resist the Japanese.

On December 9th, to celebrate the anniversary of the December 9th Movement, more than 10 thousand students in Xi'an held a demonstration and walked to Chiang's residence to demand that he halt the Civil War and turn his guns on the Japanese. Bursting with anger, Chiang ordered Zhang Xueliang to stop the students with force and to open fire if necessary. Zhang sympathized with the students. He went to them, persuaded them to retreat and promised to answer their request with facts within one week. On the very evening, Zhang Xueliang expressed the wish from the students to Chiang again, and pleaded for the decision to fight Japan and save the nation. He was once again rejected.

On the night of December 12, the two generals Zhang Xueliang and Yang Hucheng launched a coup and arrested Chiang in Huaqing Pool, near Lintong. They then invited the CPC to send Zhou Enlai to Xi'an to discuss a solution to the problem. With efforts from all sides, Chiang Kai-shek finally agreed to stop the Civil War and cooperate with the CPC to resist the Japanese invaders. Thus, the Xi'an Incident was settled peacefully. This laid the foundation for the second KMT-CPC cooperation and marked the end of the ten-year-old Civil War.

1 | 2

1. “西安事变”前，蒋介石在华清池的办公室
Chiang Kai-shek's office in the Huaqing Pool before the Xi'an Incident
2. 张学良（左）和杨虎城（右）像
Portraits of Zhang Xueliang (left) and Yang Hucheng (right)

小资料 Data

“千古功臣”

西安事变和平解决后，为了表示自己的忠诚，张学良亲自陪蒋介石回南京，从此被软禁，失去了人身自由。杨虎城后来被蒋秘密杀害。张学良于2001年病逝于美国夏威夷，享年101岁。这两位将军在民族危急关头为抗日事业作出了巨大的贡献，周恩来后来称赞他们是“千古功臣”。

"Heroes of All Time"

After the peaceful settlement of Xi'an Incident, Zhang Xueliang accompanied Chiang Kai-shek to Nanjing to show his loyalty, yet was put under house arrest by Chiang and lost his freedom. Yang Hucheng was murdered later upon Chiang's order. Zhang died in Hawaii in 2001 at the age of 101. These two generals, who had made a great contribution to the resistance against Japan when the nation was in great danger, were praised by Zhou Enlai as "Heroes of All Time".

“七七”事变

The July 7th Incident

为了实现侵占全中国的企图，日本发动了“七七”事变。1937年7月7日晚上，驻扎在北平（今北京）郊区卢沟桥一带的日本军队举行军事演习。演习结束后，日军借口有一个士兵失踪，又说好像听到宛平城内（卢沟桥附近）有枪声，要强行进入宛平县城搜查，遭到中国守军的拒绝。日军随即炮轰卢沟桥，向宛平城发起进攻。中国军队奋起还击，驻守卢沟桥的100多名士兵战斗到只剩下4人，其余全部牺牲，终于打退了敌人的进攻。由于这次事件发生在卢沟桥，所以又叫卢沟桥事变。

“七七”事变后，面对危急的形势，中国共产党发出通电，指出“平津危急！华北危急！中华民族危急！”呼吁“只有全民族实行抗战，才是我们的出路！”全国各界群众、爱国党派和团体、海外华侨也纷纷举行集会，强烈要求政府抗战。不少大城市相继组织了“抗敌后援会”，募捐了大量钱物，送往抗日前线，支持和慰劳驻守华北、积极抗日的中国军队。

在严峻的形势和全国人民高昂的抗日热情面前，蒋介石发表谈话，表示了准备抗战的决心。国共两党经过谈判，决定将共产党领导的主力红军改编为国民革命军第八路军，开赴华北抗日前线。南方八省红军游击队被改编为新四军。9月，国共合作宣言发表，全国抗日民族统一战线正式形成。

小资料 Data

卢沟桥

卢沟桥位于北京的西南郊，建于公元1192年，长266.5米，宽约7.5米，由11孔石拱组成。桥的石栏上面有485个精雕细刻、神态各异的石狮子。“卢沟晓月”曾是北京著名的风景点。

Lugouqiao Bridge

Lugouqiao Bridge is located in the southwest of Beijing. It was built in 1192. It is 266.5 meters long and about 7.5 meters wide, and is composed of 11 stone arches. On both sides of the bridge there are stone balustrades, on which there are 485 exquisitely carved stone lions with different appearances. The “Morning Moon over Lugouqiao Bridge” used to be one of Beijing’s famous sights.

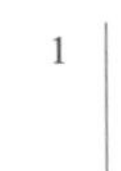

1. 卢沟桥“卢沟晓月”石碑
   The stone tablet celebrating the “Morning Moon over Lugouqiao Bridge”
2. 卢沟桥
   Lugouqiao Bridge

The July 7th Incident

To proceed with its attempt to conquer the whole China, Japan provoked the July 7th Incident. On the evening of July 7th, 1937, Japanese troops stationed in the Lugouqiao area in the suburbs of Beiping (today's Beijing) held a military exercise. Claiming to have heard gunshots in the nearby town of Wanping, and that one of their men was missing, the Japanese wanted to enter the town of Wanping to search the area. The Chinese army stopped them. They then launched an attack on Wanping and bombarded Lugouqiao. Striking back, the 100-men-strong Chinese unit stationed in the Lugouqiao area fought bravely and repulsed the enemy, but only four soldiers survived the battle. The July 7th Incident is also called the Lugouqiao Incident.

After the July 7th Incident, the CPC issued an open telegram, saying that "Beiping and Tianjin are in emergency! North China is in emergency! The Chinese nation is in emergency!" and calling upon "the whole nation to fight against the Japanese aggressors, which is the only way out". People from all walks of life, all the patriotic parties and groups, and overseas Chinese assembled, and demanded that the government mount an all-out resistance. Aid associations were organized in many big cities to collect money for the war effort and to support the Chinese armies in North China, who were fighting Japan actively.

Under these serious circumstances, facing the passionate people from all over the country, Chiang Kai-shek expressed the decision to prepare for the fighting. Upon negotiation, the CPC and the KMT agreed to reorganize the main force of the Communist-led Red Army into the Eighth Route of the National Revolutionary Army, and to dispatch it to the North China front to fight the Japanese. The guerrillas in the eight provinces of the South were reorganized into the New Fourth Army. In September, the declaration of the KMT-CPC cooperation was publicized, and the united national front to resist Japan was officially formed.

平型关大捷

The Victory at Pingxing Pass

1937年8月红军主力改编为八路军后，立即开赴华北战场，积极配合正面战场作战。

1937年9月，华北日军侵入山西，以精锐部队进攻雁门关等长城关隘，企图夺取太原。

国民政府组织太原会战，林彪（Lín Biāo）、聂荣臻（Niè Róngzhēn）率领八路军第115师在山西参加会战。平型关地形险要，是晋北交通要道。第115师利用平型关的有利地形，于9月25日伏击日军，歼灭日军板垣（Bǎnyuān）师团1 000多人，击毁汽车100多辆，缴获大批军用物资，取得平型关大捷。这是全国抗战爆发以来中国军队的第一次胜利。平型关大捷粉碎了日军不可战胜的神话，支持了国民党军队正在准备的忻口（Xīnkǒu）会战，鼓舞了全国人民抗战胜利的信心。

平型关战役形势示意图

Sketch Map of the Battle at Pingxing Pass

寒水村 Hanshui Village

老爷庙 Laoyemiao

石灰沟 Shihuigou

东跑池 Dongpaochi

关沟 Guangou

白崖台 Baiyatai

东长城村 Dongchangcheng Village

山西 Shanxi Province

八路军开进方向 The marching direction of the Eighth Route Army

八路军进攻方向 The attacking direction of the Eighth Route Army

八路军防御阵地 The defense line of the Eighth Route Army

八路军歼敌地区 The area where the Eighth Route Army wiped out the enemy

1. 平型关战斗中八路军115师指挥所
   Headquarters of Division 115 of the Eighth Route Army in the battle at Pingxing Pass
2. 聂荣臻在前线侦察
   Nie Rongzhen scouting in the frontline
3. 平型关战役缴获日军大批武器
   Weapons seized from the Japanese army in the battle at Pingxing Pass

The Victory at Pingxing Pass

The main forces of the Red Army, having been reorganized into the Eighth Route Army in August 1937, were immediately deployed in the North China battlefield.

In September 1937, the Japanese army in North China invaded Shanxi Province through Yanmen Pass and other strategic passes along the Great Wall, attempting to seize Taiyuan, the capital of Shanxi Province.

The National Government organized the Taiyuan Campaign. Lin Biao and Nie Rongzhen led the No. 115 Division of the Eighth Route Army to defend Pingxing Pass, which is the strategic spot to the north of Shanxi. On September 25th, the No. 115 Division ambushed the Japanese army and wiped out over 1 000 soldiers of the Itagaki Division, stormed over 100 vehicles and seized a lot of military materials, hence the "Victory at Pingxing Pass". This was the first victory won by the Chinese army since the beginning of the nationwide Anti-Japanese War. This win dispelled the myth that the Japanese army was invincible, and boosted the spirit of Chinese people to fight the Japanese. The victory also contributed to the preparation of Xinkou Campaign by the Nationalist Party's army.

小资料 Data

八路军

卢沟桥事变爆发不久，国共两党合作抗战。1937年8月22日，国民政府宣布，将红军主力部队改编为国民革命军第八路军，简称"八路军"，下辖三个师：第115师、第120师和第129师，朱德任总指挥，彭德怀任副总指挥。

The Eighth Route Army

Not long after the Lugouqiao Incident, the CPC and the KMT joined hands to resist the Japanese invasion. On August 22nd, 1937, the National Government announced the reorganization of the main forces of the Red Army into the Eighth Route of the National Revolutionary Army, in short "the Eighth Route Army". The Eighth Route Army had three divisions: the No. 115 Division, the No. 120 Division and the No. 129 Division. Zhu De was the commander-in-chief of the Eighth Route Army, and Peng Dehuai was his deputy.

南京大屠杀

The Nanking Massacre

1937年11月12日，日军侵占上海后，即向当时中国的首都南京进攻。12月13日上午，以松井石根为司令官的日军攻入城内，南京沦陷。日军采用极其野蛮的手段，对居民及解除武装的中国军人进行了长达6个星期的血腥屠杀。

日军在南京下关江边、草鞋峡、煤炭港、上新河、燕子矶、汉中门外等地制造了多起集体屠杀事件，还实行了分散屠杀。屠杀之后，日军又采用抛尸入江、火化焚烧、集中掩埋等手段，毁尸灭迹。据调查统计，被日军屠杀的人数总计达30万以上。日军屠杀南京人民的手段极其残忍，主要有砍头、刺杀、枪击、活埋、火烧等，还有惨无人道的杀人比赛。在日本侵略者的屠刀下，南京这座原来和平繁华的大都市，变成了阴森可怕的人间地狱。日军在南京的暴行，为现代世界文明史留下最为黑暗的一页。

1945年8月15日，日本无条件投降。中国军事法庭（于1946年12月设立）及东京军事法庭都对南京大屠杀进行了严肃认真的调查、审理，并作出判决。集体屠杀列为28案，零散屠杀列为858案。东京军事法庭对东条英机等28名日本甲级战犯进行了审判。至此，国际社会对侵华日军南京大屠杀事件定下了铁案。

1 | 2 / 3

1. 日军刺杀中国平民的情形
Atrocities carried out against Chinese civilians by the Japanese army
2. 南京大屠杀遇难同胞纪念馆前的巨型石墙
The huge wall in front of the Nanjing Massacre Memorial Hall
3. 惨遭杀害的中国平民
Tragic scene of Chinese civilians slaughtered

遇难者 VICTIMS 遭難者 300000

The Nanking Massacre

After capturing Shanghai on November 12th, 1937, the Japanese army attacked Nanking (Nanjing), China's capital at that time, on the morning of December 13. For six weeks, the occupying troops engaged in an orgy of slaughter by the most brutal means.

Massacres took place in many spots, i.e. the river bank near Xiaguan, Caoxiexia, Meitangang, Shangxinhe, Yanziji and out of the gate of Hanzhong. There were also random killing incidents. In order to exterminate the traces of massacre, the Japanese disposed of the corps in the river. They also burned or buried a large number of them. It is estimated that over 300 000 civilians and disarmed Chinese soldiers were murdered. Japanese brutality against the people of Nanjing was outrageous. Many were beheaded, thrust, shot, buried alive or burned in the killing spree. Numerous living souls were annihilated, turning the peaceful metropolitan of Nanjing into a living hell. The Nanking Massacre has gone down in the annals of history as a horrific incident and a stain on modern civilization.

Following Japan's surrender on August 15th, 1945, war crimes trials held by the Chinese Military Tribunal (set up in December 1946) and the Tokyo Military Tribunal all investigated and made judgments about the Nanking Massacre. The court came to the conclusion that there had been 28 cases of collective slaughter and 858 cases of scattered slaughter. The Tokyo Military Tribunal brought 28 Class-A war criminals to trial, including the notorious Hiranuma. Hence, the international community regarded the Nanking Massacre as an undeniable crime by the Japanese invaders against the people of China.

台儿庄战役

The Taierzhuang Campaign

台儿庄战役示意图

Sketch Map of the Taierzhuang Campaign

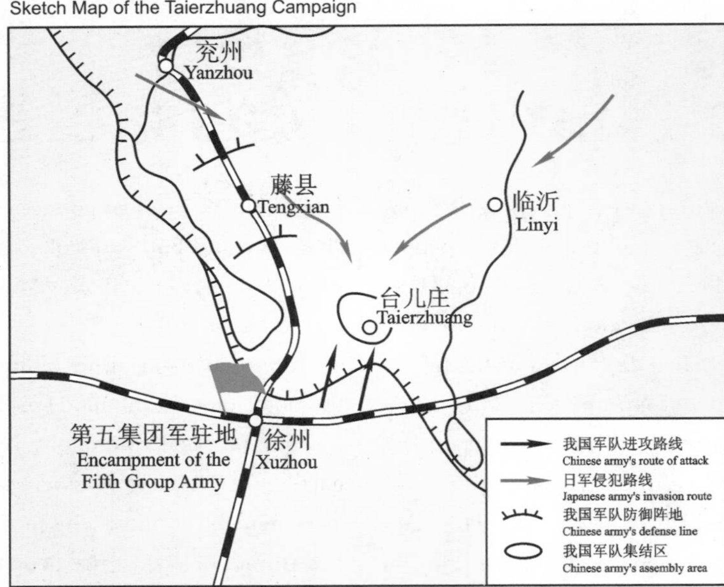

台儿庄战役是国民党军队保卫徐州的一次外围战役。

台儿庄位于徐州东北约50公里处，临近津浦铁路，同时又是运河要道，具有十分重要的战略地位。

1937年12月，日军占领南京以后，为了打通津浦路，连结南北战场，决定先夺取徐州。

1938年春，日军从山东分两路进攻徐州。国民政府第五战区司令长官李宗仁，指挥中国军队作战，将两路日军分别阻挡在山东临沂和台儿庄。

3月23日，日军约4万人进攻台儿庄，池峰城师长率领中国守军坚守半个月之久，将日军主力吸引到台儿庄附近。李宗仁调集大量兵力包围日军，形成内外夹攻之势，在台儿庄消灭日军1万余人，击毁日军坦克30余辆，并缴获大量武器，取得台儿庄大捷，这是全国抗战爆发以来正面战场取得的最大胜利。

小资料 Data

李宗仁（1891—1969年）

1891年出生于广西桂林，后成为桂系军阀首领。1948年，他在当时的国民政府选举中当选为副总统，蒋介石下野后任代总统。新中国成立后去美国治病。1965年，在中国政府的关怀帮助下，李宗仁回到北京。1969年去世。

Li Zongren (1891—1969)

Li Zongren was born in Guilin, Guangxi Zhuang Autonomous Region, in 1891. He became the chief warlord of the line of Gui. He was elected Vice President of the National Government in 1948. After Chiang Kai-shek resigned as president, Li became Acting President of the National Government. He went to the US for medical treatment after the New China was founded in 1949. In 1965, with the help and care from the government of New China, Li Zongren returned to Beijing. He passed away in 1969.

The Taierzhuang Campaign

The Taierzhuang Campaign was launched by the KMT army to protect Xuzhou.

Located about 50 km northeast of Xuzhou, Taierzhuang is a vital transportation hub, commanding the main north-south railway line and the Grand Canal.

After occupying Nanjing in December 1937, the Japanese army moved to capture Xuzhou in order to link their northern and southern forces.

In the spring of 1938, the Japanese army launched a two-pronged attack on Xuzhou from Shandong Province. Li Zongren, commander of the Fifth War Zone of the National Government, deployed his men to block both paths of the Japanese advance at Linyi and Taierzhuang, respectively, in Shandong.

On March 23rd, a Japanese army of 40 000 men began to attack Taierzhuang. Division Commander Chi Fengcheng held fast to the town for half a month, drawing the main forces of the Japanese army to the Taierzhuang area. Li Zongren mustered his main force to make a pincer attack on the Japanese. Finally, the Chinese army annihilated over 10 000 Japanese soldiers, destroyed 30-odd Japanese tanks and seized a large number of weapons. The Taierzhuang victory became the largest one on the direct front since the breakout of the nationwide Anti-Japanese War.

1. 台儿庄战役图
   The Taierzhuang Campaign
2. 指挥台儿庄战役的李宗仁司令长官
   Li Zongren, commander of the Taierzhuang Campaign

华侨与抗日战争

Overseas Chinese and the Anti-Japanese War

海外华侨有着爱国的光荣传统。孙中山领导的辛亥革命就曾得到广大华侨的积极响应和支持。

海外华侨是中华民族抗日战争中的重要力量。从1931年“九一八”事变到1945年抗日战争胜利，他们同祖国人民一起，为世界反法西斯战争作出了巨大的贡献，是中华民族的骄傲、炎黄子孙的光荣，受到世人的称颂。

在第二次世界大战期间，德、意、日结成法西斯同盟，支持日本对中国的侵略。侨居海外的广大华侨利用自己侨居

海外的便利条件，在欧洲、美洲、大洋洲以及东南亚纷纷组织起来，成立了各种爱国抗日组织，为抗日战争争取到了广泛的国际同情和援助。

他们积极捐款捐物，支持祖国抗战。他们提供的大量物资，补充了军队的给养和人民的生活费用。

他们还积极宣传抗日，支持团结抗战，反对分裂投降。“九一八”事变后，海外华侨强烈要求全国抗战，实行各党联合作战，成为推动第二次国共合作的进步力量。

美国华侨还成立了航空学校，为祖国培训航空人才。

全面抗战开始后，很多华侨回国参战。1938年10月以后，中国东南的海陆交通被日军切断，新开辟的滇缅（diānmiǎn）公路工程完成后，急需大批汽车司机和修理工。1939年，南侨总会受国民政府委托，招募约3 200名华侨机工回国效力。《南洋商报》、《星洲日报》等10多家侨报的记者联合组织“南洋华侨战地记者通讯团”，于1938年回国进行战地采访。

中国人民经过8年艰苦卓绝的斗争，终于取得了抗日战争的胜利，爱国华侨为祖国抗战作出了巨大的贡献。

1 | 2

1. 爱国华侨领袖陈嘉庚在厦门集美的墓园
The mausoleum of the patriotic overseas Chinese leader, Tan Kah-kee, Jimei, Xiamen
2. 菲律宾华侨组织的军乐队在新四军军部留影
A photo of a millitary band organized by overseas Chinese in Philippines in the headquarters of the New Fourth Army

Overseas Chinese

and the Anti-Japanese War

1. 英国伦敦华侨儿童赠送给八路军将士的锦旗
   A silk banner presented to the Eighth Route Army by overseas Chinese children in London
2. 陈嘉庚铜像
   A bronze statue of Tan Kah-kee
3. 八路军重庆办事处人员与侨胞慰劳团合影
   A group photo of overseas nationals conveying regards and bringing gifts with Staff of the Eighth Route Army's Office in Chongqing

The overseas Chinese have a glorious patriotic tradition. The Revolution of 1911 led by Sun Yat-sen received an enthusiastic welcome and support from numerous overseas Chinese.

The overseas Chinese played an important role in the Anti-Japanese War also. From the September 18th Incident in 1931 to V-J Day in 1945, overseas Chinese, together with people back home, made great contributions to the worldwide anti-Fascist war. They were part of the pride and glory of the Chinese nation, and were praised by people all over the world.

During the World War II, Germany, Italy and Japan formed a Fascist alliance in support of Japanese invasion to China. The overseas Chinese took advantage of their overseas settlement to set up united patriotic anti-Japanese organizations in Europe, Americas, Oceania and Southeast Asia, winning sympathy and aid from the international community for beleaguered China.

The overseas Chinese donated money and goods enthusiastically for the anti-Japanese cause, providing a great deal of subsidies for the military and civilian expenses in China.

They were solidly behind calls for the whole Chinese people to unite against the common enemy, especially after the September 18th Incident. The overseas Chinese were a progressive force in promoting the

Second KMT-CPC Cooperation.

Chinese people in the US established an aviation school to train flyers for their motherland.

When the nationwide Anti-Japanese War broke out, many overseas Chinese returned to the homeland to join the fighting. The Japanese army cut off marine and land transportation in southeast China in October 1938, but the Yunnan-Burma Highway was quickly constructed. A great number of drivers and mechanics were needed. In 1939, entrusted by the National Government, the "General Association of Overseas Chinese in Southeast Asia for Relieving Fellow Countrymen in Distress" recruited about 3 200 overseas Chinese mechanics to help maintain trucks that supplied the Chinese army via the new road. Reporters from *Nanyang Commercial Press*, *Sinchew Daily* and many other overseas Chinese newspapers formed the "Team of War Correspondents of Overseas Chinese from Southeast Asia" to report on the war from China in 1938.

With eight years of extreme hardship and fighting, Chinese people won the Anti-Japanese War. The overseas Chinese contributed greatly to the war of resistance in their homeland.

小资料 Data

陈嘉庚（1874—1961年）
爱国华侨领袖，福建厦门人。1910年，陈嘉庚（Chén Jiāgēng）在新加坡参加了同盟会，曾募款资助孙中山。陈嘉庚热心兴办华侨和家乡的文化教育事业，先后在厦门的集美创办中小学和师范、航海等专科学校和厦门大学。“九一八”事变后，陈嘉庚召开华侨大会，号召侨胞出钱出力，抵制日货，投身救国运动。全面抗战爆发后，陈嘉庚在新加坡成立“南洋华侨筹赈祖国难民总会”，后来他还亲自到延安慰劳抗日军民。抗战胜利后，他创办《南侨日报》，从事爱国民主活动。毛泽东曾经高度赞扬陈嘉庚先生的爱国主义精神，称他为“华侨旗帜，民族光辉”。

Tan Kah-kee (1874—1961)
A leader of patriotic overseas Chinese, Tan Kah-kee (Chen Jiageng) was born in Xiamen, Fujian Province. He joined the China Revolutionary League in Singapore in 1910, and collected money to aid Sun Yat-sen's revolutionary exertions. He also did much to spread education among the overseas Chinese and the people in his hometown. From 1913 to 1920, he set up elementary and secondary schools, teacher's colleges, maritime schools and Xiamen University in Jimei, Xiamen. Following the September 18th Incident, he convened the Overseas Chinese Conference, and called upon overseas Chinese to donate money and goods and boycott Japanese commodities in order to save China. After the nationwide Anti-Japanese War broke out in China, he founded the General Association of Overseas Chinese in Southeast Asia for Relieving Fellow Countrymen in Distress. He went to Yan'an in person to salute Chinese soldiers and civilians who were resisting the Japanese invaders. After victory in 1945, he set up the Nanqiao Daily, and engaged in patriotic and democratic activities. Mao Zedong highly praised Tan Kah-kee's patriotic spirit by referring to him as "the role model of overseas Chinese and the glory of the nation".

重庆谈判

The Chongqing Negotiations

抗日战争胜利后，蒋介石一方面准备发动内战，一方面又受到国内外要求和平、反对内战的舆论压力，于是采取了“假和平，真内战”的策略。1945年8月，蒋介石三次邀请毛泽东去重庆“商讨”国内和平问题。他的真实意图是：如果毛泽东不去，就宣传共产党没有和平诚意，把发动内战的责任加在共产党身上；如果去了，就可以借谈判逼共产党交出人民军队和解放区政权。

1945年8月28日，为谋求和平，毛泽东、周恩来、王若飞等中共领导人从延安前往重庆，与国民党谈判。国民党派王世杰、张治中、邵力子为谈判代表。

这次谈判共进行了43天。中共代表团提出了和平建国的基本方针，即坚决避免内战，在和平、民主、团结的基础上实现全国统一，建立独立、自由、富强的新中国。蒋介石不得不表面同意结束专制统治，召开各党派政治协商会议，保障民主自由，保障各党派平等合法地位等主张，并于10月10日公布了《国共代表会谈纪要》（即“双十协议”）。

这次谈判，国共双方在解放区的政权问题和军队问题上争论激烈。中共代表团要求承认人民军队和解放区民主政权的合法地位，蒋介石则要求中共交出军队和解放区。为了争取和平，中共代表团作出让步，在普遍裁减全国军队的前提下，将人民解放军减少为24个师，并自动退出广东、湖南等8个解放区。

这次谈判迫使蒋介石承认了和平建国等政治方针。同时也揭穿了国民党假和平、真备战的阴谋，使得中国共产党在政治上取得主动，国民党在政治上陷入孤立。

1. 1945年9月17日，毛泽东和蒋介石在重庆谈判期间的合影
Mao Zedong posed with Chiang Kai-shek during the Chongqing Negotiations on September 17th,1945
2. 1945年8月28日，毛泽东、周恩来等人在美国驻华大使赫尔利和蒋介石的代表张治中的陪同下前往重庆谈判
On August 28th, 1945, Mao Zedong, Zhou Enlai and other members of the CPC negotiating team left for Chongqing accompanied by the US Ambassador Patrick Hurley and Zhang Zhizhong, the representative of Chiang Kai-shek.
3. 重庆谈判旧址
The site where the Chongqing Negotiations were held

The Chongqing Negotiations

With the end of the Anti-Japanese War, Chiang Kai-shek prepared to restart the civil war. But pressure from home and abroad asking for peace forced him to adopt a policy of "Phony Peace and Real Civil War". In August 1945, Chiang invited leaders of the CPC to Chongqing, ostensibly to discuss the issue of domestic peace. His real intention was to impose the war responsibility on the CPC if they failed to show up in the negotiation, or to force the CPC to hand over their army and political power in the liberated areas if they entered into the negotiation.

Mao Zedong, Zhou Enlai, Wang Ruofei and other leaders of the CPC went from Yan'an to Chongqing on August 28th, 1945, and began the Chongqing negotiations. The representatives of the KMT were Wang Shijie, Zhang Zhizhong and Shao Lizi.

The negotiations lasted 43 days. The CPC representatives argued the principle of peaceful construction of the country, i.e. to resolve against civil war, to unite the whole country based on peace, democracy and solidarity, and to establish an independent, free and prosperous China. Chiang Kai-shek agreed to end the despotism, to convene a consultative conference of all political parties, to guarantee democracy, freedom, and the equal, legal status of all political parties. Finally, Chiang published the *Summary of Talks between the CPC and the KMT Representatives on October 10th*, hence the name, the "*Double 10 Agreement*".

However, there still remained considerable disputes over the liberated areas and the armed forces of the two sides. The delegation of the CPC demanded legal status for the people's army and the democratic government of the liberated areas, while Chiang demanded that the CPC surrender the army and the liberated areas. In order to achieve peace, the CPC delegation made concessions by reducing the People's Liberation Army to 24 divisions on condition of an overall reduction of armed forces in China, and by retreating from eight liberated areas, including those in Guangdong and Hunan.

These negotiations forced Chiang to agree to the political agenda of peaceful construction of the country. The KMT's strategy of "Preparing for War Under Phony Peace" was exposed. The CPC gained the political initiative while the KMT went into political isolation.

解放战争

The War of Liberation

1　2

1. 1949年3月25日，毛泽东在北平西苑机场检阅部队
Mao Zedong inspected troops at the Beiping Xiyuan Airport on Mar 25th, 1949.
2. 江苏南京国民党总统府旧址
The PLA occupied the Presidential Palace in Nanjing, Jiangsu Province.

1946年6月，蒋介石下令全面进攻解放区，解放区军民奋起抗击，解放战争正式开始。

全面内战爆发时，国民党政府在军事力量上占有明显优势，拥有430多万人的庞大军队，控制着全国所有的大城市和绝大部分交通干线，还得到美国在军事上和财政上的支持。

1947年2月，解放区军民打破了国民党军的全面进攻。1947年3月起，国民党政府从原来对解放区的全面进攻，改为对陕甘宁和山东两个解放区的重点进攻，但也失败了。到1947年6月，国共双方力量对比已发生了显著的变化。国民党军队总兵力下降到373万人，士气低落。国民党政府在政治上、经济上也陷入严重危机。人民解放军总兵力由127万增加到195万，装备也有很大改善，全军士气高涨，开始从战略防御转入战略进攻。

1947年7月起，解放军三支大军先后南下中原，展开进攻。到1948年8月，双方力量对比发生了进一步的变化。人民解放军的人数上升到280万，解放区面积也扩大了。从1948年9月12日至1949年1月31日，中共中央先后组织了辽沈、淮海、平津三大战役，基本上消灭了国民党的主力部队，解放了全国大部分地区，加速了全国解放战争胜利的到来。

三大战役以后，国民党政府继续在长江南岸部署兵力，妄图凭借长江天险，阻止人民解放军渡江向南进发。1949年4月21日，毛泽东和朱德下达命令，人民解放军在东起江阴，西至湖口，长达500多公里的战线上，分三路发起渡江战役。23日，人民解放军占领南京，蒋介石集团逃往台湾。到1950年6月，全国解放战争的大规模作战行动结束。

The War of Liberation

In June 1946, Chiang Kai-shek launched an all-out attack on the liberated areas. Both soldiers and civilians of the liberated areas rose as one against the enemy. The War of Liberation had started. At the beginning of the civil war, the KMT had an obvious military superiority. They possessed a massive army of over 4 300 000 men, controlled all the big cities and most of the main lines of transportation in China, and received military and financial support from the US.

In February 1947, the people and the army in the liberated areas repelled an all-out attack by the KMT army. In March 1947, the KMT began to focus their forces against the Shaanxi-Gansu-Ningxia and Shandong liberated areas, but these two areas held out against all the odds. By June 1947, the strength of the armed forces of the CPC and the KMT reversed remarkably, with the KMT troops shrinking to 3 730 000 men. At the same time, the National Government fell into grave political and economic crises. By now the People's Liberation Army (PLA), increasing in number from 1 270 000 to 1 950 000 and improving in equipment, had begun to move to the phase of strategic offensive.

From July 1947, three wings of the PLA advanced southward to the Central Plains. By August 1948, the strength of the armed forces of the two sides had changed further, with the PLA increasing to 2 800 000 men and the liberated areas expanding rapidly. From September 12th 1948 to January 31st 1949, the Central Committee of the CPC had launched three major campaigns of Liaoxi-Shenyang, Huai-Hai and Beiping-Tianjin, which basically destroyed the main forces of the KMT army, and liberated most of China.

After the three decisive campaigns, the KMT deployed its troops on the south bank of the Yangtze River, which was a natural barrier. On April 21st, 1949, Mao Zedong and Zhu De ordered the PLA to force across the river in three places along a front of over 500 km, starting from Jiangyin in the east and ending at Hukou in the west. On April 23rd, the PLA occupied Nanjing, and the Chiang Kai-shek clique fled to Taiwan. By June 1950, large-scale operations of the War of Liberation had ended.

小资料 Data

总统府

南京国民党总统府旧址位于现在南京市长江路292号。明初这里是汉王府。1912年，孙中山临时大总统也曾在此办公。在抗战前后的14年内，蒋介石把这里作为国民政府办公所在地。

The Presidential Palace

The Presidential Palace is located at 292 Changjiang Road, Nanjing. It was the residence of Prince Han in the beginning of the Ming Dynasty. Sun Yat-sen used it as his headquarters when he was Interim President in 1912. Chiang Kai-shek made it the site of the National Government for 14 years before and after the Anti-Japanese War.

北平和平解放

1949年1月，华北“剿总”总司令傅作义将军与人民解放军经过谈判，签署了和平解放北平的声明。随后，解放军举行了正式的入城仪式，具有悠久历史的文化古都北平宣告和平解放，进而大大推动了全国解放的到来。

The Peaceful Liberation of Beiping

In January 1949, General Fu Zuoyi, commander-in-chief of the KMT's North China Bandit Suppression Headquarters, signed a statement on the peaceful liberation of Beiping (today's Beijing) after negotiating with the PLA. Later, the PLA held a ceremony to enter the city, marking the peaceful liberation of Beiping, an ancient capital with a long history and rich cultural resources. This greatly propelled the liberation process of the whole China.

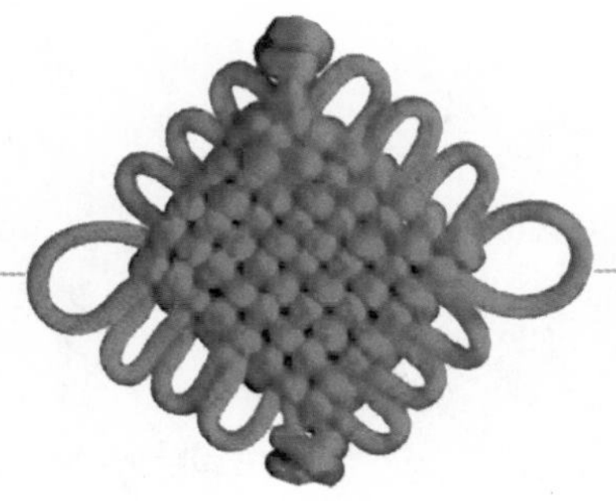

现代中国

CONTEMPORARY PERIOD

概述

Introduction

1949年10月1日，毛泽东主席登上雄伟的天安门城楼，向全世界人民庄严宣告：中华人民共和国成立了！中国人民从此站起来了！10月1日就是中国的国庆节，这一天也是中国现代史的开端。新中国成立后，在以毛泽东为核心的第一代中央领导集体的领导下，中国恢复了国民经济，建立了社会主义制度，改善了人民生活，加强了民族团结，发展了对外关系，恢复了中国在联合国和联合国常任理事国的合法席位，政治、经济面貌得到了巨大改观。

从1978年开始，在以邓小平为核心的第二代中央领导集体的领导下，在第三次科技革命的影响和推动下，中国进入改革开放和社会主义现代化建设的新时期，经济发展速度大大加快，科技、教育、文化、体育、卫生事业不断进步，国际地位迅速提高，成功地运用“一国两制”方针解决了香港问题、澳门问题。

以江泽民为核心的第三代中央领导集体，坚持改革开放政策。2001年中国加入了世界贸易组织（WTO），对中国的社会主义现代化建设产生了积极影响。

目前，中国人民正在以胡锦涛为总书记的党中央的领导下，努力构建社会主义和谐社会，加快推进全面建设小康社会的进程。

On October 1st, 1949, from the magnificent Tiananmen Rostrum, Chairman Mao Zedong solemnly declared to the world: "The People's Republic of China is founded! The Chinese people have stood up!" That day, which became the National Day, marked the beginning of contemporary Chinese history. After the founding of New China, under the direction of the CPC and the People's Republic's first-generation of leadership under Mao Zedong, the war-torn national economy was recovered, a socialist system established and people's living standard improved. Meanwhile, with the unity of all ethnic groups being strengthened within the country, China developed relations with foreign countries and resumed her legal status in the United Nations and that of the permanent membership of the UN Security Council. China took on an entirely new look, both politically and economically.

In 1978, under the direction of the CPC and New China's second-generation leadership under Deng Xiaoping, with the influence and boosting of the third wave of technological revolution worldwide, China entered a new period of reform, opening-up and socialist modernization, with her economy developing rapidly, her undertakings in the fields of scientific, educational, cultural, sports and health making constant progress and her international status increasing by leaps and bounds. Using the policy of "one country, two systems", China successfully settled the issues of Hong Kong and Macao.

The third-generation leadership of the Central Committee with Jiang Zemin at the core stuck to the policy of reforms and opening-up to the outside world. China entered the WTO in 2001, which has exerted a positive influence on China's socialist construction.

At the present time, under the direction of the CPC Central Committee headed by General Secretary Hu Jintao, China is continuing to advance steadily to build a harmonious socialist society with well-off living standard.

毛泽东与新中国的建立

Mao Zedong and the Founding of New China

1949年9月，中国人民政治协商会议第一届全体会议在北平开幕，会议决定成立中华人民共和国，选举毛泽东为中华人民共和国中央人民政府主席，朱德、刘少奇等人为副主席，决定把北平改名为北京，作为中华人民共和国的首都，以《义勇军进行曲》为代国歌，以五星红旗为国旗。

10月1日下午2时，国家领导人宣布就职，任命周恩来为中央人民政府政务院总理。

10月1日下午3时，举行开国大典。北京30万群众齐集天安门广场，毛泽东站在天安门城楼上，向全世界庄严宣告："中华人民共和国中央人民政府成立了！"在礼炮声中，他亲自升起了第一面五星红旗。接着举行了盛大的阅兵式和礼花晚会。

中华人民共和国的成立，标志着100多年来半殖民地半封建的旧中国历史的结束，揭开了中国历史的新篇章，使一个占世界人口近四分之一的大国成为独立自主的国家，人民从此成为国家的主人。

1 | 2 | 3

1. 1949年10月1日，毛泽东主席在开国大典上向全世界宣布："中华人民共和国中央人民政府今天成立了！"
On October 1st, 1949, Chairman Mao Zedong solemnly declared to the whole world at the founding ceremony of the PRC, "The Central Government of the People's Republic of China is founded today!"
2. 中华人民共和国国旗
National flag of the People's Republic of China
3. 毛泽东主席
Chairman Mao Zedong

Mao Zedong

and the Founding of New China

In September 1949, the First Plenary Session of the Chinese People's Political Consultative Conference (CPPCC) was held in Beiping. The Session decided to found the People's Republic of China (PRC), and elected Mao Zedong chairman of the Central People's Government of the PRC, and Zhu De, Liu Shaoqi and others vice-chairmen. The Session also decided to change the name of Beiping to Beijing and make it the capital of the PRC, and decided to adopt *March of the Volunteers* as the national anthem, and the five-starred red flag as the national flag.

At 2 pm on October 1st, the state leaders were sworn into office, and Zhou Enlai was appointed Premier of the Government Administration Council of the Central People's Government.

At 3 pm, the founding ceremony of the PRC was held. In Beijing, 300 000 people gathered in Tiananmen Square. Standing on the Tiananmen Rostrum, Mao Zedong solemnly declared to the world, "The Central People's Government of the People's Republic of China is founded!" He raised in person the first five-starred red flag to the accompaniment of an artillery salute. This was followed by a grand military review, and a fireworks display in the evening.

The founding of the PRC marked the end of a 100-year-old history of semi-colonial, semi-feudal society in the old China, and opened a new chapter in Chinese history. Since then, China, with nearly a quarter of the world's population within her territory, has been an independent country, and her people have become their own masters.

抗美援朝 保家卫国

The War to Resist US Aggression and Aid Korea

1950年6月25日，朝鲜内战爆发。美国随即出兵干涉朝鲜内政；同时，美国海军侵入台湾海峡。7月7日美国操纵联合国安理会通过了决议，组成以美军为主的“联合国军”，扩大侵朝战争。美国总统杜鲁门任命麦克阿瑟（sè）为“联合国军”总司令。

中国主张和平解决朝鲜问题，对于美国武装干涉朝鲜内政和侵入中国领土、领空表示强烈抗议。

9月15日，美军在朝鲜西海岸登陆，进攻朝鲜人民军，并于10月初越过北纬38度线（简称“三八线”），企图迅速占领整个朝鲜。同时，美军空军不断轰炸中朝边境的中国城乡，海军不断炮击中国船只，中国安全受到严重威胁。

10月初，中国政府根据朝鲜民主主义人民共和国政府的请求，作出“抗美援朝、保家卫国”的决策。中国人民志愿军于1950年10月19日，在司令员彭德怀的率领下，跨过鸭绿江，开赴朝鲜战场，与朝鲜人民军并肩作战，抗击美国侵略者。从1950年10月到1951年6月，连续进行了5次战役，将“联合国军”赶回“三八线”以南，扭转了朝鲜战局。1951年7月，战争双方开始举行朝鲜停战谈判。1953年7月27日，战争双方在朝鲜停战协议上签字，抗美援朝战争结束。

抗美援朝战争粉碎了帝国主义扩大侵略的野心，维护了亚洲与世界和平，提高了中国的国际威望，为新中国的建设赢得了相对稳定的和平环境。

小资料 Data

毛岸英牺牲

抗美援朝战争爆发后，毛泽东主席的长子毛岸英主动请求参加志愿军到朝鲜参战。他担任中国人民志愿军司令部俄语翻译和秘书。1950年11月25日上午，美空军轰炸机突然飞临志愿军司令部上空，投下了几十枚凝固汽油弹。在作战室紧张工作的毛岸英壮烈牺牲，长眠在朝鲜的土地上。

The Heroic Death of Mao Anying

When the Korean War broke out, Mao Anying, the eldest son of Mao Zedong volunteered to join the Chinese People's Volunteers to fight in Korea. He became an interpreter of Russian and secretary in the headquarters. On November 25th, 1950, US bombers raided the headquarters of the Chinese People's Volunteers and dropped napalm. Mao Anying died a heroic death at his working post in the campaign room. He sleeps eternally on the Korean soil.

The War to Resist US Aggression and Aid Korea

On June 25, 1950, a civil war broke out on the Korean Peninsula. The US immediately sent troops to interfere in the internal affairs of Korea. At the same time, it sent warships into the Taiwan Straits. On July 7th, the US manipulated the UN Security Council to pass a resolution to organize a UN Command, consisting mainly of US troops in order to enlarge the aggression against Korea. US President H. S. Truman appointed General Douglas MacArthur Commander-in-Chief of the UN Command.

China insisted on a peaceful solution to the Korean issue and strongly protested against the US armed interference in Korea's internal affairs as well as intrusion into China's territory.

On September 15, US troops landed on the west coast of the Korean Peninsula and began attacking the Korean People's Army. In early October 1950, US troops crossed the 38 degree of north latitude (the 38th Parallel), attempting to seize the whole of Korea. At the same time, the US air force bombed Chinese villages and towns near the Chinese-Korean border, and the US navy bombarded Chinese ships. Chinese national security was thus endangered.

In early October, upon the request of the government of the Democratic People's Republic of Korea, the Chinese government made the decision to resist the US and aid Korea, and protect our motherland. On October 19th, 1950, under Commander-in-Chief Peng Dehuai, the Chinese People's Volunteers crossed the Yalu River and marched to the Korean battlefield to fight side by side with the Korean People's Army against the US invaders. From October 1950 to June 1951, they launched five campaigns in succession, which forced the UN forces back beyond the 38th Parallel, turning the tide of the Korean War. In July 1951, the two belligerent parties began armistice talks. On July 27th, 1953, they signed the armistice agreement, and the Korean War ended.

The war to resist US aggression and aid Korea crushed the imperialists' aggressive ambitions, helped to safeguard Asian and global peace, enhanced China's international prestige and won a peaceful environment of relative stability for the construction of New China.

1 | 2

1. 中国人民志愿军跨过鸭绿江，开赴朝鲜战场
Chinese People's Volunteers crossed the Yalu River and marched to the Korean battlefield.
2. 1953年7月27日，朝鲜停战协议签字仪式在板门店举行
On July 27th, 1953, the signing ceremony of the Korean armistice agreement was held in Panmunjom, on the 38th Parallel.

周恩来与新中国外交

Zhou Enlai and New China's Diplomacy

1. 周恩来总理
   Premier Zhou Enlai
2. 1971年4月，周恩来会见美国乒乓球代表团
   Zhou Enlai receiving the American Ping-Pong delegation in April, 1971
3. 1972年2月21日，美国总统尼克松来华访问，周恩来在机场迎接
   On February 21st, 1972, Premier Zhou Enlai greeted US President Richard Nixon at Beijing International Airport.

周恩来是一位杰出的政治家、外交家，是中国共产党的重要领导人。他在北伐战争、南昌起义、遵义会议、西安事变、重庆谈判，以及中华人民共和国的创建等一系列重大历史事件中都发挥了重要的作用。他是新中国的首任总理兼外交部长，具有高超的外交艺术和人格魅力。他在外交场合的每一次出现，都会给爱好和平的人们带来希望，是成功和胜利的象征。

1954年4月至7月，美国、苏联、中国、法国，还有朝鲜战争和印度支那战争的交战各方，在瑞士日内瓦举行会议，讨论停战问题。这是新中国第一次以大国的身份参加重要国际会议。周恩来率领中国代表团出色地完成了任务，为恢复和平作出了巨大贡献。

周恩来还为中美关系的改善作出了杰出的贡献。新中国成立后，中美两国关系中断了20多年。20世纪60年代末，中美两国政府都决定改善中美关系。1970年10月1日，天安门广场举行国庆节庆祝活动，周恩来邀请美国记者埃德加·斯诺夫妇登上天安门城楼观礼，向美国发出了友好的信息。

1972年2月21日，在和中国没有外交关系的情况下，美国总统尼克松来中国进行友好访问。周恩来到机场迎接。当他们的手握在一起时，周恩来微笑着说："你把手伸过了世界上最辽阔的海洋来和我握手。"中美关系开始走上了正常化的道路。周恩来在其中发挥了关键性作用，在制定和执行这一时期中国对美国的方针方面表现了极大的创造性、灵活性，以及卓越的外交艺术。

Zhou Enlai

and New China's Diplomacy

Zhou Enlai was an important leader of the CPC. He was an outstanding statesman and diplomat who played an important role in a series of major historical events, such as the Northern Expedition, the Nanchang Uprising, the Zunyi Conference, the Xi'an Incident, the Chongqing Negotiations and the founding of the PRC. As the first premier and concurrently minister of foreign affairs of New China, he possessed superb diplomatic skills and personality charm. Every time he appeared on diplomatic occasions, he would bring hope to those who loved peace. He was a symbol of success and victory.

From April to July 1954, the US, the Soviet Union, China, France and other belligerent parties in the Korean War and the Indo-China War held a conference in Geneva, Switzerland, to discuss the armistice issue. This was the first important international conference in which New China participated as a great nation. The Chinese delegation, led by Zhou Enlai, accomplished their task at the conference with flying colors, and made a great contribution to the restoration of peace.

Zhou Enlai also made exceptional contributions to the improvement of Sino-US relations. Relations between China and the US were suspended for over 20 years after the founding of New China. But in the late 1960s, the Chinese and US governments decided to improve their relations. On October 1st, 1970, during the National Day celebrations held in Tiananmen Square, at Zhou Enlai's invitation, the US reporter Edgar Snow and his wife appeared on the Tiananmen Rostrum, sending a signal of friendship to the US.

On February 21st, 1972, US President Richard Nixon visited China, a country with no formal diplomatic relations at that time. Zhou Enlai went to the airport to welcome him, and said, as they shook hands, "You stretched out your hand across the broadest ocean in the world to shake hands with me." From that moment on, relations between the two countries began to be orbited on to the road of normalization. Zhou Enlai played an indispensable role in this process, displaying great creativity, flexibility, and extraordinary diplomatic skills in working out and implementing China's policy concerning the US.

小资料 Data

乒乓外交

1971年4月10日至17日，美国乒乓球代表队来中国进行友好访问和比赛，这是自新中国成立以来，第一个应邀访问中华人民共和国的美国代表团。美国乒乓球队访华在美国引起强烈的反响，掀起一股"中国热"，在国际上也引起了广泛的关注。1972年4月12日至29日，中国乒乓球代表团赴美进行回访。中美两国乒乓球队之间的互访，打开了两国人民友好往来的大门，"小球转动了大球"，推动了两国关系正常化的进程，被国际舆论誉为"乒乓外交"。

The Ping-Pong Diplomacy

From April 10th to 17th, 1971, a US table tennis (Ping-Pong) delegation toured China, and played matches with their Chinese counterparts. This was the first US delegation to be invited to visit China since the founding of the PRC. The visit brought about "China Craze" in the US and drew great attention internationally. From April 12th to 29th, 1972, a Chinese table tennis delegation toured the US, opening doors for the friendly communication between the two peoples. Using small balls to move the globe, this "Ping-Pong Diplomacy" named by the international media gave momentum to the process of normalizing relations between the PRC and the US.

邓小平与改革开放

Deng Xiaoping and the Reform and Opening-up Policy

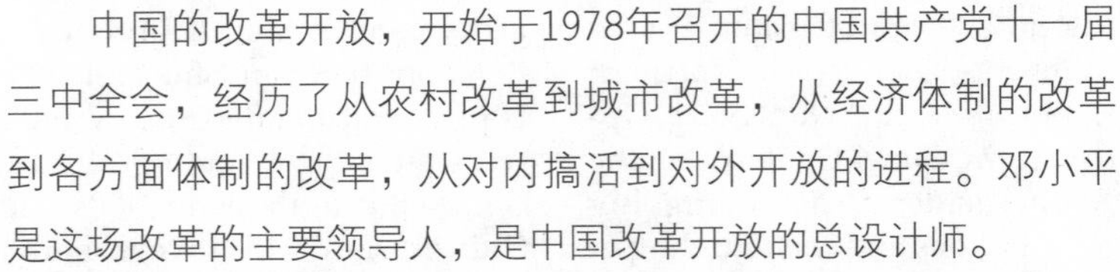

中国的改革开放，开始于1978年召开的中国共产党十一届三中全会，经历了从农村改革到城市改革，从经济体制的改革到各方面体制的改革，从对内搞活到对外开放的进程。邓小平是这场改革的主要领导人，是中国改革开放的总设计师。

邓小平提出了“建设中国特色社会主义”的理论：以经济建设为中心，进行现代化建设，在农村实行家庭联产承包责任制，在城市推行打破“大锅饭”的各种经济责任制，建立公有制基础上的社会主义市场经济体制。同时，改革政治体制，如党政分开、下放权力、精简机构、发扬民主等等。

把改革和开放结合起来，设置经济特区。1979年7月，国务院确定广东、福建两省试办经济特区。1980年，正式设立了深圳、珠海、汕头、厦门4个经济特区。又相继开放了沿海十几个城市，在长江三角洲、珠江三角洲、闽东南地区、环渤海地区开辟经济开放区，批准海南建省并成为经济特区。1984年1月，邓小平等人视察了深圳和珠海两个经济特区。1992年，又视察了武昌、深圳、珠海、上海等地，发表了重要讲话，强调改革开放胆子要大一些，要抓住时机，关键是发展经济。

邓小平提出“科学技术是第一生产力”，提出要尊重知识、尊重人才，发展教育事业，加强社会主义精神文明建设。

在解决香港和澳门回归的问题上，邓小平提出了用“一国两制”的方针实现祖国统一的构想，取得了成功。

经过20多年的改革开放，中国在经济、政治、文化、社会建设等领域都取得了巨大的成就，综合国力显著增强，人民生活水平日益提高。

Deng Xiaoping and the Reform and Opening-up Policies

The Third Plenary Session of the 11th Central Committee of the CPC, held in late 1978, saw the introduction of China's reform and opening-up policies. The process of the new policies was from rural reform to urban reform, from reform of the economic structure to structures in all aspects, and from internal vitalization to external opening-up. Deng Xiaoping was the major leader and chief architect of China's reform and opening-up policies.

Deng Xiaoping initiated the theory of "building socialism with Chinese characteristics", i.e. carrying out construction to realize modernization with economic construction as the central task, implementing the household contract responsibility system with remuneration linked to output in rural areas, practicing various economic systems of responsibility to prevent people from "eating from the same big pot"(getting the same reward or pay as everyone else regardless of one's work performance) in urban areas, and establishing a socialist market economy based on public ownership of the means of production. At the same time, the political systems were also reformed, such as separating the functions of the Party and the Government, transferring power to lower levels, simplifying the administrative structure and developing a democratic style of work.

Deng Xiaoping advocated combining reform and opening-up, and set up special economic zones (SEZs). In July 1979, the State Council decided to set up the first group of SEZs in Guangdong and Fujian provinces on a trial basis. In 1980, the four SEZs of Shenzhen, Zhuhai, Shantou and Xiamen were formally set up. Over a dozen coastal cities were opened, and open economic regions were established in the Yangtze Delta,

the Pearl River Delta, southeast Fujian area and the area around the Bohai Sea. Hainan Island was made a full-fledged province and an SEZ. In January 1984, Deng Xiaoping and other leaders went on an inspection tour of the Shenzhen and Zhuhai SEZs. In 1992, Deng inspected Wuchang, Shenzhen, Zhuhai and Shanghai, and issued instructions, emphasizing boldness in the reform and opening-up tasks, telling people to grasp opportunities, taking economic development as the key to progress.

Deng emphasized that "science and technology are the first productive forces", and urged more respect for knowledge and talented people. He also noted the need to develop education and strengthen the construction of socialist spiritual civilization.

As for the Hong Kong and Macao issues, Deng initiated the principle of "one country, two systems" to realize the reunification of the country. This principle underlay the successful reunion of Hong Kong and Macao with the motherland.

After more than 20 years of reform and opening-up, China has made enormous achievements in the economic, political, cultural and social construction. As a result, China's comprehensive national power and people's living standards have increased greatly.

1. 深圳经济特区
   Shenzhen Special Economic Zone
2. 邓小平是中国改革开放的总设计师
   Deng Xiaoping was the chief architect of China's reform and openingup policies.
3. 1992年1月，邓小平参观深圳先科激光公司
   Deng Xiaoping visited the Shenzhen Xianke Laser Company in January, 1992

香港回归

Hong Kong's Return to China

1840年6月，英国挑起侵略中国的鸦片战争。英国在1841年1月26日占领香港。1842年8月29日，清政府被迫与英国签订了屈辱的《南京条约》，将香港割让英国。

1982年9月，邓小平在会见英国首相撒切尔夫人时提出“一国两制”这一解决香港问题的方法，也就是实行“一个国家，两种制度”，“港人治港”、“高度自治”，保持香港原有的资本主义制度和生活方式50年不变。经多次协商，1984年12月19日，中英达成协议，签订了《中华人民共和国与大不列颠及北爱尔兰联合王国关于香港问题的联合声明》，宣告中国政府将于1997年7月1日对香港恢复行使主权，英国将在同时把香港交还中国。

1997年6月30日午夜，中英两国政府香港政权交接仪式在香港隆重举行。7月1日零点，中华人民共和国国旗和香港特别行政区区旗在香港升起，中华人民共和国主席江泽民在香港会议展览中心庄严宣告：根据中英关于香港问题的联合声明，中国对香港恢复行使主权，中华人民共和国香港特别行政区正式成立。之后，香港特别行政区首任行政长官董建华宣誓就职。

英国在香港一个半世纪的殖民统治结束了，香港终于回到祖国的怀抱。

小资料 Data

东方之珠——香港

香港位于珠江三角洲南部、珠江口东侧，是国际尤其是亚太地区的贸易、金融、交通、旅游中心。经济以贸易为主，制造业、金融业、房地产业、旅游业等很发达。维多利亚港是世界上最繁忙的港口之一；大屿山的香港国际机场为世界最先进的机场之一。

Hong Kong — Pearl of the Orient

Situated south of the Pearl River Delta, Hong Kong is a trade, finance, transportation and tourism center both for the Asian-Pacific region and the world. Its economy is based mainly on trade. Its manufacturing, financial, real estate and tourism sectors are highly developed. Victoria Harbor is one of the world's busiest ports, and the Hong Kong International Airport on Lantau Island is one of the world's most advanced airports.

Hong Kong's Return to China

In June 1840, the Opium War between China and Britain broke out. On January 26th, 1841, Britain seized Hong Kong. On August 29th, 1842, the government of the Qing Dynasty was forced to sign the *Treaty of Nanking* with Britain, formally ceding Hong Kong.

In September, 1982, Deng Xiaoping proposed the principle of "one country, two systems" to solve the Hong Kong issue when he met with British Prime Minister Margaret Thatcher. Under this principle, Hong Kong would be administered by Hong Kong people as a highly autonomous region, and Hong Kong's capitalist system and life style would not be changed for 50 years. After many rounds of consultation, on December 19th, 1984, China and Britain reached an agreement, and signed the *Sino-British Joint Declaration on the Issue of Hong Kong*, which declared that "the Chinese government will resume exercise of its sovereignty over Hong Kong from July 1st, 1997, and at the same time Britain will return Hong Kong to China."

On the midnight of June 30th, 1997, the hand-over ceremony was held solemnly at the Hong Kong Convention and Exhibition Centre. At zero hour on July 1st, the national flag of the PRC and the regional flag of the Hong Kong Special Administrative Region (HKSAR) were raised. Jiang Zemin, president of the PRC, solemnly declared the resumption of exercise of China's sovereignty over Hong Kong according to the *Sino-British Joint Declaration on the Issue of Hong Kong*, and the founding of the HKSAR. Then Tung Chee Hwa, the first Chief Executive of the HKSAR, took the oath of office. The one and a half centuries of British colonial rule of Hong Kong came to an end, and Hong Kong finally returned to the motherland.

1. 江泽民主席与英国查尔斯王子在香港政权交接仪式上
   President Jiang Zemin and Prince Charles of Britain at the ceremony to mark Hong Kong's return to China
2. 香港政权交接仪式现场
   A scene of the hand-over ceremony
3. 香港回归后的夜景
   A night scene after Hong Kong's return to China

澳门回归

Macao's Return to China

从1553年开始，中国澳门逐渐被葡萄牙殖民者攫取（juéqǔ）了管治权，成为西方殖民者在中国领土上建立的第一个侵略基地。

20世纪70年代末，中葡两国就澳门问题达成了原则协议。1986年至1987年，中葡两国经过和平友好谈判，最终于1987年4月13日签字发表了《中华人民共和国政府和葡萄牙共和国政府关于澳门问题的联合声明》，确认澳门地区是中国领土，中国政府将于1999年12月20日对澳门恢复行使主权。

1999年12月19日23时42分，澳门政权交接仪式正式开始，葡萄牙总统桑帕约等政府要员参加仪式。12月20日零时，中华人民共和国主席江泽民宣告，中国政府对澳门恢复行使主权。而后，澳门特别行政区首席行政长官何厚铧（Hé Hòuhuá）宣誓就职。

1. 澳门政权交接仪式现场
   A scene of the hand-over ceremony
2. 澳门大三巴牌坊
   Ruins of St. Paul's, Macau

Macao's Return to China

Macao was the first Chinese territory to fall into the hands of Western colonialists, as, starting in 1553, the Portuguese gradually asserted their power over it.

At the end of the 1970s, China and Portugal reached agreement in principle on the issue of Macao. From 1986 to 1987, after peaceful and friendly negotiations, China and Portugal signed the *Sino-Portuguese Joint Declaration on the Issue of Macao* on April 13th, 1987, affirming that Macao is a part of China, and the Chinese government would resume exercise of its sovereignty over the territory on December 20th, 1999.

At 23:42 on December 19th, 1999, the hand-over ceremony formally opened, in the presence of PRC President Jiang Zemin, Portuguese President Jorge Sampaio, and other leading governmental officials. At zero hour on December 20th, Jiang Zemin declared the resumption of exercise of China's sovereignty over Macao by the Chinese government. Then, Ho Hau-Wah, the first Chief Executive of the Macao Special Administrative Region (MSAR) took the oath of office.

小资料 Data

澳门

地处珠江三角洲西岸，面积约23.5平方公里，人口约44万，是一个中西文化交汇的地方。澳门实行的是自由经济制度，近年来，旅游博彩业以及其他服务业正逐步取代制造业而成为主要的经济支柱。

Macao

Situated on the west bank of the Pearl River Delta, Macao covers an area of 23.5 square kilometers, with a population of about 440 000. It is a place where Eastern and Western cultures converge. Macao has a free economic system. In recent years, tourism, gambling and various services and trades have gradually replaced manufacturing industry in becoming the economic mainstay.

载人航天飞行的巨大成就

Great Achievement in Manned Spaceflight

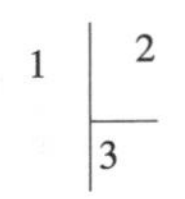

1. 神舟五号发射瞬间
   Launching of the spacecraft Shenzhou-5
2. 航天英雄杨利伟
   Yang Liwei, the Hero of Spaceflight
3. 神州六号返回舱在上海科技馆展览
   Re-entry module of the spacecraft Shenzhou-6 exhibited in Shanghai Scientific Gallery

无垠（wúyín）的太空是人类的共同财富，探索太空是人类的共同追求。中国载人航天工程于1992年正式启动实施。这是一项完全出于和平目的的伟大工程，中国人致力于通过开展空间科学实验和技术研究，对人类科学事业与和平事业作出贡献。

在先后发射4艘无人飞船之后，2003年10月15号，神舟五号将中国第一名航天员杨利伟送上太空。飞船绕地球14圈以后安全着陆。神舟五号载人飞船发射成功，标志着我国突破和掌握了载人航天的基本技术，完成和实现了中国载人航天工程第一步的计划和目标。

神舟五号成功实现了中华民族千年的飞天梦想，并使中国成为继前苏联、美国之后世界上第三个能够独立自主开展载人航天的国家。

2005年10月12日，中国自行研制的神舟六号载人飞船成功进入太空，两名航天员费俊龙和聂海胜在顺利完成各项空间试验活动后，于10月17日安全返回地面。

神舟六号的成功标志着中国在发展载人航天技术、进行有人参与的空间试验活动方面取得了又一个具有里程碑意义的重大胜利。

载人航天飞行的成功，对于进一步提升中国的国际地位，增强中国的经济实力、科技实力、国防实力和民族凝聚力，鼓舞全国各族人民紧密团结在党中央周围，不断把中国特色社会主义伟大事业推向前进，具有重大而深远的意义。

Great Achievement in Manned Spaceflight

It is a common dream of humanity to explore the vast outer space, and to utilize the common space resources of mankind. China initiated a manned spaceflight program in 1992. The program, with its peaceful nature, aims to contribute to the development of sciences and world peace by scientific and technological research and experiment in the outer space.

After launching four un-manned spaceships, on October 15th, 2003, Shenzhou-5 sent Yang Liwei, the first Chinese astronaut to the outer space, who orbited the Earth for 14 rounds and returned safely. The success of the manned spaceship Shenzhou-5 marked a breakthrough for China to grasp the basic technology of

manned spaceflight, as well as the completion of the first stage of the country's manned space program.

Shenzhou-5 is a realization of a thousand-year-old dream of the Chinese people, putting China on the list of countries with independent development of manned spaceflight, following the former Soviet Union and the US.

On October 12th, 2005, Shenzhou-6, another spaceship developed by China independently, made its trip a success by sending two astronauts, Fei Junlong and Nie Haisheng to the outer space to carry out various experiments. They came back safely on October 17th.

Shenzhou-6 became another milestone in China's development of manned spaceflight and manned outer space experiment.

The success of manned spaceflight

has tremendous impact on boosting the international standing of China and increasing the country's economic, scientific and technological, and national defense capacity, helping to raise the national morale and the solidarity of all ethnic groups around the CPC Central Committee in the great course of socialist development with Chinese characteristics.

小资料 Data

航天英雄杨利伟

随着神舟五号的飞天，全世界都记住了一个中国人的名字——杨利伟。杨利伟是中国第一代航天员。经过几年的训练，他完成了基础理论、航天环境适应性、专业技术等8大类几十个科目的训练任务，以优异的成绩通过了航天员专业技术综合考核，被光荣地选拔为中国首次载人航天飞行首飞梯队成员，成为“中国飞天第一人”。在中国首次载人航天飞行庆祝大会上，杨利伟被授予“航天英雄”光荣称号。

Yang Liwei, Hero of Spaceflight

With the launch of the spaceship Shenzhou-5, a Chinese named Yang Liwei became world famous. Yang is among the first-generation astronauts in China. After training for a few years, he finished training tasks in dozens of subjects in eight categories, i.e. fundamental theory, adaptation in outer space environment, specialized technologies, etc. He passed the comprehensive assessment of specialized space-flight technology with flying colors, and was chosen to be a member of the first team of the first manned spaceflight of China. After becoming "the first Chinese in outer space", he was awarded as the "Hero of Spaceflight" in the assembly celebrating the first manned spaceflight of China.

中国体育走向世界

China as a World Power in Sports

1924年，在张伯苓（Zhāng Bólíng）、王正廷等人的活动下，中华全国体育协进会成立了。1931年，国际奥委会正式承认中华全国体育协进会为中国奥林匹克委员会。1932年第10届奥运会在美国洛杉矶举行，中国第一次派选手刘长春参加。

1960年第17届奥运会，台湾选手参加比赛，杨传广获十项全能银牌，这是中国运动员在奥运史上取得的第一枚奖牌。1968年第19届奥运会，台湾选手纪政获得女子80米栏铜牌，这是中国女运动员在奥运会上首次获得奖牌。

1979年国际奥委会恢复了中华人民共和国的合法席位。

1984年7月，在第23届洛杉矶奥运会上，中国射击运动员许海峰夺得本届奥运会的第一枚金牌，中国运动员获得的金牌总数居第四位，中国女子排球队取得冠军，实现了世界杯冠军、世界锦标赛冠军、奥运会冠军“三连冠”。

中国又相继参加了第24届汉城奥运会、第25届巴塞罗那奥运会、第26届亚特兰大奥运会。

2000年9月，在第27届悉尼奥运会上，中国运动员共获得59枚奖牌，总数列第三名。

2004年8月，在第28届雅典奥运会上，中国运动员再创佳绩，获得了63枚奖牌，其中32枚金牌。至此中国共参加了14届奥运会的比赛。

2001年7月13日，中国申办2008年奥运会获得成功；很快又于9月成功举办了第21届世界大学生运动会，这有力地促进了中国体育事业的发展。同时也显示出中国综合国力的增强，在国际上的地位进一步提高。

1 | 2 | 3

1. 中国第一位国际奥委会委员王正廷
   Wang Zhengting, the first Chinese member on the International Olympic Committee
2. 张伯苓像
   A portrait of Zhang Boling
3. 第一位参加奥运会的中国运动员刘长春，他是1932年第10届奥运会唯一的中国运动员
   Liu Changchun, the first Chinese athlete to compete in the Olympics, in 1932

小资料 Data

2008年北京奥运会

北京获得第29届奥林匹克运动会的主办权，是中国在提高国际地位方面矗立（chùlì）起的又一座里程碑，是中华民族伟大复兴历程中一大盛事。

按照国际奥委会的要求,第29届奥林匹克运动会组织委员会在中国北京成立。中国人民以极大的热情投入到筹备工作中来。

2003年8月，2008年北京奥运会会徽“中国印・舞动的北京”向全世界公布。

2005年6月，2008年北京奥运会主题口号“同一个世界，同一个梦想”发布。

2005年11月，2008年北京奥运会吉祥物公布，吉祥物为5个福娃，名字分别为贝贝、晶晶、欢欢、迎迎、妮妮，连起来谐音为“北京欢迎你”，寄托了中国人民对于2008年北京奥运的良好祝愿和喜迎八方来客的信心。

2008 Beijing Olympics

Beijing won the bid for hosting the 29th Olympic Games. This is another milestone to enhance China's international standing, and another great event in the renaissance of Chinese people.

Under the request of the International Olympic Committee, the Organization Committee of the 29th Olympic Games was established in Beijing. Chinese people began to prepare for the game with great enthusiasm.

In August 2003, the logo for the 2008 Beijing Olympics, "Chinese seal — dancing Beijing" was publicized.

In June 2005, the theme slogan of 2008 Beijing Olympics, "One World, One Dream" was announced.

In November 2005, mascots of the 2008 Beijing Olympics were unveiled. Five of them in total, they are called Fuwa, namely Beibei, Jingjing, Huanhuan, Yingying and Nini. When the rhyming two-syllable names are put together, they say in Chinese, "Welcome to Beijing." The mascots embody good wishes of Chinese people for the 2008 Beijing Olympics, and warm welcome to people all over the world.

China as a World Power in Sports

In 1924, the All-China Sports Association was founded, with the efforts of Zhang Boling, Wang Zhengting and others. In 1931, the International Olympic Committee formally recognized the Association as the Chinese Olympic Committee. China was represented for the first time, by runner Liu Changchun, at the Olympic Games when the 10th Olympics were held in Los Angeles in 1932.

China won its first Olympic medal when Yang Chuanguang from Taiwan won the silver

medal for the decathlon at the 17th Olympics in 1960. In the 19th Olympics in 1968, Taiwan athlete Ji Zheng won the bronze medal in the women's 80-meter hurdle, which was the first Olympic medal won by a Chinese female athlete.

In 1979, the International Olympic Committee restored the PRC's legal seat on the committee.

In July 1984, Chinese marksman Xu Haifeng won China's first gold medal at the 23rd Olympics held in Los Angeles. At this Olympics, China ranked fourth in the gold medal standings. The Chinese women's volleyball team also won a gold medal, attaining three successive Championships for the sport (the other two being the World Cup and the World Championships).

China attended the Seoul (24th), Barcelona (25th) and Atlanta (26th) Olympics.

At the 27th Olympics held in Sydney in September 2000, Chinese athletes won 59 medals, ranking China third in the medal standings.

At the 28th Athens Olympics in August 2004, Chinese athletes won a record of 63 medals, among which 32 were gold. By then, China had been represented at 14 sessions of the Olympic Games.

On July 13th, 2001, China's bid for the 2008 Olympics was successful; in September that year, China hosted the 21st Universiade, which vigorously promoted the development of China's sports, demonstrated the increase of China's overall national strength and enhanced China's international status.

1. 2008年北京奥运会吉祥物——福娃
Official Mascots of Beijing 2008 Olympic Games — Fuwa
2. 2008年北京奥运会会徽——中国印·舞动的北京
Logo for Beijing 2008 Olympic Games — Chinese Seal - Dancing Beijing

小资料 Data

"东方玫瑰"

中国女子足球自20世纪80年代组建国家队以来，在国际比赛中取得了很好的成绩，如1986—1999年女足亚洲杯7连冠；亚运会女足3连冠；1996年亚特兰大奥运会女足亚军；1999年第3届女足世界杯亚军等等，被人们誉为"东方玫瑰"。

The Oriental Roses

The Chinese women's national football team has achieved very good results in international matches since its founding in the 1980s. Its achieve-ments include seven Asian Cup championships in succession—from 1986 to 1999; three Asian Games championships in succession; runner-up in the 1996 Atlanta Olympics; and runner-up in the third Women's Football World Cup in 1999. The women players are popularly known as the "Oriental Roses".

附 录
Appendix

中国历史年代简表		A Brief Chronology of Chinese History	
中国古代史	约170万年前—1840年	**Ancient Period**	c. 1 700 000 years ago—1840 AD
旧石器时代	约170万年前—约1万年前	Paleolithic Period	c.1 700 000 years ago—c.10 000 years ago
新石器时代	约1万年前—4 000年前	Neolithic Period	c.10 000 years ago—4 000 years ago
夏	约公元前2070—前1600年	Xia Dynasty	c. 2070 BC—1600 BC
商	约公元前1600—前1046年	Shang Dynasty	c. 1600 BC—1046 BC
西周	约公元前1046—前771年	Western Zhou Dynasty	c. 1046 BC—771 BC
春秋	公元前770—前476年	Spring and Autumn Period	770 BC—476 BC
战国	公元前475—前221年	Warring States Period	475 BC—221 BC
秦	公元前221—前206年	Qin Dynasty	221 BC—206 BC
汉（西汉、东汉）	公元前206—公元220年	Han Dynasty (Western Han and Eastern Han)	206 BC—220 AD
三国（魏、蜀、吴）	公元220—280年	Three Kingdoms (Wei, Shu, Wu)	220—280 AD
晋（西晋、东晋）	公元265—420年	Jin Dynasty (Western Jin and Eastern Jin)	265—420 AD
南北朝	公元420—589年	Southern and Northern Dynasties	420—589 AD

中国历史年代简表	A Brief Chronology of Chinese History		
隋	公元581—618年	Sui Dynasty	581–618 AD
唐	公元618—907年	Tang Dynasty	618–907 AD
五代	公元907—960年	Five Dynasties	907–960 AD
辽	公元907—1125年	Liao Dynasty	907–1125 AD
宋（北宋、南宋）	公元960—1279年	Song Dynasty (Northern Song and Southern Song)	960–1279 AD
西夏	公元1038—1227年	Western Xia Dynasty	1038–1227 AD
金	公元1115—1234年	Jin Dynasty	1115–1234 AD
元	公元1206—1368年	Yuan Dynasty	1206–1368 AD
明	公元1368—1644年	Ming Dynasty	1368–1644 AD
清（鸦片战争以前）	公元1616—1840年	Qing Dynasty (before the Opium War of 1840)	1616–1840 AD
中国近代史	公元1840—1949年	**Modern Period**	1840–1949 AD
清（鸦片战争以后）	公元1840—1911年	Qing Dynasty (after the Opium War of 1840)	1840–1911 AD
中华民国	公元1912—1949年	Republic of China	1912–1949 AD
现代中国	公元1949—	**Contemporary Period**	1949 AD–
中华人民共和国	公元1949—	People's Republic of China	1949 AD–

《中国历史常识》

主　　编　王　恺
编写人员　李　华　张美霞　徐正龙　夏小芸　钱玉莲
　　　　　赵　玉　王　浩　唐晓丹　薛蓓蓓
责任编辑　金　红
英文编辑　林美琪
美术编辑　阮永贤　刘玉瑜

《中国历史常识》（中英对照）

改编人员　张　轶　贾　宇
中文审稿　叶蓁蓁
英文翻译　许德金　巩　华
英文审稿　杨纳让　孙亦丽

策　　划　刘　援　祝大鸣
项目负责　祝大鸣　梁　宇
项目编辑　梁　宇
责任编辑　宋亚昆
版式设计　高等教育出版社美编室
美术编辑　张志奇　张　志
封面设计　王凌波
责任绘图　朱　静
插图选配　宋亚昆
责任印制　朱学忠
图片来源　高等教育出版社　全景图片公司　ChinaFotoPress

郑 重 声 明

图书在版编目(CIP)数据

中国历史常识/国务院侨务办公室，国家汉语国际推广领导小组办公室．—北京：高等教育出版社，2007.4 (2010重印)

ISBN 978-7-04-020717-0

Ⅰ．中... Ⅱ．①国...②国... Ⅲ．①汉语－对外汉语教学－语言读物②中国－历史－基本知识－汉、英。Ⅳ．①H195.5 ②K2

中国版本图书馆CIP数据核字(2006)第128489号

出版发行	高等教育出版社	**购书热线**	010－58581118
社　　址	北京市西城区德外大街4号	**免费咨询**	800－810－0598
邮政编码	100120	**网　　址**	http://www.hep.edu.cn
总　　机	010-58581000		http://www.hep.com.cn
		网上订购	http://www.landraco.com
经　　销	蓝色畅想图书发行有限公司		http://www.landraco.com.cn
印　　刷	北京信彩瑞禾印刷厂	**畅想教育**	http://www.widedu.com
开　　本	787×1092　1/16		
印　　张	17.75	**版　　次**	2007年4月第1版
字　　数	400 000	**印　　次**	2010年1月第13次印刷

本书如有印装等质量问题，请到所购图书销售部门调换。

ISBN 978-7-04-020717-0

06500

物 料 号　20717-00